Race to the Swift

STUDIES OF THE EAST ASIAN INSTITUTE
COLUMBIA UNIVERSITY

Studies of the East Asian Institute
Columbia University

The East Asian Institute is Columbia University's center for research, publication, and teaching on modern East Asia. The Studies of the East Asian Institute were inaugurated in 1962 to bring to a wider public the results of significant new research on modern and contemporary East Asia.

A STUDY OF THE EAST ASIAN INSTITUTE

Race to the Swift

State and Finance in Korean Industrialization

Jung-en Woo

COLUMBIA UNIVERSITY PRESS *New York*

Columbia University Press
New York   Oxford

Library of Congress Cataloging-in-Publication Data
Woo, Jung-en.
Race to the swift : state and finance in Korean industrialization
/ Jung-en Woo.
p. cm.—(Studies of the East Asian Institute)
Includes bibliographical references and index.
ISBN 0-231-07146-9
ISBN 0-231-07147-7 (pbk.)
1. Industry and state—Korea (South)   2. Monetary policy—Korea (South)
I. Title. II. Series.
HD3616.K853W66   1991
338.95195—dc20
90-2600
CIP

FOR MY FATHER AND IN MEMORY OF MY MOTHER

Contents

Preface

A PREFACE turns up first but is written last. It thus forces upon the author a recuperation of what it was that she had intended in the first place, after knowing the final outcome. My intent was to explain the rise of the developmental state in Korea in the last half century. For many analysts, Korea's cultural proclivities predict the economic outcome: it all seems to have been predetermined. Twenty years ago culture was the explanation for the absence of development, however, and forty years ago inviability was supposed to be the natural state of the Korean economy. I wanted to privilege a different Korea, whose economic growth could be seen as neither a miracle nor a cultural mystery, but the outcome of a misunderstood political economy—poorly enough understood to require this book. I wish to merge Korea with the stream of world history by discovering universal aspects of its development. The political economy of finance seems a useful way to do that.

Financial structure is the mechanism guiding the flow of savings and investment, determining the options of industrial policy, and managing financial flows to different sectors. In this sense, all states are potentially "developmental" whether they exist in Europe, Latin America, or East Asia. Depending on the type and degree of financial control, money can be turned into a mechanism for political control, and for restructuring the economy and the society, as well. Just as the monopoly on the use of violence is the first requisite of a strong state, so the monopoly on financial resources can govern a strongly developmental trajectory. The main thesis of this book is that the political logic of the Korean financial structure offers us the best explanation of Korea's swift industrialization.

I will show how the state deployed financial resources at home and abroad to accumulate power unto itself, in order to force rapid industrialization and to create—out of a historical vacuum caused by colonialism and war—a new class of entrepreneurs. This is also a state that has moved from a dependent, penetrated status to one of relative autonomy, from mendicant to world-competitive status.

My inquiry took a good bit of excavation and reexamination, more than I had bargained for. Much of modern Korean history is buried in idiosyncratic official lore, and I often had to start from scratch, discover new materials, and winnow out truths from half-truths and myths. I had to rethink the colonial configuration in the 1930s in order to specify the developmental model available to Korea, to place Korea's import-substitution industrialization in the 1950s in the context of America's East Asian policy, to understand Korea's 1960s take-off and the belabored policies of the 1970s in terms of the regional reintegration in East Asia, and finally to grasp why a model of the mercantilist or developmental state is inevitably a finite one, one whose historical role is being eclipsed by new demands of the world economy and world politics. The result is a different periodization and interpretation of Korea's political economy, and a different way of conceptualizing Korea's relationship to the world.

This book had several patrons. My first acknowledgment is owed to Gerald Curtis, my adviser at Columbia, who supported my dissertation work from start to finish, and who ran interference so that I could transform it into a book. I was so happy that he first thought the project interesting; later, he read and commented on various drafts, and provided me with a year of residency at Columbia University's East Asian Institute. Richard Nelson was an inspiration, and I would be very pleased if he deemed this book a successful outcome of our many talks, and his friendly guidance. Yoonje Cho, my brother-in-law and an economist, had to grin and bear my many questions, and I am deeply grateful to him. Stephan Haggard took special pains to read my manuscript with care and insight. I would also like to thank Carter Eckert, Mark Kesselman, James Kurth, and Gari Ledyard, for reading this manuscript at various stages, and for improving this book with helpful comments. Carl Riskin gave me the compliment of a very close reading for which, entre nous, I am very grateful.

I have benefited from discussions about my work with Valerie Bunce, Daniel Chirot, Douglas Chalmers, Fred Chernoff, Thomas Ferguson, Gary Gereffi, H. D. Harootunian, Barbara Helfferich, Ronald Herring, Michael Johnston, Michael Loriaux, Ben Page, Engelbert Schucking, and John and Evelyne Stephens. This would have been a lesser book without the insights they imparted to me. Jay Casper, my department chairman at Northwestern, provided many facilities so that this book could be completed. A summer grant from Colgate University was most helpful, as well. Kate Wittenberg of Columbia University Press was always enthusiastic in helping to bring this book to fruition.

My family in Seoul, and Adam and Regina Doi, have been the mainstays in my life, and I thank them for their love. Bruce Cumings is my husband, friend, colleague, discussant, and sounding board; without his love and jokes (good and bad), this book would not have been possible. Our son, Ian Woo Cumings, arrived between dissertation and book, adding delight (and delay) to the project.

1

Theoretical Considerations

SOUTH KOREA has had one of the fastest-growing economies in the world for a quarter-century. In December 1985 *Business Week* proclaimed that "the Koreans are coming," heralding the unexpected emergence of another East Asian competitor in the world market, like Japan earlier: Korea is a celebrated parvenue. Like other parvenues that preceded Korea, the success is said to have been orchestrated by a ubiquitous and interventionist state. Yet we have little understanding of how this strong, ubiquitous state has come about, and of what it does to stimulate the economy. Unraveling the riddle of the Korean state would enlighten us not only about the political economy of rapid industrialization, but about the nature of the state in general.

This study seeks to contribute to the literature on the theory of the state through an examination of finance and development in Korea. The Korean state has recently been seen as strong, interventionary, and autonomous—to such a degree that scholars speak of "Korea, Incorporated," with the state as maker and breaker of big firms. I propose that the political logic of the financial structure in Korea offers us the best explanation of the origin and development of this state.

In any market system, even the most liberal ones, monetary arrangements fall within the purview of the state. A stable monetary framework is not something that the market can provide by itself, and even Milton Friedman emphasized state supervision of the money supply as an essential prerequisite for a market economy.[1] Marxists likewise argue that money is a special commodity that capitalists cannot manage for themselves, and hence requires state intervention.[2]

In the process of regulating and guiding the market, however, the state accumulates rents from the market. Depending on types and degrees of monetary control, the state is in a position to decide how national resources are mobilized and allocated: who gets what, when, and how. At the *core* of state power, therefore, is its channeling of the flow of money. As such, money is not merely a medium of exchange but also a political tool. No wonder, then, that monetary and financial policy remain the most zealously guarded realms of any state—combined with, of course, centralized control of the military. But this is not well recognized in the literature.

The usual conception of a "strong" state embodies three dimensions: coercive capacity, comparative independence from particular groups and classes, and an interventionism capable of restructuring society, or substituting for other structures, such as the market. With the eclipse of functional behaviorism as the dominant mode of analysis in political science, scholars of diverse perspectives have sought to explain one or another of these three facets of strong states. Huntington focused on an organizational accumulation of power through institution-building, Skocpol reinterpreted the strong states that emerge with modern revolutions as a function of state-building by revolutionary elites, and Krasner and Stepan have defined a strong state as one that is insulated from outside pressure groups, and capable of reordering society.[3] This literature on the state has a linage to the continental tradition of Otto Hintze and Max Weber. From Hintze comes the conception of the state as an actor conditioned by historically-changing transnational contexts, and from Weber the concern with coercive or repressive capacities (i.e., a legitimate monopoly on administrative and military control of a given territory.)[4] When this literature turns to state and economy, the emphasis is often on welfare and fiscal policy. Fiscal policies are seen as the nexus between state and economy, and between the state and the restructuring of society.

In the Marxist literature, too, the instrumental conception of the state has given way to a theory of "relative autonomy," sharing many of the same arguments about what makes for a formidable state. For Poulantzas, the state's relative autonomy from class interests is an integral part of the effective functioning of a class state. Poulantzas' structuralist argument, however, has spawned a critique by Miliband, Offe, and Therborn, among others, which asserts that the relative autonomy argument is tautological, has no way of specifying degrees of autonomy, and lacks a sense of mechanisms which manifest state power or show how states "reproduce" social structures.[5] To demystify the process whereby the capitalist state conceals its role in aiding accumulation, Offe, Wolfe, and O'Connor focus on bureaucracy, tax and welfare policies—much like the Weberians cited above.[6] Both the Marxist and the bureaucratic literature rarely look at financial structure.[7]

The notable exceptions would be those who study the organization of capital, labor, and the state to see how that has a determining influence on economic policies adopted in the advanced industrial nations. As a result of organizational variation, for instance, finance capital seems better able to influence the state in Germany than in France, and the ability of the state to bargain with the union movement is greater in Germany and Britain than in France. It is little wonder then that people like Loriaux and Zysman (who both study France) have produced studies on state and finance.[8]

The theory of the state has most often been a theory of the advanced industrial capitalist state. If not that, then it is the theory of the more or less dependent Latin American state. This produces a curious regional bias, and a hiatus between the two bodies of theory, giving us theories of the European or the Latin American state at distinctly different levels of development. In the Latin American examples, for years the dependency paradigm overwhelmed and muffled alternative conceptions of the state, so that nearly all scholars took up the question, how dependent is the state? In one form or the other, the dependency perspective has been incorporated into critical political economy accounts of Latin America, starting from the work of those associated with the Economic Commission for Latin America, to theses on unequal exchange, underdevelopment, dependent development, imperialism, and even post-imperialism.[9]

The emphasis is on external shaping, so the question of finance becomes, for example, a function of the "debt crisis," which is seen in the framework of external challenge and domestic response, as if all Latin American states were at some residual "receiving end," ever the victims of metropolitan capital. The critical problem becomes the relationship between stabilization, repression, and authoritarianism. Kaufman has shown, for instance, how different responses to austerity are rooted in enduring features of Latin political systems—but his conception remains one of how to impose an austerity program originating in the metropole. O'Donnell and Frenkel examine how—in the periphery—IMF policies benefit sectors in primary production and finance capital, and Stallings shows how politics—at the core—shape the lending pattern, leading to a tidal wave of changes in the periphery. This emphasis on external debt problem is less a structural analysis of finance than another elaboration of the mendicancy of Latin America in the world system.[10]

Somehow, in East Asia, both conceptions give way to one of the "developmental" state, even though we are still in the presumably dependent semi-periphery (with the exception of Japan). This approach, however, is theoretically impoverished, relying on little more than impressions about how the state guides industrialization, or pursues "handwaving" to influence the market mechanism, with causality emerging from residual categories called culture and historical evolution. At the least sophisticated end, scholars have attributed economic development in East Asia to "post-Confucianism," "aggressive Confucianism," and even to "*samurai* Confucianism."[11]

The Japan field fares better, but the study of Japan's political economy remains caught between an old "statist" conception (starting with E. H. Norman), and a specifically American perspective that wants to uncover pluralism everywhere. Lineages of the statist conception trace back to Norman and to (the earlier) Lockwood, but the most representative writing is Chalmers Johnson's *MITI and the Japanese Miracle.* His preferred method for unlocking the secret of Japanese neomercantilism is an institutional analysis, combined with a genealogy of prominent bureaucratic careers. Samuels's theory of the "politics of reciprocal consent," on the other hand, conceives of Japanese state and society (e.g., MITI and the firm) as occupying overlapping arenas of mutual appropriation, and the state becomes just another cluster of interests. Hence, Japan becomes "a web without a spider."[12] Any number of arguments ("patterned pluralism," "the societal state," "state-led capitalism," and "adaptive communitarianism") seek to fine-tune the existing theories, but the terms of debate oscillate between statism and pluralism.[13] We still lack a conception that both grasps the idiosyncrasy of Japan's political economy and contributes to state theory.

The Korean literature is even less rich, yet Korea partakes of the same problems. Here the "developmental" conception mires itself in a unique East Asian configuration, attributing too much similarity to Japan, South Korea, and Taiwan, and reinforcing the compartmentalization of the state theory literature. The regional solipsism of such conceptions is most often found in the literature on economic development in the East Asian "Gang of Four," NICs that include Korea.[14]

Some more theoretically conscious scholars have begun to pay attention to Korea and Taiwan, it is true, such as those at the Institute of Development in Sussex, who analyze Korea in the context of late development and mercantile tendencies. They have tried to provide a corrective to the notion of the triumph of liberal economic philosophy in Korea by showing, for instance, the level of domestic market protection at home, combined with the export-led strategy for trade. But such work is still embryonic and eclectic, with the exception of a recent book by Alice Amsden, which examines the process of learning—the advantages of backwardness—in the Korean context.[15]

Given its position in the global economic hierarchy and its domestic regime structure, Korea finds a natural point of reference in the Latin America experience—issues of "late-late development," bureaucratic-authoritarian politics, and dependency on the metropole are not foreign to Korea. But, the rate and the pattern of Korea's economic growth, not to mention geographic and cultural proximity, also make Japan a useful referent. So, study of Korea must inevitably partake of the discourses within the two regions—East Asia and Latin America—and do so in such a way that it is *in* but not *of* the mainstream debate: a stranger often observes strange things, things hitherto unnoticed.

Second, Korea's promontory position in the cold war requires an analyst to mesh domestic with international politics. Korea makes no sense without paying attention to the world system and to security structures. Yet, the neorealist conception of the state as an international actor does not account for the domestic accretion of state power, and state theory in comparative politics treats security matters in passing, almost as an afterthought. We obviously need a dialectical conjoining of comparative and international politics, something this study seeks to do.

Third, financial structure can be used to test state efficacy because it is the overarching mechanism guiding the flow of savings and investment, delimiting the options of industrial policy, and managing financial flows to different industrial sectors. It is this that makes all states potentially "developmental," whether they exist in Europe, Latin America, or East Asia. But the existing literature buries this insight, so that we get the fiscal crisis of the advanced industrial state, the dependency paradigm for the Latin American state, and the developmental model of the East Asian state. Herein is the bias—both regional and theoretical—of the existing literature, and here is where we can contribute to bridging these discrete, encapsulated theories.

We must first define what we mean by the state. The state-centric literature has given us a definition that accentuates state autonomy in the domestic context: the state is "the continuous administrative, legal, bureaucratic, and coercive system" that is capable of restructuring its relation to social groups, as well as relations among those groups.[16] The strength of the state depends on how effectively the state alters these structures, and in this context, Korea is a "strong state." There is little differentiation among states that occupy different positions in the world system.[17] The state also stands, however, between the international system and the domestic society. Yet the world system literature informs us that states in the periphery, no matter how strong at home, are ipso facto "weak states." A fuller and more comprehensive definition of the state would help us avoid such antinomies.

We agree with the state-centric definition, in part: the state is the rational-legal, administrative agency of coercion. But we also posit the state as poised between the world system and the domestic system. Depending on the autonomy or the strength of the state, it can either be a *lumpen*, dependent state or it can engineer a movement upward in the international system, wresting away power from the external system. Unless we understand the full complexity of the state's relationship to the outside world and domestic sectors— the "give-and-take," for developing states are not merely "takers"— we cannot understand how the international system is constituted, how it is both made and remade.

The central hypothesis of this study is that an examination of the state and the financial structure can explain different developmental outcomes, in particular the comparative developmental success of South Korea. The Korean state has moved from a dependent, penetrated status to one of relative autonomy by positioning itself astride the flow of foreign capital, refracting capital in a prismatic fashion to fund rising industries, create mammoth firms, buttress its social support, and in dialectical fashion wrest national autonomy from the external system. Its very openness to the outside world (especially in contrast to Latin America's residual import-substituting pattern), combined with its remarkable insulation at home, give it a dynamic, pivotal role in moving from mendicant to world-competitive status. This could never be understood without grasping the political logic of the Korean financial structure.

Most treatments of finance are static, missing the Gerschenkronian developmental perspective which would tell us that a credit system based in equity and securities markets is an artifact of early industrialization, and that the model of state or bank-influenced industrialization (Germany, Japan) is a consequence of "lateness" in world time, viz., the absence of abundant capital in the private sector. Latin American theories differentiate a "late-late" model, where capital comes from direct foreign investment or, more recently, foreign lending.[18] If Gerschenkron is right in citing the "feudal" advantages of "late" development, usually meaning the virtues of a strong state and a partial bourgeois revolution at a particular point in industrialization, we would cite the Korean "advantages" of a colonially bequeathed strong state, the virtual absence of a local bourgeoisie (thus avoiding many of the domestic conflicts of the Latin American states), and the post-1965 external environment of widely available loan capital.

The Korean model of the state will become more apparent when we look at the categories of financial *mobilization* and *allocation*, and their *social consequences*. In the literature on the theory of the state, these categories are isomorphic to state power, interventionism, and relative autonomy vis-à-vis social forces. By mobilization, I mean the gathering together of foreign and domestic resources by the state, thus enhancing its capacity. By allocation, I mean the modalities by which the state directs these resources in terms of its own goals. By social consequences, I refer to the state's capacity to restructure society, and to resist or be insulated from domestic social forces.

Mobilization of Financial Resources and State Power

In regard to mobilization, an essential point is that no consideration of the relative autonomy of the Korean state can proceed without mention of its position as a security state in the global system.

Whether we speak of Japanese industrialization in Korea in the 1930s and 1940s, or the postwar development of Korea, security concerns have always justified the logic of industrialization and created an environment very different from Latin America. But at the same time, this is not so different from the pattern of nineteenth century continental industrialization, in the context of British hegemony. The big difference in the Korean case is the role of outside guarantors like the United States and Japan who, so intent on preventing South Korea from being another domino, opened a realm of opportunity for Korean action (this is true from the first days of the Rhee regime, however weak it was at the time). The main point is that this security environment showers benefits on the guaranteed state in the form of bilateral aid or multilateral loans, and enhances Korean maneuverability—such as, for example, justifying in security terms the adding on of heavy industrial capacity in the 1970s.

Security concerns can thus be utilized to mobilize resources for development. Because of the promontory strategic position of Korea, the United States has historically been willing to pump financial resources into the country; the Koreans first used munificent bilateral aid to build a social basis of support for a strong state in the 1950s; later on, multilateral lending was used to finance ambitious developmental projects. Sources of funding have important political implications. Here, in both cases, the effect was to augment state power. In Latin America, by contrast, the source of funding was usually multinational corporations; foreign capital possessed its own investment and market goals and bypassed the state, thus emerging as a formidable domestic force which hamstrung the state; in Korea, the opposite occurred, thereby building state power and reducing foreign goal direction. Thus, a generation of scholars can take dependency theory as their focus, yet give us little more than a parochial, local, theory; it could never explain how Korea, or for that matter Taiwan, has "triumphed" over dependency.

The point is not that this sort of external financing (foreign aid and multilateral loans) is free from foreign interference. Quite the contrary. Taiwan and Korea in the 1950s and the early 1960s were penetrated states, often approximating the situation in Central America. The aid missions of the United States would often keep the largest branch offices in these nations, closely monitoring their use of funds. Taiwan's turn toward market liberalization in the late 1950s, and Korea's in the mid-1960s, cannot be understood apart from the pressure of USAID, which used aid as a bargaining chip. How, then, could Taiwan and Korea escape the abuses that might arise from a quasi-colonial situation and turn the external situation to their advantages?

The answer is that the penetration was not one way but both ways, because of the cold war milieu. The promontory strategic positions of the ROK and ROC, poised on the geopolitical fault lines, gave the two states remarkable leverage on the big ally; thus, for example, they were able to influence the Congress through lobbying activities (here, the China Lobby was particularly successful; Korea notorious in its failure, with "Koreagate"). Both were able to manipulate the bureaucratic cleavages within the United States government. Korea was perhaps more successful in its access to the Pentagon than was Taiwan, because of the heavy American troop commitment in the peninsula. It was effective in playing off the Defense Department against USAID and the State Department. It is little wonder then that theories on the power of the "small allies" would often use Taiwan and Korea as the model.[19]

The Korean financial structure, along with the external source of finance, also helped to cement a social coalition; again, there was a back-and-forth dialectic at work, in this case between the state and business. In a nation with a dearth of accumulated capital, business has had to rely on credits from banks that were controlled and, until recently, owned by the state. Since the firms are highly leveraged, much more so than is the case in Mexico or Brazil, business has had to maintain good relations with the state so as to avert the possibility of severance of credit. Public records show remarkable expenditures not found in Western corporate experience. A glance at the annual reports of firms listed in the Seoul Stock Exchange catches an entry called "voluntary contribution" to the government. Typically, the voluntary contribution of the big business amounts to some 22 percent of the corporate net profit, taking third place only after the operating cost and financial cost of the firm.[20]

This exemplifies strong business support for the state; but pursuing this question further brings us into the shady realm of political contributions, kickbacks, and corruption. Corruption can have a detrimental effect on state building if the yield from corruption exceeds the rate of return on investment, thus aborting economic growth. In the Korean instance, the effect of corruption (a concrete manifestation of the state-business coalition) was on the side of augmenting the power base of the state. We might therefore see corruption as a propitiatory offering of big business toward the state in order to be an allocatory beneficiary of low-cost foreign financing and bank credit; but the main point is that foreign lending enhanced state capacity and reduced the organized political power of business vis-à-vis the state.

State mobilization of credits on preferential terms drove down bank interest rates, which had a dire effect on household savings, causing them to flee mostly into an unregulated financial market, called the "curb." Channeling resources from the curb into institutionalized financial intermediaries, without altering the interest structure, would prove most taxing for the state. Thus, it is no coincidence that the first and major economic decree of the *yushin* state—belonging generically to the bureaucratic authoritarian structure—was a moratorium on corporate debt to the curb, intended to coerce curb investors into placing savings in banks, as another aspect of the mobilization of finance. The state and business were the beneficiaries, and the casualties were the citizens who had stayed away from the banks. This type of decree—and many to follow—is most symbolic of the economic policies of an authoritarian state with the financial structure we are describing. The periodic crackdown on the curb, insofar as the pronounced aim was to restore effectiveness of monetary policy and to recoup the lost revenues of the state, will receive some attention in this study as constituting the ultimate parameter of state power and intervention in the market system.

Allocation of Finance, State Interventionism, and Industrialization of Korea

Contrary to what liberal economists may say in their panegyrics about Korea's open economy and its pursuit of comparative advantage, Korea maintained a strong import-substitution regime for target industries and consumer goods.[21] Further, its industrial policies in the 1970s hardly conformed to comparative advantage and international competitiveness; instead, the 1970s were marked by a conscious attempt of the Korean state to protect infant industries—the second or "deepening" phase of import-substitution—and to enhance military preparedness by an excessive investment in heavy industries. Notwithstanding considerable protest from international development agencies, the Korean state has heavily intervened in the financial allocation process so as to direct resources into heavy industry sectors; it provided incentives in the form of "policy loans," interest rates, and other subsidies, and showed willingness to share the risk of default for those firms willing to conform to the state policies. The concern of the state became long-run, future international competitiveness and industrial transformation.

The rationale for such industrial strategy was primarily political and security-oriented, an economic nationalism that coincided with the perception of the decline of the United States as an hegemonic power: the Nixon Doctrine, the first major troop withdrawal, the fall of Vietnam. President Carter's threat to withdraw the remaining ground troops from Korea, his human rights salvos, and "Koreagate" further provided the impetus and context in which Korea began to push for heavy industrialization associated with the goal of national self-sufficiency. Investment in heavy industries, often implemented without regard to actual or future demand, or the international market situation, resulted predictably in waste, idle capacity, and overall inefficiency, producing a storm of protest from international agencies and economists.

Yet, it often happens that considerations of efficiency loom large only in the minds of economists; efficiency, as Susan Strange argues, rarely, if ever, commands priority in the national economic policies of *any* nation.[22] Rather, the top priority is national efficacy. Such was the case historically in European continental and Japanese "late" industrialization. (The lack of external security concern may partially explain why, comparatively speaking, the convulsive élan, or the spurt of industrialization geared toward the production of capital goods did not take place in Latin America with the same intensity and compression.) Investment in lumpy projects with a long gestation period, and with an uncertain future market to boot, cannot be undertaken by the private sector, unless, of course, accompanied by the state's willingness to shoulder the risk, or to provide significant subsidy.

The argument here is that the credit-based financial structure made possible such industrial sectoral upward mobility. In such a structure, according to John Zysman, firms rely on bank credit—to the extent that the banks are the main suppliers—for raising finance beyond retained earnings.[23] The banks may be autonomous of the state, as in Germany, or might themselves be dependent on the state as in East Asian countries such as Japan, Taiwan, and Korea. The Korean banking system exhibits the most extreme case of dependence on the state; unlike the privately owned Japanese banks, identified by T. J. Pempel as "among the most centralized and controllable in the world,"[24] the Korean banks do not enjoy even the limited autonomy with respect to criteria of lending and response to "nonperforming" loans. Nor are the Korean banks "pawnshops" with high collateral requirements as in the Taiwan case.

The advantage of the credit-based system is that the state can exert influence over the economy's investment pattern and guide sectoral mobility; another element aiding this is the highly leveraged nature of business firms, which is a logical consequence of state-mobilized credit. When compared with Brazil or Mexico in the 1970s, where the debt-equity ratio of firms averaged around 100 percent to 120 percent, Korea showed a rate of 300 percent to 400 percent and Taiwan, 160 percent to 200 percent in the same time period. Thus, even small changes in the discount rate or in concessional credit rates between sectors can have dramatic effects on resource allocation, because the effect of such changes on the firms' cash flow position is much greater than where the firms have smaller debt-equity ratios.[25] The Korean firms would exhibit, therefore, higher propensity to conform to the macroeconomic policy goals of the state.

On top of this basic financial structure, the Korean state has erected a complex incentive structure to further facilitate sectoral mobility. The best example perhaps would be *policy loans;* at the end of 1981, there were some 221 types of policy loans among the total of 298 types of bank loans.[26] Policy loans refer to those earmarked to specific sectors or industries at lower rates than the already highly subsidized bank loans. Banks were allowed no voice over the allocative decisions, and had to passively accomodate the loans irrespective of their portfolio strategies. Moreover, in a milieu where real interest rates were negative (inflation is higher than interest rates) and where the state exercised ubiquitous control over all allocative decisions, all institutional loans should have been considered policy loans. In this situation, the state may then give large manufacturers greater access to bank loans than that of small and medium manufacturers, push the export sector rather than the domestic market, and favor heavy industrial sectors over light manufacturing.

So far we have only discussed the advantages of the Korean variant of the credit-based system. But the Korean financial system is also intrinsically unstable. Three reasons may be traced, two of which arise directly out of the incentive system of the financial structure, and one of which is due to the structural condition of Korea's open economy. First, the incentive of a virtual interest subsidy was so attractive that those firms with access to the loan window tended to resist going public, preferring to remain highly leveraged. But, then, bankruptcy was a perennial threat since highly leveraged firms were vulnerable to declines in current earnings to below the levels required by debt repayment, a fixed cost, compared to payments on equity, a share of profits. Banks often ended up carrying a huge amount of "nonperforming" loans, and if these are incurred by mammoth firms, known as the *chaebôl* in Korea, the state often has no choice but to bail them out through loans from the Bank of Korea, in turn fueling inflation. (A *chaebôl* is a family-owned and managed group of companies that exercise monopolistic or oligopolistic control in product lines and industries, isomorphic to the Japanese *shinko zaibatsu* (the new *zaibatsu*) of the prewar era.)

Second, since this system is perennially in a situation of what Theodore Lowi calls the "state of permanent receivership," whereby any institution large enough to be a significant factor in the community shall have its stability underwritten (the system promotes bankrupcy, but the state cannot let big firms go bankrupt),[27] it is in the interest of the firms to expand in size, to become large enough that the possibility of bankruptcy would pose a social threat. While the state is chary of the expansion mania of firms, once credit is allocated, it is difficult to track down the actual use of the funds since various bookkeeping devices can hide it. Thus, the excessive concern of the chaebôl with expansion rather than with the soundness of their financial base breeds instability for the Korean financial system.

The third point is that since Korea has a small domestic market and thus relies excessively on export (more so than, say, Japan), Korean firms are tested in the fires of international competition and are more vulnerable to external shocks. A slowdown in the global economy can shake the economy from the bottom, and firms can collapse like a house of cards, creating instability in the financial system.

Thus, state interventionism in the market is necessarily Janus-faced. The state can achieve its goal by manipulating the financial structure, but once it does so, it has to socialize the risk, either through inflationary refinancing (monetary means) of the nonperforming loans to bail the firms out, or through expansion of the state equity share of the banks (essentially fiscal means) so as to write off the bad loans. The former is indirect taxation on the populace, and the latter, direct.

It is in this sense that state intervention and manipulation of the financial structure illustrate the redundancy of the debate in the state literature, i.e., between the instrumentalist approach (the state as the executive committee of the bourgeoisie) and the structuralist argument about relative autonomy. States do pursue goals autonomous of various interest groups; in the Korean case and other historical instances, the goals may be security (something that is rarely spoken of in the capitalist state literature), and related to it, industrial transformation. But, the state does so in ways that favor the capitalist class. In the instrumentalist argument, it is merely tautological to say that the state favors the capitalist class, for such is merely a matter of definition of the "capitalist state". For the problematics of the "relative autonomy" argument, however, a concern with financial structure can specify for us the mechanism and the extent of the state's relationship with capital.

Social Consequences: The State, Finance, and Rise of Big Business

In referring to the state in Korea, scholars use various adjectives ranging from interventionary, discretionary or—wrongly, since it confuses Korea with Japan—guiding. Lately, entries such as the state as the "senior partner" or "Korea Inc." have circulated.[28] The silent counterpart of this concern with the state, however, is the absence of countervailing social power. Korea's historical development corresponds to Barrington Moore's third path to modernity: all other things being equal, the weakness of the bourgois impulse, as in China, should have led to a peasant revolution. This did not occur, for reasons that need not concern us here.[29] Capitalist development in such a social milieu, however, comes to resemble capitalism without the capitalist class or, in Gerschenkron's terms, a striking substitution of the state for the "natural" historical process of development. The Korean state has met comparatively little resistance in transforming the industrial structure of the nation because domestic resistance has been feeble. Not only that, what powerful group exists today in Korea, mostly the chaebôl, had to be built *by* the state. As such, the historical mission of the Korean state is not so much the "reproduction" of social relations as the state theorists argue, but the "production" of such: abortion of organized labor power through repression, and nurturing big business by supplying financial resources.

While Latin American and East Asian (Korea and Taiwan) countries all share experiences both of colonialism and phases of import substitution industrialization, the differing nature, duration, and intensity of the colonial and ISI phases made the social consequences radically different. Under Japanese colonialism, domestic capital was given neither the time nor space to develop; this was more true of Korea than Taiwan. Colonialism only deepened the weaknesses of the Korean bourgeoisie, placing practical and even legal impediments in the way of commercial and industrial investments, preserving landed capital as the main arena for Korean owners, and thereby locking them to the land and to their relative backwardness as a class. Thus, in the two Asian countries, but especially in Korea, powerful agrarian export interests did not emerge to play havoc with the state's industrialization attempt, in contrast to Latin America, nor did a protected domestic sector militate against the attempt to turn the economic structure toward export of manufactured goods. This has both opened more space for state autonomy, and made transition from one industrial phase to another more fluid.

But perhaps the most important consequence of this historical development has been the modal type of capitalist firm in Korea: the chaebôl. Three of these (Hyundai, Daewoo, and Samsung) are now so large as to be in the top fifty corporations in the world; fully one-third of the ROK's GDP was accounted for by twenty top chaebôl in 1978. Ostensibly, therefore, they bring a powerful force of concentration into the economic realm, and therefore a formidable competitor to the state. In reality, they are creations—productions and not reproductions—of the state and the Korean financial structure. This is true to the point where one asks if there is an important distinction in Korea between public and private, between state and civil society.

Most of the chaebôl existed as firms by the immediate postwar period, but they were small enterprises milling rice or repairing automobiles. Daewoo did not even appear until the late 1960s. The others did not grow into anything big until the 1970s; thus, the conglomerates are a very recent phenomenon. Furthermore, the characteristic of the big chaebôl groups is their concentration in heavy manufacturing, meaning that—by definition—they could not exist before the "deepening" of the early 1970s. Our argument about the Korean financial system, financial policies, and the role of the state would lead us to predict precisely such an outcome. Interest rate subsidies, preferential lending, and other such devices have been the energy fueling the growth of these firms.

We will see that the agenda of the 1980s has introduced some alterations in our picture. But we have now sketched some of the most important theoretical concerns of this study, and illustrated them with Korean examples. In this detailed analysis, we pursue historical contours through chapter four, not because of concern for a descriptive rendering of facts and dates, but because—without a developmental perspective on how things got the way they are—one misses the whole point about the *context* in which a strong state came about, and misses the specific developmental model available to Korea, that is, the colonial configuration of the 1930s. The literature on Korea written by economists rushes through the colonial period, if it is covered at all, as an appetizer to be done with quickly to get to their *pièce de résistance,* export-led growth and its manifold successes. This is a function of the immanent positivism and empiricism idiosyncratic to that discipline today. For our purposes, history is not just an important background, but a tissue connected to the living present, without which the present makes no sense whatsoever. The past two decades of "development" in Korea cannot be abstracted from the earlier decades of this century without distorting our understanding, much as a photograph sliced from a film would excise the film's meaning and perspective.

Chapter 2 is a retrospective on colonial industrialization. Originally, the decision to look into the 1930s and 1940s was made based on the suspicion that the substantial industrialization of that period might have served as the model for Korean development in the 1970s. Then a logic emerged, tying together the type of the state structure, its mode of intervention, and its relationship to private capital in both eras—that is, a logic tying together a strong, repressive state, rapid industrial transformation, credit-based system, and emergence of the shinko zaibatsu as the industrial leader.

The third chapter deals with the period of import-substitution industrialization of the 1950s. This is easily the most maligned era of Korean economic history. But, this was an important decade for understanding how the ROK, using U.S. backing, began developing a strong state structure on a post-colonial basis. Superficially the Rhee state was a captive of the United States, but Korean economic policy made use of American indulgence by pursuing an import-substitution strategy (however fitfully) that the Americans resisted, and it siphoned off developmental funds to the political tasks of creating a social constituency for the state. Rhee knew better than did the Americans the weakness or absence of backing for his regime in the class structure of the 1940s. This was the rationality in the irrationality of Rhee's political economy.

The 1960s, the subject of the fourth chapter, were the beginning of the switch from abject dependence on the United States to relative autonomy; one element making this possible was the normalization of relations with Japan. This normalization also occasioned the possibility of a reincorporation into a Japan-led East Asian regional sphere on a new basis, but one that, by instituting a dual hegemony, also instituted a peculiar version of dependence, which could be turned into advantage. The advantages were manifold: a flow of capital from Japan in the form of suppliers' credit, technology transfer, and articulation with the Japanese industrial structure, viz., being a receptacle for the declining industries. Politically, it bolstered the power base of the dominant party. But, the Japan connection was also double-edged: a turn to "debt-led growth," and the beginning of accumulating short-term commercial credits.

We will also discuss the financial reform—controlled liberalization—of 1965–1972, which was intended to mobilize domestic household savings, and why the experiment had to be halted. The Korean attempt, spearheaded by USAID and designed by American academics, to get the "financial prices right" has been often celebrated as one of the most successful case of proselytising by the global "money doctors," and used at times as the best model in relating financial development to overall economic growth. The lessons from the failure of this reform would seem a timely contribution to the current debate regarding the proper path of financial liberalization in developing countries.[30]

The third emphasis will be on the buildup of tensions, caused partially by the crisis in foreign debt payment, that eventuated in the inauguration of a bureaucratic authoritarian regime. It was often said that Guillermo O'Donnell's argument did not fit the Korean context, since Korea never had a real populist phase—ISI did not bring about a populist coalition, and export-led development therefore did not lead to a crisis of deactivation and could not have caused the turn to authoritarianism. But, in Korea, the critical link with regime change is not with the domestic sector, but with the outside world: a simultaneous crisis in the security structure that gave the ROK its strong bargaining position in the first place (meaning the Nixon opening to China), and a crisis of foreign debt repayment, threatening national bankruptcy. The bureaucratic authoritarian regime resulted from external restructuring and the "financial crisis of the state," both of which threatened the ROK.

Heavy industrialization (the Big Push) under the BA regime is the topic of the fifth chapter. The political rationale for industrial transformation has been ignored by most observers, especially the economists. I will discuss the Korea variant of nationalism, that is, a nationalism which, unlike that of the nineteenth or the early twentieth century, can no longer be truly nationalistic in the interdependent milieu of the 1970s; the more the regime pushes economic nationalism through industrialization, the more it gets into debt by virtue of the structure of financing. The rest of the chapter discusses the process of industrialization, with particular focus on five basic industries. We find that the Big Push of the 1970s resembles, both in the ambience and substance of industrialization, "late" development in Japan and continental Europe rather than "late-late" development in Latin America.

In chapter 6, we turn to the state mechanism for the Big Push through a nuts-and-bolts analysis of the financial structure and its policies in the 1970s. We examine interest rate policies, types of "policy loans," the plight of the banking system, policies of credit allocation, etc., and the strain on the state of this type of policy.

We also discuss the impact of financial policies on class structure. The result demonstrates overwhelming favoritism toward the large manufacturers, that is, the chaebôl, and the heavy industries. It will show how the rapid growth of the chaebôl were related to their rapid move into sectors favored by the state, for which concessional loans were available.

The last chapter assesses the political and economic impact of American policy, which finally led to regime change in Korea. It also assesses financial liberalization, which was in many ways the critical issue of the late 1980s. The liberalization crawled at a snail's pace throughout the decade, as state and business confronted the central problem of power in the Republic of Korea.

2

Soldiers, Bankers, and the Zaibatsu in Colonial Korea: Prologue to the Future

*T*HE FIRST problem one faces in discussing the role of the state and finance in the industrialization of Korea is that of locating the beginning. A spurt of massive industrialization occurred during the last half of the Japanese imperium, yet many assume, a priori, that the beginning of economic development in Korea should be traced to the Liberation, or even more commonly, to the inauguration of a growth-oriented regime in the early 1960s. One reason for this anachronism is that very little dispassionate work exists in either Korean or English on industrialization during the colonial era, and virtually none on the role of state and finance during the period.[1]

This remarkable displacement of attention assumes no visible connection, no sign of historical continuity in the accumulation of capital and human resources from the colonial period through to an independent Korea. Instead, the literature assumes a continuous deformation, making reference to the suppression of native entrepre-

neurial drive (leaving post-colonial Korea ill-prepared for an economic takeoff), or the massive and regionally concentrated industrial
plants which lay inaccessible north of the Parallel after 1945, or the
destruction of physical assets in the Korean War.[2] Much of the light
industry that existed in the South was, indeed, either a smoldering
ruin by the end of the Korean War, or abandoned for lack of both
operating capital and market demand in the post-colonial milieu.[3]
Of course, what was carried into the post-colonial era—the semi-
proletarized labor force and the extensive communication and transportation network—found their most immediate utility in political,
not economic, mobilization, leading eventually to war and instability[4]:
hence, more contributions to economic *de*-construction, not *recon*-
struction. Thus, the entire colonial period takes on an aberrational
quality in the literature, and the era of national independence marks
the proper beginning of an economic development sui generis.

Although the nationalist thesis on capitalist underdevelopment
in the colonial period has been exaggerated, still the economic impact of the national division was devastating. It is wrong, however,
to go from there to assert no historical continuity at all; in fact, it
would be truly amazing if the strong industrial push of the 1930s left
no mark in post-1945 South Korea. The analytical concern in this
chapter is different: if we do not see a linear historical continuity,
we nonetheless seek to discover, through the study of the colonial
era, a *pattern* (or model, or template) in Korean industrial development.

The first discernible pattern, it will be argued, is one of national
industrialization determined to a significant degree by an East Asian
regional economic integration, led by Japan. Whether understood in
terms of a regional division of labor, or dovetailing with the product
cycle as Bruce Cumings has argued, the Korean industrial structure
has historically exhibited a high degree of articulation with that in
Japan.[5] We find the genesis and the prototype of this articulation in
the colonial experience.

The second pattern is the state's role in the comprehensive and
semicoercive channeling of capital to target industries. We find an
uncanny parallel to the 1970s in the state's manner of financing
industrialization in the last decade of colonial rule—both periods of
military-related heavy industrialization—and in state creation and
utilization of new breeds of conglomerates (the *zaibatsu* in the former instance, and the *chaebôl* in the latter) as the spearheads of
industrial mobilization. There are, of course, serious obstacles, both
political and methodological, in assessing the extent to which such

colonial policy was consciously and assiduously emulated in later years. Yet, insofar as the gestalt of the colonial state and industrialization reappears, mutatis mutandis, with the inauguration of the bureaucratic-authoritarian regime in the 1970s, the colonial experience is well worth investigating.

To facilitate our analysis, we will divide the colonial period in two: the first half, a more or less a generic form of colonialism, with some differences stemming from the peculiarly Japanese—and German—approaches to colonialization: and the second half, a period of rapid industrialization that would leave a significant imprint on the future course of state action and industrial development in Korea. It is in the latter period that we see the interplay of a strong state (both the Japanese imperial state and the colonial Government-General), specific patterns of industrial financing, and a zaibatsu-concentrated private sector, all combining to bring about the industrial transformation of colonial Korea.

Regional Integration and Underdevelopment: 1910–1930

From as early as the 1880s, the Japanese interest in Korea sprang from regional security concerns, broadly conceived. In the words of Marius Jensen, the compass of Japan's strategic concern was in concentric circles radiating from the homelands: the "cordon of sovereignty" encompassing territory vital to the nation's survival and under formal occupation, and the "cordon of advantages," an outer limit of informal Japanese domination, seen as necessary to protect and guarantee the inner line.[6] The territorial contiguity of Japanese imperialism and this security concern, when combined with the fact that Japan was still a developing country itself, meant that Japanese policy in its colonies would be significantly different from that of, say, Britain. Whereas the globe-girdling British imperium left open the possibility of autonomous development of its various components (hence, the emergence of the Chinese entrepreneurs in Singapore and Hong Kong, etc.),[7] Japanese control and use of the colonies were much more extensive, thorough, and systematic; the economic structure of the colonies had to undergo radical and brutal transformation tied to the needs of the rapidly growing Japan.

In the first phase of Japanese imperialism in Korea the latter served as a breadbasket, its economic structure geared toward exporting agricultural commodities to Japan. In some ways, Japanese policy exhibited a pattern parallel to the one that Albert O. Hirschman describes for Germany vis-à-vis its trading partner prior to

World War I: namely, the attempt to prevent the industrialization of its agricultural partners, thus to create export markets for the colonizer's goods, and to destroy competitive industries already established.[8] In both the German and Japanese cases, there was remarkable coherence in the planning and execution of this policy. Detailed scientific analysis preceded the implementation, coupled with stringent financial control over foreign enterprises. The common link in Japanese and German foreign economic policy was a pattern of "late development," of having to protect and expand the market for nascent industries in the face of sharp competition from earlier industrializers. The Japanese case also was a function of capital shortage; unlike other colonizers searching for investment opportunities for excess capital, Japan had little capital to export to its colony. Rather, its concern was mercantilist,[9] maximizing resource extraction from the colonies and creating captured markets for Japanese goods.[10]

Japanese policy aborted Korean industrialization in two ways: a cadastral survey and agricultural reorganization to transform Korea into an exporter of rice, and later, a Corporation Law that empowered the colonial government to control, and to dissolve if necessary, both new and established businesses in Korea. In the absence of an urban economy, the immediate effect of the first policy was the classic manorial reaction as occurred east of the Elbe: an intensified seignorial repression, with a strong dose of violence from above pumped into social relations, primarily and inevitably in the *new* form of the "absolutist state"[11] (the Government-General, here). The power of local landlords had to be firmly grounded to discipline peasants and prevent the type of peasant mobilization that occurred in Korea at the end of the nineteenth century. What the loose, decaying agarian state of Yi could not provide for the landlords, political control over the restless peasantry, was now provided by a colonial state possessing considerable repressive capacity—through establishment of a nationwide gendarme (the *kempeitai*) and the military.[12]

The effect of the cadastral survey, which established the system of capitalist ownership in the countryside, was as devastating for Korea's peasants as it was gainful for the Japanese colonists and the Government-General. Peasants were stripped of the motley benefits guaranteed them by feudal arrangements, and the propertied farmers often found their land confiscated in a flurry of land registration which they hardly understood, let alone agreed with. When the decade-long cadastral survey was over, the ratio of independent farmers to the total agrarian population skidded downward, and that of landless peasants went up; various categories of lands owned by the Yi state were transferred to the Government-General and the Oriental Development Company; and vast amounts of unclaimed land were snatched up at firesale prices by Japanese colonizers, most of them *pied noirs* from Kyushu.[13]

The decrees limiting Korean ownership aimed at insuring a monopoly position for Japan's manufactured goods, and severely curtailed investment in the nonagricultural sector; no Korean was permitted to start a factory without permission (and the permission was almost always denied) and direct private Japanese capital inflow was discouraged, lest colonial industries compete with those at home. Through 1919, therefore, those industries that thrived in colonial Korea were mostly household industries that did not require company registration, and large-scale factories employing more than fifty workers numbered only 89 (and were mostly Japanese owned), even as late as 1922.[14] Industrial production accounted for only 13 percent of agricultural production as of 1920, and this was mostly in cottage industries such as dyeing, papermaking, ceramics, leather processing, rice milling, soy sauce making, brewing, rubber shoemaking, candles, etc.[15]

World War I, however, brought Japan unprecedented prosperity, transforming it from an economy with a labor surplus to one with capital abundance: a debtor nation with capital account deficit of Y1.1 billion in 1914, Japan was a creditor nation with Y2.7 billion surplus in 1920—a reversal on the order of Y3.8 billion.[16] About half of the foreign reserves built up during this period went for imperialist warmongering and political expansion abroad: military expenses in the general account rose from 26.4 percent in 1914 to 49.0 percent in 1920.[17] These years of surplus also started the industrialization of the colonies and other spheres of influence, with an estimated Y1.8 billion of Japanese private capital invested overseas in 1914–1924—most of it in China, Manchuria, and Korea.[18] It is in these years that the barriers to capital exports were significantly relaxed, and finally the Corporation Law was repealed so that Japanese companies could freely invest in Korea if they so wished.

This change came but slowly to Korea, however. A combination of land tax and other measures still ensured a higher return for investment in land ownership than in other sectors: conspicuously lacking was any colonial state mechanism for financing capital formation for industrial development. Return on investments in land therefore remained more lucrative than alternative uses of capital. Thus, all through the 1920s, industrial development remained sluggish, save a sudden injection of economic vitality in northern Korea occasioned by the establishment of Noguchi's hydroelectrical and chemical combines, which became the stepping-stone for the large scale industrial boom in the 1930s (more of this later.)[19] At any rate, as of 1929, the bulk of manufacturing output still remained in foodstuffs at 63.5 percent, followed by textiles at 10.9 percent; gas and electricity were at 4.7 percent, ceramics at 2.6 percent, and machine and machine tools at a pitiful 1.3 percent.[20] Small firms employing fewer than fifty persons constituted a 94.5 percent of the total, with large firms (more than 100 persons) at only 2.1 percent.[21]

Significantly, one domestic industry was given breathing space during this period: rice milling. But this should not surprise us, given the colonizer's desire to substitute Korean rice for upwards of twenty percent of Japanese production. In contrast to Japan, where rice hauling was done largely by the farmers themselves, a division of labor was established in Korea to speed the massive handling and channeling of rice into Japan. This process, with benefits shared by merchants and mill owners, is said by one economic historian to be the first example of dualism in the Korean economic structure: household production of the bulk of nonagricultural products, in parallel with the production of rice as an export commodity through the modern facilities of these mills.[22] Thus, the configuration that emerged during this period of the Japanese governace would appear fairly typical of colonial development, say, in Latin America: an economy geared toward the export of agricultural commodities, an incipient dual economic structure, and resulting uneven development.

What was less typical was the political machinery that was imposed on top of this agrarian economy. The colonial state was not only unaccountable to social groups in Korea (merely a matter of defining a colonial state). But it was also exempt from the supervisional scrutiny of both the Japanese cabinet and the parliament. This resulting separation both from Korean society and from superordinate Japanese influence was reinforced by the highly articulated, well organized, and bureaucratized nature of this state machinery.[23]

The remarkable autonomy of the colonial state was reinforced by the mechanisms available for financing colonial expansion, that is, an assortment of highly effective colonial banks and state-owned development enterprises; in the first decade of colonial rule, foreign capital was mostly used, acquired through the issuance of foreign bonds in the period immediately following the Russo-Japanese War. Most typically, the Industrial Bank (Shokusan Ginkō) of Japan would issue bonds to be purchased by the Deposit Trust Fund, which would then extend loans to colonial banks and enterprises.[24] At other times, the bank would underwrite foreign issues of colonial enterprise bonds. In this way, it was said that "about 46 percent of the foreign capital imported by the Industrial Bank of Japan during 1902–1913, that is, 46 percent of Y384.2 million, was used for capital export."[25] In that short period after the Russo-Japanese war when foreign loans exceeded domestic loans (foreign loan of Y1,165 million versus domestic of Y1,088 million in 1907, and Y1,427 million versus Y1,066 million in 1912), Kobayashi computes that 55 percent of the loans were used for war, armament and colonialization.[26]

Politically, these sources of funding meant that capital export to colonial territories merited little attention or investigation by the parliament or the political parties. Strategic decisions regarding colonial investment were taken by a coterie of military leaders, politicians, and bureaucrats, and operational administration lay with the Ministry of Finance, which oversaw the activities of the colonial banks and the Deposit Trust Fund.

Thus, in contrast to Japan proper, where financing policies—say, between the Sino-Japanese War and the Hara era—reflected political struggles of the time between the clan-*genro* and the bourgeoisie, often manifested in the Diet, financing *of*, as well as *in*, the colony would take on an apolitical character. Once the economic raison d'être of the colony was established, the rest was a mere matter of administration.

Banks and development enterprises moved swiftly and *sequentially* in administering changes in the Korean economy. The architect for such sweeping transformation was Megata Tanetarō, a Harvard-educated bureaucrat from the Japanese Ministry of Finance, who had come to Korea in 1904 to serve as the court's financial advisor. With the enormous political and military power of imperial Japan stiff-arming the Yi court, Megata created almost overnight the entire modern fiscal and financial system in Korea (a system that in some ways persists to this day). He built institutions of state finance, first by separating the finances of the court and the government, and then by creating a budget office, a tax agency, and later, a whole panoply of state-sponsored special banks as well as the central bank.[27]

The most controversial of the Megata reform was the "currency reform": a euphemism for what Lenin had called the debauchery of the currency, the most powerful act of subversion. The agents provocateurs here were the Korea branches of the Dai Ichi Bank (first established in 1876).[28] An ordinary bank in Japan, it was a bank extraordinaire in Korea, collecting customs and postal savings, procuring gold and silver for the Japanese treasury, and financing the trade between the two countries; it was also a depository of military finance during the Sino-Japanese and the Russo-Japanese wars, both of which were staged in and around Korea.[29] In spite of protests against wartime transactions in yen, and advocacy of native currency reform by Koreans like Yi Yong-ik, the Dai Ichi Bank soon began issuing notes to be circulated without limit in any transaction, making it by 1905 a de facto central bank and the mint for Korea.[30] The old currencies—the "mischievous" nickels and coppers, as the Japanese would call them, which had been exceptionally stable as large-scale inflation was impossible with these metals—were eventually withdrawn from circulation, but not without causing depression: exchange rates were adverse for holders of the old Korean currency, and the Japanese also refused to redeem the lower grades of nickel (paekdonghwa) and most of the copper (yôpchôn) currencies. Monetary assets were thus transferred from Koreans to the Japanese, and in the ensuing depression, many merchants "closed their shops and absconded, or committed suicide by poisoning themselves."[31] Thus, the currency reform became a vital instrument in the Japanese acquisition of the Korean property and labor.

With the dissolution of the old monetary system, the multifarious functions of the Dai Ichi Bank were apportioned and relegated to a set of specialized and commercial banks: to the Oriental Development Company went the reorganization and purchase of land and agricultural settlement, central banking to the Bank of Chosen, medium- and long-term loans to the Agricultural and Industrial Bank (later to be reorganized as the Industrial Bank of Chosen), deposit banking to commercial banks (as well as to the specialized banks), and small loans for productive purposes to local financial cooperatives (kinyū kumiai) and mutual credit corporations (mujin kaisha).

The resulting financial system was one of rare sophistication, overly so for a nation as unmodern and impoverished as Korea. In fact, after the initial flurry of activities related to agricultural reorganization and settlement, mostly done by the energetic Oriental Development Company, inertia set in; the groundwork for reforming the agricultural sector was now done, mobilizing domestic savings both of business and households was never in the equation because of capital paucity in Korea, and given the imperial policy of discouraging manufacturing industries in the colony, industrial loans could not be advanced. As can be seen from table 2.1, loans for industrial

use never exceeded 8 percent of the total institutional loans throughout the period 1910–1930, and were only 4 percent and 6 percent in
1920 and 1930, respectively.

It was not until Manchuria became another Japanese lebensraum
that the colonial banks could engage in activities congruent with
their capacity and potential. And then it was the Korean financial
system that provisioned capital throughout the newly acquired realm,
mediating Japanese capital to Manchuria. In their own way, then,
the colonial banks in Korea were, to use Hugh Patrick's term, "sup-
ply-leading";[32] their financial assets, liabilities, and related financial
services were created in advance of the industrial demand for loans
and other financial services in the colonies.

In the years following the First World War, the Bank of Chosen
and the Oriental Development Company sprinted to Manchuria, the
Russian Far East, and China, rerunning on a wider stage the earlier
performance of the Dai Ichi Bank in Korea. The Bank of Chosen
would arrogate to itself the authority of the central bank in Manchuria, circulating its own notes without limit.[33] The use of Korean
currency in Manchuria became so widespread that it was hard to
know whether there was more currency in Korea or outside at any
given time, a factor which significantly undermined the conduct of
monetary policy.[34] The international operation of this "central bank"
of Korea soon eclipsed the domestic one; it developed twenty branches
in Manchuria, as well as an agency in New York to secure American
loans to finance colonial expansion. It also served as a fiscal agent

TABLE 2.1. Total Institutional Loans by Types of Use
(Korean Y1000)

Year-end	Agriculture	Industrial	Commercial	Miscellaneous	Total
1910	743	1,808	18,165	2,237	22,953
	(3)	(8)	(79)	(10)	(100)
1920	22,865	10,420	132,196	16,968	182,449
	(13)	(6)	(72)	(9)	(100)
1930	173,735	16,953	154,704	59,592	404,984
	(43)	(4)	(38)	(15)	(100)
1937	181,321	165,928	319,922	142,401	809,572
	(22)	(20)	(40)	(18)	(100)

SOURCE: Government General of Chosen, Chōsen kinyū jijō sankōsho.

NOTE: Figures in parentheses are percentage share.

for the Kwantung army, conducting currency operations on their behalf and financing puppet regimes and companies on the continent. It also trafficked in opium, silver, and textile smuggling to Tientsin, trying in 1935–1936 to demolish the Chinese administrative authority in the area. But the Bank of Chosen's biggest claim to fame (or notoriety) really rested with the nefarious Nishihara loan, payola to a military clique in Peking in order to consolidate Japanese influence in China after the twenty-one demands—which, when it defaulted, forced the Japanese government to pay off creditors to the tune of Y156 million.[35]

The Oriental Development Company was even more protean. Founded in 1908 with an initial capital of Y10 million, this omnibus company was to finance any activity it saw fit, to increase the production and export of food stuffs. In the process, it became, by hook or crook, the largest landlord in Korea. Reorganized in 1917, the company then began to concentrate on mortgaging activities, extending loans to merchants, enterprises, banks, and trading posts in both Korea and Manchuria. By 1923, only 35 percent of its total investment was found in Korea, in contrast to 47 percent in Manchuria.[36] Later on, it would establish in Southeast Asia a branch called the Dutch East Indies Colonization Company, for development of rice, coconuts, and rubber; it financed the Hainan Development Company for producing sugar in the Mandated Islands; it funded the production of cotton in China and electric power in Manchuria. In the late 1930s, the Oriental Development Company began again to concentrate on the region of its origin, Korea, mostly directing its capital to steel and power development, making substantial investments in Chosen Hydroelectric, Kokai Hydroelectric, Chosen Steel, Southern Chosen Hydroelectric, and other firms. Only in the period of the 1920s was the ODC relatively idle in Korea.[37]

The retrenchment of the above financial intermediaries in Korea (as a proportion of total business) left a vacuum, however temporary, in the center of the banking network in Korea. The Bank of Chosen —now occupied with issuing debentures to finance the Southern Manchurian Railways and the Kwantung government, and usurping central bank functions in Manchuria and, later, North China—had all but abandoned the crucial function of supervision and control in Korea that a central bank would exercise under ordinary circumstances. The lacuna was eventually filled by the Shokusan Ginkō, otherwise known as the Industrial Bank of Chosen (IBC).[38]

Formed in 1918 through the merger of six regional agricultural and industrial banks (Nōkō Ginkō), and modeled after the Nippon

Kangyō Ginkō, the IBC was to finance industrial—and public—projects with long-term loans at low interest rates. This primary function, however, was not vigorously pursued until the 1930s when it procured enormous funds in the Japanese money markets—Y344 million through industrial bonds by 1937 and Y1 billion by 1945—to finance the machine-building industry, munition plants, and other heavy industries. Earlier, its real forte was diversity: consolidating the banking network in Korea; acting as an agent of, and selling debentures and bonds issued by, the Kangyō Bank; practicing general banking in competition with other commercial banks; handling provincial and city treasuries; advising the Oriental Development Company on real estate financial problems; financing the purchase of raw materials to small- and medium-scale industries; extending emergency loans for rice purchase to keep the price high in periods of rural depression in Japan, and the like.

Unlike the Bank of Chosen, the IBC was clearly a bona fide institution for industrial financing, especially toward the last two decades of the Japanese imperium. As such, it was the inevitable referent for those men who plotted economic development in postcolonial Korea: the similarities in the operation of the IBC (in the next section) and the manner of industrial financing in independent Korea (chapter 6) are quite remarkable. Given that, it is not surprising that by the end of the Second World War, more than half of the IBC's regular personnel had been Koreans, while one-third in the Bank of Chosen were Koreans, and not all of them were in clerical positions. Such remarkable upward mobility for colonial subjects was undoubtedly an artifact of wartime expediency, but even in peacetime, the number was never less than a third of the total bank personnel.[39] Men who went from the IBC to economic and financial decision-making positions in independent Korea are numerous and included men like Chang Pong-ho, Im Song-bon, Kwôn Sôk-sin, Chang Kyông-hwan, Kim Chin-hwan, Kim Po-yông, Kim Kyông-jin, An Yi-sang, and Yi Tôk-yong, to name a few. Former employees of the Bank of Chosen who were hoisted to responsible financial positions included Yun Ho-byông, Ku Yong-sô, An Myông-hwan, Na Chông-ho, Kim Yu-t'aek, Pak Sûng-jin, Choe Sun-ju, and Chôn Byông-gyu—but probably the most celebrated is Chang Ki-yông, who was the head of the Economic Planning Board and Deputy Prime Minister in the 1960s.[40]

The legacy of the IBC is important in another way: under the presidency of Ariga Mitsutoyo (1919–1937), it played a role in jump-starting Korea's first industrial and commercial entrepreneurs, men such as Min Tae-sik, Min Kyu-sik, Pak Hûng-sik, and Kim Yôn-su. For instance, annual subsidies from the IBC helped Kim's Kyôngsông Spinning Company weather the first decade and a half of slow growth; the IBC provided loans equal to equity investment for the South Manchurian Spinning Company (also owned by Kim Yôn-su) and then handled 90 percent of its business; it also gave many medium-term loans for Pak Hûng-sik's Hwashin Chain Stores.[41]

Now, if an important theme were to be singled out in the foregoing discussion of the Japanese conquest of Korea—with banks as condottieri—it has to be that of the dehermitization of the Hermit Kingdom, or in the terms of dependency theory, the incorporation of Korea into the capitalist world market. This is a fact embarrassingly obvious, and almost tautological given the *colonial* context, but worth repeating as a corrective to the prevailing academic thinking in which 1965 is permanently inscribed as the annus mirabilis, a turn to the world market. Not only was colonial Korea firmly articulated into the Japanese imperium—and through it, the world market—it showed progression upward through the world-system hierarchy: from the "peripheral" activity of producing basic food stuffs, plus some textiles when Japanese producers were not in protectionist moods, to the locale of war-related heavy manufacturing. The key mechanism inhered in financial institutions remarkably developed for such an "underdeveloped" colony.

The State, the Industrial Push, and the Zaibatsu: 1930–1945

The 1930s was a period of epochal change. Ironically, the global depression relieved the Korean landscape of its stagnant monocrop export economy, and thrust it fully into the Japanese industrial complex as an integral part. The precipitating factor was the deterioration of the Japanese rural economy, which, to reverse the trend, required a halt in the expansion of Korean rice production.[42] More important, however, was a complex set of policy changes occurring in Japan as a response to domestic crisis and the rapidly fluctuating international environment: the decision, following the boycott of Japanese products by other nations through tariffs and quotas, to pursue autonomous development, to create a self-sufficient economy within its bloc of influence: the closing of the "Open Door."

This de-linking from the liberal world economy proceeded, as elsewhere, with the abandonment of the gold standard and the adoption of a control-based monetary system, including exchange controls, which is said to have been emulated later by Germany, England, and the U.S. The advantage of such a system was obvious: it protected the domestic economy from the ravages of international economy and global depression, allowed for fiscal expansion at home through easy money, and made possible the promotion of exports through devaluation. The fiscal portion of the closed door policy was Keynesian: farm village relief and military buildup—with the latter overtaking the former at the approach of the war.[43]

Military expansion in the wake of the Manchurian Incident required that war-related heavy industries be developed as fast as possible. Korea, as an entrepôt between Manchuria and Japan and as a natural supplier of an abundant variety of mineral resources, cheap labor, and hydroelectricity, was one of the logical locations for the crash industrialization program: hence such slogans as "Chosen as a base of war supplies," and "Chosen as a base of penetration."[44]

Ugaki Kazushige, the Governor-General of Korea from 1931 to 1936, personified the natural leadership for the kind of industrial task ahead: an ultra-nationalist, he deeply believed in the need for a Japanese imperium of economic autarky and industrial self-sufficiency.[45] Thus in the 1930s, the real growth of Korea's manufacturing production and value-added would average over 10 percent per annum, a much greater rate than the one achieved in Taiwan (less than 6 percent); the real value-added from Korea's mining sector increased at an annual compound rate of 19 percent, more than 4 times the growth rate achieved before 1927, also remarkable in comparison to Taiwan (a mere 3.5 percent).[46] In other words, these were the first years of Korean "double-digit growth," although Koreans, who were ruthlessly exploited, found it rather less than "miraculous."

Colonial Korea was, in ways that Japan proper was not, a "capitalist paradise"; taxes on business were minimal in order to attract the zaibatsu, there was nothing equivalent to the "Law Controlling Major Industries" that regulated business in Japan proper, legislation for protecting workers was nonexistent, and wages were half of what they were in Japan. The Government-General of Korea granted financial priority and preferential treatment to the zaibatsu with respect to capital, materials, and equipment procurements; for mining firms, there was subsidy in prospecting activities and in the processing of low grade iron ores. For the producers of synthetic petroleum, subsidies ranged from Y19 to Y77 per kiloliter; 93 percent subsidy for every ton over the 1937 level for florspar, 65 percent for tungsten and mica, and 97 percent for aluminum.[47]

The colonial state also offered big business the two most fundamental preconditions in business engagement and practice: guarantee of political stability and of state investment in infrastructure necessary for industrialization—political and social overhead, so to speak.[48] Relying on Y1,400 million set aside for a five-year industrial plan for Korea, and other subsidy funds and revenues from bond sales in Japan, the colonial government invested heavily in railways, ports, roads, communications, and "other activities," the last one being the cost of maintaining law and order, subsidized through the Japanese government to the tune of Y15 million a year[49] (and something that the Taiwanese Government General, comparatively speaking, did not have to worry about). Energy was also critically deployed. While power generation remained in private hands, the Governor-General, along with four government-run electrical companies, controlled the transmission and distribution of electricity and thus guaranteed the zaibatsu cheap hydroelectric power for industrial use.[50]

Unlike the case with Taiwan, the government intervened in the economy extensively, taking upon itself the leading role in creating the "spurt" of industrialization; the government share of capital formation in Korea was consistently high, becoming more than half of total investment during 1930, and declining slightly thereafter as the Japanese zaibatsu began moving into the peninsula. In terms of assets, the colonial administration and its associated agencies owned close to 20 percent of the total Japanese assets: Y14.9 billion out of a total of Y88.6 billion of real estate and plant investment on the peninsula by 1945.[51] And again, unlike Taiwan which became a net creditor to Japan, Korea showed a huge deficit in current account, extremely low domestic savings, and low fiscal revenue owing to the immiserization of the populace, leading to reliance by the Government-General on capital inflows and subsidies from Japan.[52] The long term capital inflow from Japanese government spending would in turn be used in Korea to provide incentives for the private sector willing to relocate to Korea. Many young and venturesome zaibatsu, often blocked in the Japanese domestic market, responded to such enthusiasm and incentives, and came to establish their fortunes in Korea.

Most critical in the Japanese private sector's decision to invest in Korea, however, was the financial incentives created by the Japanese government and the latter's willingness to share the risk should the investment turn unprofitable. The fist half of the 1930s had been the most unusual in Japanese financial history, when deposits were rising and loans falling, and plant and equipment investment was largely financed by equity and not by borrowing. The situation changed by 1936, with a rapid increase in corporate borrowing; this should have tightened the financial market, but the state intervened to lower the interest rate so as to make fund-raising easier even in the face of the deteriorating balance of payment.[53] In a situation of excess demand for money, the government began intervening heavily in the bank credit allocative process, at first with respect to the Industrial Bank of Japan, and then later the private, commercial banks as well. The Temporary Funds Adjustment Law, enacted from 1937 to the end of the Second World War, directed 68 percent of that total fund allocation to the "military and related field," and if the allocations to industrial sector are broken down, 31 percent to machinery, 21 percent to metal, 11 percent to the chemical industry, as versus, say, 1 percent for food.[54] Through trial and error the Japanese government devised, over time, ways of channeling capital and credit into war-related heavy industries, and drying up the flow into nonessential industries.

The older and better established zaibatsu could depend on their own banks, insurance, and trust companies. But, for the *shinko* (new), the most adventurous zaibatsu, the source of capital was the Industrial Bank of Japan (IBJ) and the government. The former, organized in 1900 to meet the industrial sector's demand for long term capital in the absence of a developed and widely based capital market, was by the 1930s financing government-sponsored munitions and overseas projects, heading syndicates distributing and absorbing issues of the South Manchuria Railway Company, the Manchurian Heavy Industries Development Company, Nippon Iron, Coal and Transport Companies. After 1937, however, the Industrial Bank began to handle a large part of financing of the new zaibatsu. The Ministry of Finance might order the bank to advance funds to these zaibatsu, or to subscribe, underwrite, or buy securities so as to further essential industrial production. The government would in turn make good any loss incurred by the IBJ in the process, and also restricted corporate dividend payments in order to encourage reinvestment. Under the Bank Fund Utilization Order, the Ministry of Finance was able to arrogate the power to compel commercial and private banks to lend to specific companies in the target sector.[55]

Business and financial interests were not reluctant to go along with the financial policies of the state, for again, any loss suffered by the banks through the nonperforming loans would be indemnified by the state, which might pay in government securities. In this manner, even short-term credit came under the control of the state.

In the decade preceding the end of the Second World War, the Bank of Japan violated every tenet of central banking. Prudence in monetary policy was abandoned, and the bank took on every conceivable financial chore, even including long-term industrial financing. An "easy money" policy accelerated government bond absorption by commercial banks and enabled money market institutions to obtain a greater volume of credit at lower cost; various rediscount rates were progressively lowered, and the bank also relaxed its rediscounting eligibility requirement. Now eligible were special drafts, issued by essential armament-producing corporations and accepted by the Industrial Bank of Japan, and second-grade debentures were also upgraded and made eligible as collateral. Thus, through 1939 to 1941, the rise in bills discounted by the Bank of Japan recorded a whopping 578 percent.[56]

Yet, in some ways, this should not be so surprising. While financial matters may assume great importance in peacetime and draw attention and publicity, no war belligerent is ever kept from exploiting its resources to the hilt simply by financial limitations. In fact, of all factors of production, capital, in the financial sense, poses the least obstacle for the state in a security-related development rush. Time and time again, we see how warring states, especially if the war happened to be unpopular, resort to inflationary financing. As early as 1795, Kant noted an uncanny coincidence between the British financial revolution and her war victories of the eighteenth century, and argued for the abolition of standing armies and paper money to bring about the "perpetual peace."[57] The most recent example of the inflationary war financing would be the U.S. monetary policy during the Korean and Vietnam wars. At any rate, Japan—unlike England or the United States, who relied on either taxation financing or bond ownership by the people—chose to balloon the financial structure to create resources for the war; it was far simpler and more productive to create an internal financing circuit, and it did yield, for a long while, the same results with much less trouble. As Kaya, Japan's finance minister at the time, pointed out, the state's management of finance prevented the collapse of the wartime economy, but it also made a long war possible and opened the road to war with the U.S.[58]

By the middle of 1940, private banking institutions showed signs of reaching the limit of their ability to expand credit further. Lack of funds forced a number of banks to resort to the Bank of Japan for help, and even several of the "Big Six" banks, which had traditionally abstained from contact with the central bank, broke their custom and resorted to it. Once the financial structure became over-stretched, the state resorted to centralization. In August of 1940, commercial banks were ordered to form the Emergency Accommodation Syndicate under the leadership of the Industrial Bank of Japan, providing loans to essential industries on joint account. In the process, not only banking activities but also private capital became concentrated. According to E. H. Norman, given that Japan did not want and could not afford outside capital, and possessed insufficient capital at home, the state had either to utilize its resources or encourage the centralization of private capital in the hands of financial oligarchs for more efficient use. The effect of this was clearly visible in Korea.[59]

In a relatively short period of time, the grip of zaibatsu groups on the Korean economy became tight and concentrated, and they substituted, by the 1930s, for the national policy companies as the spearhead of industrial expansion drive. Three quarters of the total capital investment in Korea was estimated to have been made by the leading Japanese zaibatsu in 1940, the roster containing names like Mitsubishi, Mitsui, Nichitsu, Nissan, Asano, Mori, Riken, Sumitomo, and Yasuda.[60]

The prewar Japanese zaibatsu, especially the new ones like Nichitsu, really formed the mold from which the latterday Korean chaebôl was cast—in fact, the term chaebôl, the Korean transliteration of the Japanese counterpart, had been in circulation as early as 1932, to refer to Korean moneybags like Kim Sông-su and Pak Hûng-sik.[61] Despite the gradual transformation since the Meiji period of the zaibatsu from family-owned firms to joint stock companies, the prewar zaibatsu retained dominant ownership and often management control by a family or kinship group (such as the Iwasakis of Mitsubishi) and diversification into many industries and oligopolization through mergers and cartels. The dominance of these groups was such that the ten largest zaibatsu, along with their affiliated firms, came to hold 35 percent of the total paid-up capital in Japan in 1945.[62]

The most notable zaibatsu operating in Korea was Japan Nitrogen Fertilizer Company (Nihon Chisso Hiryō Kabushiki Kaisha), Nichitsu for short, of the Noguchi interest. In contrast to Nissan, which faced stiff competition in Manchuria from the subsidiaries of the Mantetsu, the Noguchi group emerged as the instrument of imperial policy and an "industrial ruler" of Korea. By 1945, the estimated assets of Noguchi Jun's empire in Korea was Y4.5 billion, accounting for some 35 percent of total Japanese direct investment, monopolizing fertilizer, mining, synthetic fuel, and electric power industries and commanding a substantial presence in other heavy industrial sectors. Included in this empire were Chosen Magnesium Corporation, Chosen Coal, Chosen Explosives, Chosen Aluminum Manufacturing, Chosen Synthetic Oil, Chosen Zinc Products Corporations, Soybean Chemical Industry, etc.

Nichitsu, with capital of Y62.5 million, was the second largest chemical complex in the world, and its operation was not only larger but much more profitable than its counterpart in Japan; with the cost of electric power at one half of that in Japan, labor cost and construction expenses at 15 percent less, Noguchi's Korean plant brought in a net profit of 31–33 percent while his Japan Nitrogen was only making the net profit of 11–13 percent.[63]

Electric power development in Korea was also in Noguchi's hand; 90 percent of it, including dams on the Pujôn, Changjin, and the Hoch'on rivers, and the Suiho Power on the Yalu, the second largest reservoir in the world, took place under his auspices.[64] The mainstay of Noguchi's industrial empire was, then, a huge electrical-chemical complex in Hûngnam, composed of twenty-eight subsidiaries and armament factories, and employing some 20,000 laborers by 1945.[65] It is no wonder that the Japanese atomic bomb project was, in the last stages of the war, transplanted to the willing hands of Jun Noguchi.

Mitsui was earlier involved, through Mitsui Bussan, in commerce, but soon began to branch out to light industries such as silk, cotton, flour milling, textiles, brewery, fats, oils, and paper production, and then joined in heavy industrial projects toward the end of the colonial period. Mitsubishi invested in railways, blast furnaces, chemicals, and machine tools, but its real strength was in mining. Nissan interests also deeply penetrated the mining of tungsten, copper, and gold; and Sumitomo, light metals.[66]

By 1940, industrial production was almost equal to agricultural production. In terms of the production ratio, heavy industrial output, slightly more than a quarter of the light industrial output in 1930, suddenly jumped to equal it by 1943. This remarkable change is illustrated in table 2.2.

The chemical industry showed the most impressive growth: accounting for only 5 percent of industrial production (including food production) in 1929, it quickly became the leading sector, claiming a whopping one-third of the total industrial output by 1939,[67] and between 1930 and 1943, chemical production would make a ten-fold jump.[68] Chemicals are the preeminent industry of autarky. Both

Japan and Germany, resource-poor at home, sought relief in the fabrication of synthetic products. Some of the chemical factories, particularly those making fertilizer, were comparable to the best in the world, and larger in scale than those in Japan. The Chosen Nitrogen Fertilizer Plant in Hamhûng was the second largest in the world.

The textile industry also recorded significant growth. The historical importance of this is not so much in the share of its output in the total (14 percent), but in its employment of over 20 percent of the work force in Korea by 1937. The number of spindles in Korea was 15,000 in 1934 but increased to 213,000 by 1939.[69] Unlike the heavy industry plants of the North, these were concentrated in Pusan and Seoul. Along with the hydroelectric and chemical complexes in Hûngnam and Hamhûng, textile factories in the Seoul-Inchôn area became the main pull for industrial growth in 1930–1936.

By contrast, food production showed a precipitous decline: from 64 percent in 1929 to 24 percent by 1938. In trade, Korea became a net exporter of fertilizers, explosives, pulp, gold, hard oils, and other manufactured goods.

The steel industry in Korea was less of a success than chemicals, but this was less for lack of attention than for failure at implementing policies. It was recognized at the outset of the Pacific War that the most fundamental limiting factor in the Japanese war economy would be its low level of iron and steel production capacity. To rectify the situation whereby iron ore, high-quality coking coal, scrap iron, and steel were mostly imported from abroad, Japan began emphasizing the growth of steel industries in Korea and Manchuria. To build a large stockpile of iron ore, scrap, manganese and other ferro-alloys, Japan launched a five-year plan to increase steel output in Korea, Manchuria and Japan proper.

The five-year plan was a resounding failure; its ambitious aim of building innumerable small-type blast furnaces never materialized to the level of professed goals. (We might say this was another

TABLE 2.2. Production Ratio of Heavy and Light Industries

Year	1930	1936	1939	1943
Heavy industries	20.7%	33.2%	46.1%	49.5%
Light industries	79.3%	66.8%	53.9%	50.5%

SOURCE: Park, "The Emergence of Factory Labor Force in Colonial Korea," p. 51.

"Great Leap Forward" that failed.) Nonetheless, Korea's importance as a supplier of iron ore became critical toward the end of the war, primarily because the cost of shipping was minimal and crossing the Japan strait was relatively safe. In 1930, Korea provided 8 percent of Japan's total supplies of iron and steel materials,[70] but by 1944, Korea was supplying Japan with 37 percent of its iron ore imports.[71]

Production of synthetic fuel received particular attention during the war. Noguchi's Korean Synthetic Oil Company, operating on coal tar and churning out 180 barrels a day, received a great boost with the "Synthetic Oil Industry Law" in 1937, with projected production of 14 million barrels by 1943. This, however, was another failure in crash industrialization, just as with the steel industry: it absorbed materials and manpower excessively, and was thus more of a liability than an asset in the war.

In magnesium production, Korea provided 50 percent of total output in the empire in 1944–1945, and coal production increased 131 percent in Korea in 1937–1940.[72] Korea was the most important hydroelectricity producer in the empire; its hydroelectric capacity was more than 50 percent of the empire total. In the last year of the war, Japan even moved its fledgling atomic bomb project to northern Korea, taking advantage of hydroelectric facilities that by then produced twice the total Japanese domestic output.[73]

Politically, economic transformation and reorganization of this magnitude demanded of the state a vast strengthening of its major functions: repression, legitimation, and intervention with the aim to restructure social relations. This phenomenon of a ubiquitous state was not, of course, confined to Korea. It occurred in Japan proper, and in Taiwan. Yet, it was more accentuated in Korea, in part because the populace proved particularly recalcitrant, and in part due to both the suddenness and magnitude of change, which certainly was not the case in Taiwan: hence, permanent deployment of two of Japan's best divisions as well as wide distribution of gendarmerie units all over Korea.[74] The extent of state repression and the failed efforts at legitimation are well documented, from the chilling details of massacres to harsh labor controls, to the unleashing of a classic police state for the politics of forced conformity: obliteration of the Korean national identity, language, and surnames, the institution of emperor and Shinto worship, and so on.

The legacy of state corporatism (as distinct from societal corporatism) that was implanted during this period is less well understood than are the details of industrialization that we have just surveyed, but it made mass mobilization for industrialization possible.[75] This "mobilization from above" sought to structure nearly every aspect and every unit of Korean life to serve Japanese interests; included here were efforts like the National General Mobilization Law (for labor control), the General Mobilization of the National Spirit (to enforce the *naisen ittai*—Japanese-Korean unity—policy), the Special Volunteers Corps, the Korean Anti-Communist Association, the Korean Youth Special Training Law, and various forms of conscription and participation in work details, "patriotic organizations," and the like. Koreans were subject to mobilizational scrutiny even when they went abroad, hence the Naisen kyōwakai (Japan-Korean Harmony Society) for Koreans in Japan, "Youth Protective Corps,"and "Patriotic Corps" for Koreans in Manchuria.[76] This sort of rapid and thorough social engineering caused Koreans untold suffering, and the pressure built up in this process would eventually explode into the Korean War.

This colonial experience, so painful that many Koreans would prefer it expunged from the memory, makes a feeble reappearance in the 1970s with the launching of the *Saemaûl undong* which mobilized the populace for rural industrialization, para-militarized places of work and study (turning students and other able-bodied males into reserve forces), and inculcated through an extensive campaign and school indoctrination the virtues of nationalism, anticommunism, and industry. Thus, the Korean state in the 1970s, (and perhaps the North Korean state as well) is consanguineous with the earlier corporatist state in much the same way that, say, the corporatist state of Brazil in the 1930s made an atavistic return in 1964 with the inauguration of the Castello Branco regime. What makes such a return visitation possible still remains, on the theoretical level, moot: after all, nothing attests to the failure of comparative politics more than its resounding failure to understand *causality* in particular political regime formations. Some writings do, however, possess heuristic value; O'Donnell zeroes in on the seeming complementarity between the need for "industrial deepening" and the emergence of authoritarian—often corporatist—regimes, and Gerschenkron, albeit of a different discipline, points to external factors, mainly war, in accelerating the commingling of crash industrialization and the illiberal state.

If, in fact, the political requisite for rapid industrialization and sovereign security favors the emergence of an authoritarian regime, that would explain, in part, the similarity between the colonial form of corporatism-cum-authoritarianism and the 1970s version. In both cases, heavy industrialization took place in bold disregard for comparative advantages in factor endowment—in the earlier instance, through the imperative of war mobilization, and in the latter, prompted by defense considerations following the Nixon Doctrine, or in President Park's word, "Big Power politics," which requires dependence on "only our own power to safeguard security and independence."[77] That meant the economics of *chaju*, i.e., the Southern equivalent of the North Korean *chuch'e*, both of which connote self-reliance and self-sufficiency.

The most edifying memory for the latter day industrializers, however, was that the colonial industrialization pattern *worked*, and that its success was based on close collaboration between the state and the zaibatsu, and on the building of economies of scale. Perhaps nobody knew and appreciated this better than President Park Chung Hee (1961–1979), a military cadet in Manchuria in 1940 and a lieutenant in the Kwantung Army—the architect of industrialization in Japan's continental territory—when war came to a halt in 1945.

This wartime economy of vast scope and daunting augury for the future seemed terribly formidable, but it had a devastating effect on the development of that class which has carried all before it in the modern world, the entrepreneurial fraction. Certainly there were Koreans who did quite well under the Japanese, then parlayed their capital and entrepreneurial skill into a fortune in postcolonial Korea, men like Park Hûng-sik, Yi Pyông-chôl, Ku In-hoe, Kim Yong-ju Kim Sông-su, Kim Yôn-su, Min Tae-sik, and others. But the Japanese presence in Korea was much too overbearing for one to argue the case of successful entrepreneurial continuity. By 1945, Japanese ownership, most of which was in the hands of the zaibatsu, constituted 81.7 percent of the paid-up capital of all industrial enterprises in Korea; 97 percent in chemical industry, 93 percent in metal and machinery, 97 percent in cement, 94 percent for lumber. Even in light manufacturing such as textiles and flour mills, the ratios were 80 percent and 81 percent, respectively.[78] So, of all the NICs today, Korea had the weakest domestic capital, combined with the most powerful industrial push. A ruthless state deployed Korean social classes in its own imperial interests, and saw no need to incubate Korean entrepreneurs. Singapore, Hong Kong, and Taiwan were exploited, true, but were allowed a significantly wider realm for domestic capital growth.

The division of Korea that followed the Japanese surrender also denied the South Koreans much of the fruits—at least in the physical sense—of the formidable industrialization of the war years. War-related and heavy industrialization, as we know, occurred in northern Korea, in complexes in Hûngnam, Kyomip'o, Ch'ôngjin, Najin, Sôngjin, and Wônsan. In contrast, southern Korea possessed superiority vis-à-vis the north in production of food and consumer goods, as table 2.3 reveals. Surprisingly, the table also shows that the southern half surpassed the north in machine building; manufacturers of machines and machine tools for mining, and of heavy vehicles, electric machinery, even airplane parts were housed in Seoul and Inch'on, and huge clusters of Korean subconstractors for machine parts lined the streets of Yôngdûngp'o and Yongsan.[79] The regional cast of the industrialization effort is shown in table 2.3

History does not repeat itself, it is true, and to the extent that it does, it is not necessarily first time tragedy, second time farce in the Brumairean sequence. It is also possible that a bad seed can produce a good harvest. South Korea in the 1960s could not see itself finding a usable past in the wartime industrialization of the 1930s; indeed the very idea is anathema to Korean patriots. But sometimes history proceeds as a straightforward text, and at other times important forces appear—as it were—in the parentheses. The 1930s bequeathed a set of patterns, a model, that could be the silent companion of Korean development, the parenthetical unspoken force that brings home the truth that people make their own history, but not in circumstances of their own choosing. The Janus-faced legacy of Japanese imperialism was to make of the Korean suffering of the 1930s a usable past for the 1960s onward. Although this is by no means the whole story of the 1960s, it is the part almost neglected in the literature.

TABLE 2.3. Regional Concentration of Industries

Industry	Percentage	
	North Korea	*South Korea*
Food Production	35	65
Coal	80	20
Iron and steel	95	5
Hydroelectric power	90	10
Chemicals	85	15
Machinery	35	65
Consumer goods	20	80

SOURCE: Edwin Pauley, *Report to President Truman.*

We do notice something uncannily similiar about the colonial experience and the later industrialization—the type of state and its role in the economy; the state's relationship to business, especially the conglomerates; the financial mechanisms peculiar to Japanese development, then, and Korean development, now. The constant variables are a mode of industrialization connected to security needs and, more broadly, to the harsh requirements of industrialization in a world that the Western powers dominated; and a domestic social situation making the mobilization of capital difficult without heavy state intervention, and consequent state direction of funds. Once these two structural constraints are enunciated, the regime type would oscillate within relatively narrow parameters. If mountain climbers are wont to say that they climb Mount Everest "because it is there," we may say that Koreans used a model of the 1930s "because it was there," and *why* it was there flows from what we have just said. Instead of being the miraculous model of the triumphant procession of neoclassical economics into the mysterious East, the Korean model limns its origins in the relatively ruthless neomercantilism of prewar Japan.

3

A Method to His Madness: The Political Economy of Import-Substitution Industrialization in Rhee's Korea

THE CHIAROSCURO of Korean historiography, as we have it, curiously whites out the period under consideration in this chapter. Perhaps it is the war that raged for three years, blinding us with its gleaming light, or maybe it is the refraction of the critical transition of the Rhee regime through the idiosyncratic prism of American developmental theory, which leaves so much in the shadows because Syngman Rhee does not fit. Rhee's failures—inflation, corruption, stagnation—draw all the highlighting, while the successes remain unpainted, because there is no theory with which to appreciate them, or because existing theory grows aphasic when confronted with successes that are not supposed to happen. Perhaps the best proof for the point is that Rhee's preferred developmental scheme, import substitution, is itself, ipso facto, seen as a failure, a part of the problem.[1] Thus this pause, the 1950s, is precisely that, a blank hiatus between the predatory developmentalism of the Japanese period and the benign miracle of export-led success; nothing remains but an olio of unflattering and contradictory images.

Korea was a "client" state, led nevertheless by a recalcitrant, putative nationalist. It had a political system where autocracy commingled with party politics and semifascist mobilization, thriving on a system-wide corruption, but this pastiche still carried the U.S. cachet of liberal democracy. Said to be an economic failure, the ROK was still an unaccountably expensive one, making unprecedented inroads on the U.S. treasury in the form of billions of dollars in aid. Political scientists have an epithet for this type of a system, *political decay* (another means to explain away the 1950s);[2] the economist's menu is full of reasons to dismiss the belabored economics of the Rhee period: wrong policy choices, the absence of native technology and technocracy, and the tried-and-true catchall for everything that does not fit, irrationality.[3]

Yet, cognitive dissonance is more often suffered by social scientists with their theoretical sclerosis than by the politics they purport to explain. It was once said that Syngman Rhee could play poker with two deuces and bluff his way to victory—an "Oriental bargainer," and "master of evasion," according to John Foster Dulles.[4] Outraged Eisenhower, too, complained of Rhee's "blackmail,"[5] but Rhee's point was to suck in the American hemorrhage of a billion dollars a year to bolster Korea's security, to finance reconstruction, and to build a powerful state structure. We will present here a tableau of a destitute nation that, using its geopolitical situation as both leverage and mortgage, managed to extract maximum "rents" from the global hegemon; of a leadership which parlayed a very short hand to operate a strong, and this time around, native state; and of an economic policy with method to its madness. What we do here is reverse the conventional images and discourses in the international relations discipline, and pursue, in Peter Gourevitch's terms, "the international sources of domestic politics,"[6] the contradictions and strains in U.S. foreign policy that could be manipulated by the client state for its own political end. Only when the image is thus reversed can we begin to grasp the rationality behind the seeming irrationality in Rhee's political economy, a peculiar version of import-substitution industrialization amid a dizzying set of arcane financial policies. We do not argue for sterling success, only for bringing to light the Korean agency and purpose that has long dwelt in the shadows of existing historiography.

The Political Economy of Alliances: The United States, Japan, and Import-Substitution Industrialization in Korea

Korea in the 1950s presents an archetype of import-substitution industrialization (ISI) supported almost entirely through direct aid, yet scholars have paid scant attention to it, and we have little understanding of how such financing is related to domestic class formation. André Gunder Frank argued that there were basically two ways of financing ISI, the first through bilateral and multilateral lending agencies like USAID or the World Bank, and the other through multinational corporations, and that the varying methods of financing can have serious consequences for relations between the state, domestic capital, and foreign capital in developing countries.[7] The best analysis of the state and its relationship to capital is perhaps that of Peter Evans on Brazil, emphasizing a *"tri-pé"* with the state as the mediator between the foreign and local capital.[8] Korea, through the 1950s and well into the second half of the 1970s, had its own *tri-pé:* American resources, local capital, and the state, the last serving as the broker and mediator. Unlike Latin America, however, this *tri-pé* functioned simultaneously within frameworks of political economy and tense geopolitics. We can begin to get at these differences and underline the meaning of "aid-led development" simply by perusing the record of American aid to Korea, and comparing this to Latin America and other cases.

From 1946 to 1976, the United States provided $12.6 billion in American economic and military aid to Korea (for Taiwan, it was $5.6 billion), with Japan contributing an additional $1 billion, and $2 billion coming from international financial institutions. The total, well over $15 billion, for a country with a population of 25 million in the midpoint year of 1960 gives a per capita assistance figure of $600 for three decades (Taiwan, $425 per capita). No other country in the world received such large sums in per capita terms, with the exception of Israel and South Vietnam.[9] The Korean total of $6 billion in U.S. *economic* grants and loans, 1946–1978, compares to $6.89 billion for all of Africa, and $14.89 billion for all of Latin America. U.S. *military deliveries* to Taiwan and Korea in 1955–1978, (i.e., excluding the Korean War) totaled $9.05 billion, whereas all of Latin America and Africa combined received $3.2 billion. (One might add that Soviet economic aid to LDCs, 1954–1978, was $7.6 billion in drawn aid, a little more than American aid to Korea alone.)[10]

The magnitude of US aid to Korea becomes pellucid when we look at the figure for the 1950s only. Table 3.1 shows U.S. economic assistance to Korea at an average of $200 million or more a year, with the peak of $383 million in 1957. Such figures are equivalent to 70 percent of Korea's domestic revenue in, say, 1958, when it stood at only $456 million.[11]

But the total cost to the United States of supporting Korea was really more like $1 billion a year: in 1956, for instance, economic aid was more than $326 million, military aid more than $400 million, and $300 million covered the costs for U.S. troops in Korea.[12] (In terms of military aid only, Korea received more than $325 million in FY 1959, in contrast to $83 million for all of Latin America; $259 million for all of Europe, $226 million for Taiwan, $246 million for Turkey, and $118 million for Greece.)[13]

Assessing the impact of this munificent aid is not easy, for what we face here would be an old methodological conundrum in social science: the lack of a reliable counterfactual, that is, a plausible scenario for Korean growth in the absence not only of aid, but more importantly and intractably, of the disincentive for growth that economic assistance of this magnitude breeds.[14] The verdict most often heard at the time was that aid did nothing for economic development, or even worse, doused Koreans with a welfare mentality. Thus, American development agencies found Korea a nightmare, an albatross,[15] a "rat-hole,"[16] a bottomless pit; even in the middle of the 1960s, some American academics despaired of the "dawn" of the day when Korea might become anything more than a permanent U.S. "ward."[17] But the truth of the matter is that Korea did show something for the money; it recorded an average annual growth of 4.5 percent in the period between 1953 to 1962. This was of course less than half of the world historical rate that Korea would later

TABLE 3.1. Grant Foreign Economic Aid Received by Korea (in U.S. $1000)

Year	Total Value	Year	Total Value
1951	106,542	1956	326,705
1952	161,327	1957	382,892
1953	194,107	1958	321,272
1954	153,925	1959	222,204
1955	236,707	1960	245,393

achieve, but the point is that it was not terribly meretricious in comparison to other countries at the time.

Another way to evaluate U.S. aid is in terms of fulfilling one of its most crucial objectives: financial stability as a condition for growth. Aid financed the major part of commodity imports, and the macroeconomic implication of this import flow was supposed to dampen inflationary pressure. Yet, we know ex post facto that the decade of the 1950s was wracked by an inflationary spiral caused by enormous budget deficit, and notwithstanding American protests, arm-twisting and occasional stabilization programs enacted by aid agencies, inflation did not subside significantly. The aid program was, in this sense, a failure in bringing its intent into fruition; instead of containing what was repeatedly pointed out as the bête noir of Korean development—massive government spending—it ended up buying a tumescent state structure and a fitful program of import-substitution industrialization.

This was not for want of either the expertise or the capacity for control of the aid agencies; they were staffed by competent economists ("surveying the Korean economy to death," as the Nathan Associates put it), and their unique "jawboning" power grew naturally out of sharp controls on the purse strings. How, then, do we explain Rhee's remarkable ability to sabotage the sagacious efforts of development economists, a practice described in the old Spanish colonial adage as *se acata pero no se cumple* (one obeys but one does not comply)?

We argue that Rhee found his space for maneuverability in the logical contradictions inherent in the U.S. foreign policy design toward Korea, playing one off against another. First and foremost, Korea in the minds of American foreign policy architects was a test case of great political and psychological importance (if not of military importance in a general war), and by virtue of its lines to Japan, a key to the entire American position in the Far East.[18] Here, the logic of containment called for a "forward defense state" capable of staving off the threat from within—and that meant a strong state. Yet, the logic of economic developmentalism in the 1950s, on the theoretical level and in the ICA policy thrust, postulated that the state should be decentralized, leaving the economic realm to market forces— hence a small, if not a weak, state. P. T. Bauer's attack on India's Second Economic Plan and his—and ICA's—belief in the use of foreign aid to maximize the role of the private sector, especially small business, is a particularly good example of this tendency.[19] Finally, the logic of regional recovery placed Japan at the core of trade and as the centerpiece of American East Asian policy, which meant that Korea had to be a market for Japanese goods, with open trade and export promotion (and not ISI), as Korea's overall economic policy; in this scenario, Korea was to be a dependent state. This was another reason why Rhee's turn toward ISI in the 1950s raised American eyebrows, even as the same was tolerated, even encouraged, in, say, the Philippines, Turkey, and Argentina.[20]

The first two components described above constituted twin pillars of the overall U.S. foreign aid policy under the rubric of the Mutual Security Act; the third was a geopolitical obsession by architects of the postwar global order, like Acheson, Kennan, and Dulles, which lasted right through the 1960s. While the three tenets together formed a coherent whole in a peculiarly American solipsistic liberalism, Rhee saw them as antinomies-cum-opportunities, the ensuing contradictions opening a small ally's realm for maneuver.

He sought to use the American's tolerance for a *strong* containment state to thwart their domestic project of a *liberal, dependent* state—for example, the forward defense state could be strong not just against communists, but against the market, and against the backwash of "regional recovery," which looked like neocolonialism to Rhee. This could work only if America were politically and militarily mired in Korea, and Rhee's favored method of manacling Americans was constant threats to blitzkrieg into North Korea and frightening Americans into maintaining their troops in Korea as a force of stability and moderation. Rhee's tricks worked because, since the armistice in 1953, many discussions on Korea during the National Security Council meetings were laced with handwringing about Rhee making a northward ho.[21]

To better grasp the dialectics of U.S.-Korean relations, we need to go back to the Liberation and the three-year American Occupation that followed it. The first phase of the Occupation—between liberation and the emergence of separate regimes, i.e., between 1945 and 1947—was a political phase in which Americans and Koreans under the Occupation sought mainly to contain an internal threat from the Left.[22] What is more interesting to us is the later turn toward cold war developmentalism, with its twin perched military and economic design, and the renewed interest in Korea's economic relationship with its old enemy, Japan.

Korea was a de facto Truman Doctrine country from early 1947 on, placed in tandem with Greece and Turkey. Between 1948 to 1950, the Marshall Plan concept was transferred, through the machinery of the Economic Cooperation Administration (ECA), to East and Southeast Asia.[23] Although Congress balked at putting up the money, Dean Acheson and his allies at the State Department went ahead with a fullblown ECA and military advisory program for Korea anyway, which ended up—by 1949—being larger than their counterparts in Greece and Turkey. While there were parts of the world where the United States could not do anything effective, "(in Korea) the line has been clearly drawn between the Russians and ourselves," Acheson testified in March 1947,[24] expressing the logic that inaugurated a comparatively huge call on American resources for this little peninsula, and gave the Rhee government the chance to display "the big influence of a small ally."[25] Acheson and the State Department determined that successful American ministrations in Korea were essential to the prestige and credibility of American foreign policy, which, in turn, joined power and plenty in a cold war developmental effort.

Congress and the Pentagon, however, never quite grasped such logic, being intent at best on relief programs for Korea rather than recovery aimed at development; at worst, they wanted to get out. ECA budget requests for Korea in 1949 faced stiff opposition, and the first third of the appropriation (in the form of aid bill H.R. 5330) failed to pass by one vote. Congress was curiously wrapped up with the remarkably big power of another small state, Taiwan, and put Korea behind Nationalist China in its hard-argued but shortsighted priorities. Even so, Acheson got the aid funds he wanted for Korea, by hook or by crook.

The military's narrow conception was well represented by General Albert Wedemeyer, who told Truman that only "political and strategic considerations of the highest order" could justify a rehabilitation effort bringing South Korea to a minimal subsistence level, let alone seeking to touch off rapid growth. "The possibility," he reported to the President, "of South Korea financing a program of investment and rehabilitation out of the proceeds of exports is not worth considering in detail. Although South Korea is primarily agricultural, it is unlikely that it will be able to export foodstuffs, even under the most favorable circumstances."[26] The real issue, though, was that the Department of the Army could not conceive of Korea's worth apart from the question of whether to fight there or not in time of global war.

Acheson had contempt for such thinking. He thought that global war was unlikely, and that a conjoining of power and plenty was the essence of turning a country away from communism. So, Korea became an object of American attention not so much because of "strategic considerations of the highest order," but because it was an important test case in the cold war, like Greece and Turkey, a state perched on the fault lines of the new global conflict, threatened both from without and from within. Containment as Truman and Acheson conceived of it was not primarily military, but rather founded on a developmental theory that assumed a direct correlation between political stability (absence of communism) and economic growth. In a directive to John Muccio, the U.S. Ambassador to Korea, Acheson specified that "military assistance must be viewed . . . in light [sic] proposed ECA and KMAG programs, as merely one aspect of overall U.S. support."[27] This remained essentially true all throughout the 1950s, with America pouring in $1 billion a year in combined military and economic aid to prop up the war-devastated country.

Thus, by late 1947, the logic was there, and by 1949, the institutions were in place to make South Korea a key containment country. The first was the Korean Military Advisory Group, 500-strong and deeply involved in containing the communist threat at the 38th parallel and in the mountainous interior. Another was the U.S. embassy in Seoul, the largest in the world: on the eve of the Korean war, it had a staff of 2,000 (and replete with, for some inexplicable reason, a huge mortuary icebox.)[28] More important for our purposes was the Economic Cooperation Administration (ECA), which had its biggest operation in the world headquartered in Seoul—again, well before the Korean War.

The ECA head was an archetypal liberal developmentalist, Arthur Bunce. During the Occupation, he had been a gadfly for General Hodge, the head of the U.S. Occupation in Korea, arguing that in fighting communism economic reform was more effective than bashing heads. But once the Occupation ended, the State Department and ECA ran the American effort in Korea, and it became a key demonstration country for liberal developmentalism. The 1949 ECA reconstruction program promoted investment, not relief, thus becoming an incipient huzzah for the miracle on the Han, Paul Hoffman being a cheerleader for a Korea that he thought poised on the ramparts of "takeoff."[29]

But, while power and plenty might sometimes conjoin, the interests of power and plenty may not always coincide: the goal of state building often competes for resources with the goal of stable economic development. The most obvious example is the drumbeat of rebukes to Rhee for not controlling inflation, a staple of the 1950s; but state-building costs money and if money is not there, you print it out against the backdrop of aid imports as the wet blanket over incendiary inflation. A flabbergasted Bunce at the ECA thought the remedy was to limit executive power over the economy, in the belief that only a well-functioning legislature could stop the reckless spending on defense and police—one of the main causes of inflation.[30]

Arthur Bloomfield's *Banking Reform in South Korea* serves as an illustration of the conflicts between development and state-building, the recurrent clash of American liberal developmentalism with idiosyncratic Korean praxis. An economist with the Federal Reserve Board of New York, Bloomfield came to Korea to create a financial system with a "genuine central bank," akin to the U.S. Fed, and therefore different from the old colonial system. The Fed had already engineered such in Guatemala, Paraguay, and the Dominican Republic, and sought to use the same blueprint in Korea. It would be an entity that could, once and for all, control the supply of money and credit to achieve and maintain monetary stability and moderate inflationary, speculative tendencies in the national economy. This reform proposal (which became the *Act Establishing the Bank of Korea*) is noteworthy because it singled out—as the chief culprits in inflation—advances and loans to the state and its various agencies, and stated that the only solution lay in decentralization, dilution of the power of the executive, and a strengthened legislature—i.e., good liberal logic. In the ROK, it had the additional logic of bolstering the opposition, not the Rhee forces.

As Bloomfield put it,

> To place the responsibility for bank borrowings by government agencies where they properly belong, namely, in the National Assembly, and to assure that all such borrowings have in fact been approved by it, we provide in our statute that all central bank loans to such agencies must be duly authorized, and that repayment must be guaranteed, by the National Assembly. ... The statute does at least place the responsibility for the loans in the hands of the one entity that has the real ability to control them.[31]

Privatization was the prerequisite of this Banking Reform—"getting most of the banks as rapidly as possible out of government hands into the hands of private owners."[32] All this is merely interesting for what it says about American plans; the Act would remain by and large a curiosity on paper, and bank privatization was not enacted until the end of 1957. In 1961, military leaders scrapped the Act for the farce it had been, and renationalized banks. Even today,

Korea lacks an autonomous, independent central bank, the state having retained full authority in matters of banking, and the legislature remaining as irrelevant as it always had been.

So, one could not have cold-war state building and a political system with checks and balances at the same time. During an era of hegemonic indulgence in the 1950s, security would come before proper economics, even for American liberals. The wrenching stabilization program of 1957–1960 was an adumbration, the beginning of the end for Rhee. It was only in the 1960s that the switch began to American directed program aid, with preponderant emphasis on total reorientation at the system level, articulating hegemonic and peripheral economies, or what Hirschman might call "a meeting of minds." So, all in all, Rhee saw clearly that cold war and developmentalism did not make comfortable bedfellows, and that when push came to shove, he would win over the cranky U.S. aid officers, even at the cost of periodic rebukes by the likes of Bunce.

While the primacy of geopolitics over developmentalism was a general thrust in the scheme of U.S. foreign policy, there was also a back-and-forth dialectic at work to assure it. Throughout the late 1940s and 1950s, Rhee flaunted hyper-loyalty to the hegemon by offering, among other things, the dispatch of troops to Vietnam and Laos, formation of a Pacific Union, a defense alliance modeled on the Atlantic Pact.[33] But once the Korean war was over, with the United States unequivocally committed in Korea, Rhee switched from obsequiousness to recalcitrance, a luxury that envious Chiang Kai-shek, for instance, could not afford. Of the three states to enjoy strong support by the American right—Taiwan, South Korea, and South Vietnam—Chiang was to suffer the deepest penetration by American aid agencies and to implement therefore the most far-reaching economic and social reforms. Rhee and Diem were more successful in using the presence of American armed forces or their precarious political and military position to play off one American bureaucratic actor or interest against another.[34]

Liberalization of finance was not the only thing Rhee resisted. He disliked the very idea of a stable economy and maximum exploitation of its presumed comparative advantage. Instead, he insisted on crash building of factories, an ISI program that ultimately sought to make of Korea an overnight Japan. In one sense, he had to make the most of the aid money while it was available, but there was something else: defensiveness vis-à-vis Japan, or more especially, American plans for Japan. "Comparative advantage" here meant linking a subordinate Korean economy to the revival of Japan. The existing literature is conspicuously silent on this aspect (it is quite possible the literature has not understood the relationship), but it is in this hitherto unstudied realm that we find the logic for the Korean variant of ISI. This requires some elaboration.

Economists have difficulty explaining Korea's ISI phase, its duration, and extent. Gustav Ranis asserts that the first phase of ISI was successfully completed (i.e., exhausted) by the end of the 1950s,[35] while Anne Krueger says that, to the extent that it existed, it failed.[36] Yet, the reasons for Korea's choice of ISI are never made clear in the literature, except for paying lip service (with vaguely disturbing automacity) to theories on stages of economic development. This silence stems in part from the absence in Korea of ideological proselytizers, the likes of Raul Prebisch and Celso Furtado in Latin America, or even Miguel Cuaderno and Salvador Araneta in the Philippines, who could powerfully articulate the logic of economic nationalism. But, that only begs more questions: if, in fact, Korea never had its own theorists, and what is more, given that economic advisers at aid agencies were intellectually and openly adverse to the logic of ISI (at best, it was a necessary and temporary evil before global equilibrium and growth could be resumed), how did this practice happen without theory?

The puzzle is more complicated when we look at it as follows: while prolonged ISI in the Third World was anathema to economists, it is true that the same could not be said for some U.S. protectionist interests (especially agrarian products) or to big business that could invest behind the tariff barriers in the Third World. U.S. tolerance, if not encouragement, thus contributed to the longevity of ISI in the Third World—until recent years, that is.[37] But, none of these were applicable to Korea in the 1950s. Its main exports—like tungsten— were not the sort to get anyone's dander up, and American multinational business did not wish to touch a place like Korea with a ten-foot pole: militarily volatile, politically unstable, it also had a very limited domestic market. In fact, Korea had "little or no economic value to the United States."[38] So, again how did ISI happen in Korea, without prominent domestic advocates, without ECA encouragement, without the support of U.S. protectionist interests, and without the connivance of U.S. business?

The answer is that the Korean choice of ISI was political, as it so often was with ISI elsewhere. But unlike Latin America, the political consideration was not in the domestic sector,[39] but outside, and the force to reckon with was the old enemy, Japan. Korean ISI was a defensive industrialization, to keep Japan at arm's length by sabotag-

ing the American effort to coordinate postwar reconstruction policies through recycling aid resources in the regional political economy of North East Asia. This was not the only reason for ISI, but it
was a very powerful reason; with the same dollar, it makes infinitely
more sense to build Korean industries than to purchase Japanese
goods.

Rhee was not so wrong about this. When American policy-makers
such as Acheson and Kennan thought about East Asia, they thought
about Japan: it alone had a modern industrial structure and it alone
had to be an assured containment state. Elsewhere, they operated on
the principle that containment could work only with continent regimes, and that meant potentiality both for political cohesion and
for economic growth. Nationalist China had neither, at least in its
mainland incarnation, and thus they opposed substantial aid for
Chiang's regime until June 1950. South Korea, however, had displayed its relative political prowess by suppressing a strong internal
communist threat (by early 1950)[40] and had a previous structural
relationship to Japan's industrial economy. Acheson's cold war logic
for Korea of 1947 was matched in the same year by the "reverse
course" in Japan. This carried an obvious logic for Korean development. In a memorandum to Acheson, Kennan wrote:

> [Dulles'] inquiry reminded me that I have never really set forth to
> you my feelings about Far Eastern policy in general, and has made
> me feel that perhaps I ought to try to summarize them for you. . . .
> From the standpoint of our interest it is preferable that Japan
> should dominate Korea than that Russia should do so. But, Japan,
> at the moment is too weak to compete. We must hope that with
> the revival of her normal strength and prestige, Japan will regain
> her influence there. But the interval will probably be too long to
> be bridged over successfully by any of the expedients we have
> employed in the past. . . . It is important that the nominal indepen-
> dence of Korea be preserved, *for it provides a flexible vehicle
> through which Japanese influence may someday gradually replace
> Soviet influence without creating undue international repercus-
> sion.*[41] [Italics mine]

This line of thinking was a curious anachronism: Kennan referred
back to turn-of-the-century politics. Yet the ideas really referred
forward to the 1960s and 1970s, in a prescient if rudimentary tri-
lateral concept, based on the revival of Germany and Japan. The
central problem vis-à-vis Japan in this regard was the resurrection of
the Co-Prosperity Sphere as the "natural" economy. Although various revisionist historians have linked this Japanese trade sphere to

Southeast Asia, they err in neglecting to point out that Japan's links with Korea and Taiwan were far older, thicker, and easier to revive.[42] Senator Elbert Thomas of Utah nailed it down in a question put to Edgar A. J. Johnson of the ECA, in June 1949:

> If you are going to restore the [Korean] economy you have to restore the economy in connection with the type of trade . . . that has been going on for the last 40 or 50 years. Is that not right?[43]

The answer to that was yes. In the years immediately preceding the Korean War, Americans revived in the old colony the classic pattern of unequal trade in which Korea would export to Japan rice, tungsten, ores, fish products, animal hair, and the like, and import from Japan cement, sheet glass, radios, machinery, and transportation equipment.[44] This was possible because Korea in the late 1940s was a thoroughly penetrated regime, where few important economic decisions were left to Korean themselves. But all of this is really very thoroughly documented elsewhere, leading to the inevitable and perturbing question: the relationship between the restoration of the colonial empire and the origins of the Korean War.[45] What concerns us here in Rhee's economic policy once he handcuffed Americans in Korea after 1950, and its relationship to Japan.

The Korean War was a deus ex machina for Japan's economic take-off. As Chalmers Johnson notes, it was the equivalent for Japan of the Marshall Plan, the United States having spent close to $3 billion in Japan for war and war-related supplies between June 1950 and 1954: "a gift of the gods," according to Yoshida Shigeru.[46] Dulles, noting that Japan was "living to a great extent off U.S. expenditures for the prosecution of the Korean War," worried about the Japanese need for U.S. aid in the event of a truce in Korea.[47] In fact, the truce —so traumatic that it caused a freefall in the Tokyo Stock Exchange —reopened for America the whole issue of regional economy. The problem was the viability of the Japanese economy in the absence of its "natural market" in the Greater East Asia Co-Prosperity Sphere, especially Manchuria and North China. Eisenhower thought that Japan had no future without access to the Asian mainland, whereas Dulles gave it five years,[48] and the Japanese reinforced the fear by threatening to establish diplomatic and economic ties with Communist China.[49]

The American solution to Japan's economic problem was, once again and predictably, increased trade with Korea, Taiwan, and Southeast Asia—i. e., restoration of a truncated Co-Prosperity Sphere. The idea of allowing Japan to trade with Communist China was bandied about in 1954–1955 but quickly squelched,[50] and the American market was out of the question because, as Dulles told Yoshida, "the Japanese don't make the things we [the United States] like," and so they should not look for "a big U.S. market."[51] American design for Japanese economic supremacy in the region was later crystallized in NSC 5506, which called for the reduction of the U.S. financial burden by increasing Japan's "trading capabilities with other free nations of Asia," to which end, the U.S. ought to use its good offices.[52] NSC 5516, which spelled out U.S. policy toward Japan, noted that Taiwan was enthusiastic about such trade but that the Japanese, looking nervously over their shoulders at China, did not particularly welcome it: South Asian nations were uninterested in Japan's economic problem. Thus, the United States had to work on Korea to open up to Japan.[53] Then in 1955, Chou En-lai made overtures to Japan, which so alarmed the United States that it intensified the effort to cajole Korea back into the Japanese trade sphere.[54] But most importantly, it forced American policy makers into contemplating an Asian economic bloc (and the Asian Development Fund) so as to delay Japan's economic rapprochement with China.[55]

Rhee was well aware of the American conception of the postwar East Asian order, and fought tooth and nail against it.This is terribly important, for the struggles generated by differing conceptions of the East Asian order—Korea as the economic appendix of the Japanese recovery in the American conception, versus Korea as an independent and soon-to-be self-sufficient nation (if only enough American resources could be pumped into the economy)—significantly shaped the orientation of Rhee's political economy.

Rhee balked especially at the American attempt to coordinate the aid program for all of East Asia: to wit, showering aid on Korea, but simultaneously forcing the Koreans to use these financial resources to procure goods from Japan. Recycling aid resources for the entire East Asian region was the "major part of the solution" to America's financial burden in Asia, and the Japanese, for their part, conducted intense lobbying to get the United States to spend its Korean aid money to purchase goods from Japan.[56] Americans repeatedly assured the Japanese that their policy of procuring Korean aid goods from Japan was intact, but noted that there were "practical difficulties."[57] The greatest difficulty was, of course, Rhee. Rhee called the scheme "the American policy to secure two dollars of benefit—one for Japan and one for Korea—from every dollar expended."[58] What this mercantilist wanted instead was all dollar benefit to Korea alone, to nurture Korean industries with U.S. aid in a zero-sum game. Rhee thought expansion of Korean industry should have its counterpart in suppression of Japan's. In other words, he would refuse to have a part in the long-run global solution for the "dollar gap", which, to rectify the massive structural disequilibrium in world trade, required rebuilding the economies of Europe and Japan.

Thus when the truce was reached in 1953, with Eisenhower calling for massive economic aid to Korea since "all eyes would be on South Korea after the armistice,"[59] Rhee did precisely what the Japanese industrialists in their "Korean peace scare" dreaded: he insisted on banning United Nations Rehabilitation Agency orders for Japan. American officials had already given general assurances to the Japanese that the Korean peace settlement would not drastically reduce procurement: an example is the Robertson promise to Ikeda of $100 million in offshore procurement in fiscal year 1954. But, the Korean rehabilitation orders, long expected to substitute for war orders, were not forthcoming, and the amount was now slashed to $64 million. The Japanese bitterly protested this shortfall to the Americans in the U.S.-Japan Consultation Meetings in August and December 1954. They also pressed Americans to get Koreans to use at least a quarter of U.S. reconstruction aid on Japanese goods, and to let Japanese traders into Korea for the FOA bidding; the American Embassy in Tokyo also got into the act, making a pitch for Japanese industries and rebuking home government for "disillusioning" the Japanese.[60] Eisenhower himself told General van Fleet that he was going to inform Rhee that "we have got to get Japan backing up Korea as a 'big brother.' "[61] But Rhee could not be persuaded: he already had a different design, a reactive industrialization.

Rhee complained in the same year to Eisenhower that "high U.S. authorities are of the opinion that Koreans cannot defend their country without aid from their neighbors and that the neighbor that would help them is Japan," and asked him to reverse priorities in the regional aid program.[62] Elsewhere, Rhee wrote in a personal appeal to Eisenhower:

> What [aid coordination] means is that [Korean] recovery is slowed as we are expected to buy more from Japan, and accordingly to use less to build up our own productive facilities. This has an immediate effect of once more placing our economy at the mercy of the Japanese.[63]

Ten years later, the same "high U.S. authorities" that Rhee dreaded—most visibly, Dean Rusk—would have the chance to translate the idea into reality: normalization of the Korea-Japan relationship, and the resurrection of Japan as a regional core. Thus, the period 1945–1960 is not so much a blank page, but more a breathing space, a period of keeping Japan at arm's length on borrowed time, utilizing what Dulles called "interim measures" before the solution for Japanese recovery could be found—even if that meant "a terrific drain on [U.S.] gold," according to the Secretary of Treasury Humphrey.[64]

The extent of Korean ISI may be illustrated through a comparison with Chenery's estimates of the "normal" structure of countries at differing stages of development and capital inflows. While this type of comparison requires much qualification—the "norm" being affected by geography, population, size of the market, among others—it does suggest a decided inward orientation, above and beyond country expectation at the same level of development. For the ROK, exports, manufactured exports, and imports all had shares of GDP well below the "norm": 1.7 percent, 0.4 percent, and 10 percent of GDP in 1955 as versus 9.8 percent, and 1.4 percent and 17.6 percent, respectively.

The bias toward import substitution may also be noticed in the growth of the manufacturing sector: the direct contribution of export expansion to manufacturing growth was 5.1 percent, while import substitution accounted for 24.5 percent. Yet, drawing attention to Korean industry's share of GDP in comparison to the "norm" (see

TABLE 3.2. Korea's Actual Structure for 1955 and 1960 versus the Norm for 1955

	1955 Actual	1960 Actual	1955 Norm
Per capita GNP	$79	$86	$79
Per capita inflow as percent of GDP	7.7	8.5	7.7
Percent of exports in GDP	1.7	3.4	9.8
Industry percent of GDP	13.0	15.6	17.0
Percent of manufacturing exports of GDP	0.4	1.2	1.4
Imports as percent of GDP	10.0	12.7	17.6

SOURCE: Charles Frank, Kwangsuk Kim, and Larry Westphal, *Foreign Trade Regimes and Economic Development: South Korea*, p. 96.

table 3.2), Anne Krueger argues that Korea's ISI was a *failure* in that manufacturing had not become a dominant sector.[65] That seems too premature an indictment. ISI is a tightly sequenced program of long duration, judging from the Latin American experience. Notwithstanding the rhetoric, rapidity is not its forte.[66] Even so, the Korean annual average growth rate for industry in the 1950s (10.8 percent) was far greater than that for growth in the primary sector of 2.5 percent, or for the service sector total at 3.9 percent, not to mention the fact that large-size investments in sectors such as chemical fertilizers had not yet borne fruit in 1960. Rhee also succeeded in channeling U.S. project aid preponderantly into manufacturing, transportation and electric power.

According to one estimate of the dollar value of production in different sectors over 1953–1960, the value of manufacturing output, just over half that of the primary sector in 1953, became nearly equal to it in 1960. Heavy and chemical industries increased threefold during this period, while light manufacturing recorded a growth of 250 percent.

Clearly, the Rhee era is not synonymous merely with economic degeneration and stagnation. At the same time, it is also true that the record is fairly meretricious when compared with the brutalizing industrialization under the Japanese or with the post–1965 achievement. The reason had less to do with wrong policy choices than with inauspicious beginnings and unquestionable calamities. Since Korea

TABLE 3.3. The Dollar Value of Production in Different Sectors, 1953–1960

Year	Primary Industry	Light Manufacturing	Heavy and Chemical Industries
1953	997	417	109
1954	942	564	146
1955	1,106	632	144
1956	1,210	684	151
1957	1,310	732	179
1958	1,318	811	205
1959	1,232	893	264
1960	1,343	976	330

SOURCE: Suh Sok-tai, quoted in Anne Krueger, *The Developmental Role of the Foreign Sector and Aid*, p. 65.

was a smouldering ruin in 1953, the economic agenda was survival and respite from the ravages of war; from 1945 to 1950, the upward spiral of wholesale prices was 70,000 percent, a figure that might properly belong in the same league as the Shanghai Inflation; the war damage was equivalent to wiping out nearly three years of GNP (annual average extrapolated from the GNP of 1952 and 1953,) not to mention the lingering wartime psychology that fed hoarding and speculation. Simply, economic miracle-mongering was neither the agenda nor the aspiration of the 1950s.

So far, we have explored the circumstances that give substance to Rhee's political economy: to recap, being a beneficiary of the Mutual Security Act meant that external and internal security took precedence over either economic development per se or political decentralization. The push for ISI was an attempt to resist regional domination by Japan. The dislocation of liberation and the devastation of war, all things considered, makes the sluggish growth of the era more understandable, perhaps even more respectable. But the major achievement of Rhee lay elsewhere: state building. We will see in the next section how the byzantine financial structure came to aid the process of state building.

Financial Policies and State Building

No nation can afford to leave matters of money and finance entirely to the market. Some nations are more active than others, however, in substituting and supplementing for the market, setting financial prices by fiat. Such interventions are often termed "financial repression," and take the form of establishing unattractive yields on domestic financial assets and allocating scarce capital to select groups of favored entrepreneurs and government agencies. This phenomenon, widespread throughout capitalist economies of the Third World, is said to further fragment the capital market, induce inefficient resource allocation, and, in the opinion of more militant monetarists, to be the very definition of underdevelopment.[67]

Korea in the 1950s was a textbook case of financial repression. The real interest rate charged by banks was almost always negative; savers reduced their money holdings, leading to a low ratio of money to GNP; bank credit was a de facto subsidy for licensed importers, mineral exporters, import substitution industries, government agencies, and covered government deficits. The financing of the rest of the economy was left in the hands of the private moneylenders.

Government preoccupation was with spending and lending:

spending for police and military, which were dominant apparatuses that brought electoral victory for Rhee, a president with a small social basis of support; and lending to selected new businesses which would back and replenish the treasury of the dominant party. There was one other key element of Rhee's program: keeping the foreign spigot open. Domestic resource mobilization, so important in other systems, was simply not an overriding concern. A state that lacks a sound fiscal base given immiserization of the populace, often resorts to manipulating the nation's financial system. Korea could do so without incurring national bankruptcy because Rhee could also manipulate foreign savings, using America as the "giver" of last resort. The gap between investment plus government current expenditure on the one hand, and domestic savings plus government revenue on the other, would be taken care of, it was hoped, by a mixture of fresh printings of nominal money and the ever-present U.S. aid, which Rhee knew how to wheedle better than any other Korean politician.

The Bank of Korea was used not so much for formulating monetary policy as for covering the budget deficit. Rediscount policy, reserve requirements, and open market operations were largely ineffective, and the only method of monetary control that was meaningful in any way was the imposition of ceilings on commercial bank credit to the private sector. But, here, too, evasion prevailed, and important categories of loans were not covered: loans guaranteed by the government, that is, to nationalized corporations and vested enterprises, and loans to traders purchasing imported aid supplies.[68]

The specialized banking system, established under the Japanese, was no longer functioning; all specialized banks now concentrated on short-term commercial transaction. The only exception was the Industrial Bank of Korea, but its long term lending for investment, too, was small in comparison to deposit activities.[69] Solvency of banks was always precarious, given the extremely small size of their capital and surplus. Operating with remarkably narrow margin of cash reserves, they were heavily reliant on the Bank of Korea for reserve replenishment as indicated in table 3.4. Improvement in the 1957 to 1960 period corresponds to the privatization of commercial banks and period of low inflation.

The government insistence on rigid and unprofitable bank interest structures was often contested. As early as 1951, and on many occasions thereafter, the Monetary Board of the BOK would recommend the repeal of the Interest Restriction Act in favor of a flexible interest rate policy; when the *monthly* interest rate in the unregulated curb market fluctuated as much as 15 to 20 percent at the

TABLE 3.4. Dependence of Commercial Banks on the Bank of Korea Credit

Year (A)	Loans and Discounts	Money Borrowed from Bank of Korea (B)	B/A (%)
1951	193	71	36.7
1952	578	327	56.5
1953	1,541	997	64.7
1954	1,844	830	45.0
1955	3,038	1,302	42.9
1956	5,403	2,693	49.9
1957	5,474	1,364	24.9
1958	6,917	1,050	15.2
1959	8,508	1,005	11.8
1960	10,447	2,667	25.5

SOURCE: The Bank of Korea, *Economic Statistics Year Book.*

highest point (the early 1950s) and 4 to 6 percent thereafter, the legal prescription of 29 percent maximum in *annual* interest rate could only fuel speculative demands for bank loans (see table 3.5). Nonetheless, the Interest Restriction Act remained intact to the end.

Given excessive demand for credit generated by inflation and low interest rates, monetary authorities had to devise rules of credit allocation. Broadly, two types of measures were invoked: the first was a quantitative one, placing credit ceilings on commercial bank loans, and the second was qualitative, giving priority to industries

TABLE 3.5. Interest Rates on Loans and Discounts of Banking Institutions

Effective Date	Discount on Bills	Loans on Bills (% per annum)
July 1, 1950	14.24	14.60
April 1, 1951	17.52	18.25
July 15, 1959	13.87	17.52
April 1, 1962	13.87	16.43
Dec. 1, 1962	13.87	15.70

SOURCE: Byông-kuk Kim, *Central Banking Experiment in a Developing Economy,* p. 125.

deemed either important or productive. Commercial bills for "productive" industries—coal, marine goods, textiles—were discounted at 12.78 percent per annum, some 5 percent below the ordinary rate of discount. Just what constituted "important" industries would change rapidly. Thus, in the early 1950s, loan priority went to those related to defense, relief, and reconstruction: production of military supplies, food production, loans for purchasing aid goods, government agencies and public institution, enterprises guaranteed by the government, and fishery and marine industries.

In the late 1950s, "important" metamorphosed. The Bank of Korea experimented with what was said to be one of the most elaborate systems of selective discount policy ever tried by a central bank; here, all private sector loans were divided into three: those eligible for rediscount, those eligible only under tortuously specific conditions, and those merely ineligible. Manufacturing in chemicals, textiles, machinery, metal mining, and food figured prominently in the category eligible for the Bank of Korea rediscount; ineligible were various and somewhat curiously designated "nonproductive" activities, such as service industries and consumer goods like beverages, finished textile goods, furniture, fixtures, cosmetics, retail trade, and so on. All the rest hung in a limbo of byzantine specifications and intricate negotiations.[70]

Loan ceilings for these categories, redetermined on a quarterly basis, were expected to be strictly kept. Exceptions were granted, however, for those industries in the rediscount-eligible category that were favored by the government (read: enterprises with "government loan guarantee.") It turned out that the range of exception was truly exceptional, and was often the fulcrum of complaint registered by U.S. authorities and domestic opposition on government credit allocation policy.[71]

The most acrimonious debate, however, developed around the exchange rate. Overvalued currency was a means of increasing the real value of the dollars received in exchange for won advances, and of maximizing the volume of aid imports received. It was also an integral component to Rhee's ISI: keeping the cost of imported capital and intermediate goods low as an inducement to investment and production. As for the charge that overvaluation militates against exports, a countercharge could be advanced that exports of primary products that Korea specialized in at the moment were inelastic, and that low exchange rates would lead to lower prices without stimulating sales.[72] Besides, more egregious effects on exports could be eliminated by instituting a catch-as-catch-can multiple exchange rate, i.e., various lower values of currency for different categories of export items and destinations. The silver lining in all this was that import licensing and other restrictive activities were a relatively efficient method for the government to control economic activities of the nation, not to mention the rent that could be garnered: tariff and other duties ranging around 10 percent to 24 percent of imports, as well as premiums from the disparities in official and real exchange rates.

Americans pressured hard for devaluation, succeeding in 1953 and 1955, but no official reduction took place thereafter until 1960, just before the regime toppled. In fact, defense of the overvalued exchange rate seemed almost a matter of life and death for the Rhee government. In 1957, for instance, the official exchange rate was 500 won to a dollar when the real value of the dollar was estimated to hover around 800 to 1,000 won. The opposition and the press—especially the *Tonga ilbo* which was owned by the textile interests of Kim Sông Su—bombarded the government to devalue and institute a single exchange rate system. The net result of domestic and foreign pressure was to force the government into forming a laager. Rhee issued a directive that "all necessary economic adjustment" would be made in order to keep foreign exchange at the current level, and the Ministry of Reconstruction (forerunner of the Economic Planning Board) declared at the same time that the "defense of 500 won to a dollar" would remain on the national agenda.[73]

The full tale of why overvalued currency, or for that matter the whole gamut of the "financial repression" structure, became so important cannot be complete without some understanding of the political support—or the lack thereof—for Rhee. There was something more than "misguided Keynsianism"[74] and fear of inflation by cost-push, something deeper than the often heard complain that "the market doesn't work here, therefore . . ." Reasons of politics were infinitely closer to the heart of the matter.

Syngman Rhee had next to no ties to the Korean body politic, having pounded the pavement in Washington for nearly four decades. Yet in many ways this was an asset; he was not embedded in the clan and patronage politics that hamstrung other political leaders, and could put together a coalition by engineering from on high, the executive as the entrepreneur of a new politics. But whence would come this coalition?

Throughout the occupation period, the two most numerous classes—workers and peasants—were arrayed against him and his American patrons in the quasi-revolutionary circumstances of the late 1940s, and a redistribution of agrarian assets that would quiet peasant land hunger was impossible because of landlord obstructionism.[75] Furthermore, Rhee's perferences for an ISI program to create "little Japan" on the peninsula meant that agricultural investment would take a back seat.

Korea's powerful landed class could have been a coalitional candidate in the late 1940s (and, in general, supported Rhee because Americans supported Rhee, and Americans guaranteed their property against revolutionists), but they really preferred the opposition Korean Democratic Party, arrayed around Kim Sông-su and commanding the central bureaucracy. This grouping was the most powerful in southern Korea, especially in its control of the ubiquitous National Police, but it was tainted by its associations with Japanese colonialism. So, Rhee's initial and really solitary virtues were his free-wheeling suspension above the stuff of Korean politics, and his patriotism—won in forty years of exile.

The Rise of Political Capitalists

Rhee emerged in 1948 as the first president of the new republic in South Korea. He now commanded the executive and a state with vast resources: a strong bureaucracy and police, plus an army that became increasingly bloated with a shower of American military aid; the vested colonial enterprises; the running sore of U.S. aid money which he knew how to wheedle as well as any national leader; and ubiquitous interventionary power over economic activity in the nation. Using these extraordinary assets of the state in the economy, he would build a powerful patronage constituency, comprised of a select group of old and new entrepreneurs. The old included the much-maligned Pak Hûng-sik, fresh from a raunchy collaboration with Japan that had made him a rich and vibrant industrialist; the new included Yï Pyông-ch'ol, who turned one or two vested properties into a huge chaebôl that made him Korea's best candidate for Rockefeller status. But Pak, Yi, and a slew of others who parlayed small beginnings into overnight conglomerates could not exist without the state and its ebullient, utterly political president, nor could they overlook the state's access to very scarce capital.

What they gave in return was what they had: bucks. These were entrepreneurs, but their enterprise was in and through the state; the best way to maintain access was to cough up cash for party coffers. The process had its embarrassing moments. For example, before the

1956 presidential campaign the Commercial Bank of Korea loaned 17 million won to twelve industries, which then kicked back, upwards of 100 percent of the loans to Rhee's party.[76] In 1960 things got worse, with the finance minister and the vice president arguing over which method best assured the funds necessary for Rhee's reelection: the 1956 path of whirlwind circulation from state to chaebôl to party, or the tried and true method of auctioning off a few more state properties.[77] The compromise reached was to do both, and even the Industrial Bank got in on the act, issuing a 4.3 million won bond to nine enterprises and getting 1.7 million back.[78] It all cost Rhee his residency in the Blue House, and he once again pounded the pavements (in Hawaii this time), but it illustrates the assets he deployed in fifteen years of coalition building.

One outcome of Japan's intense, overbearing, and brutal colonial development policy, as we discussed in the last chapter, was the smothering of native entrepreneurial talent and the birth of a capitalism without any significant participation by Korean capitalists: Korean ownership was almost nil in heavy and chemical industries, and even in light manufacturing such as flour milling and textiles, Korean ownership was less than 20 percent. A few entrepreneurs, like Pak Hûng-sik and Kim Yôn-su, managed to garner commercial capital by collaborating with the Japanese, some of the first and better-known instances of the Korean *comprador*, or in André Gunder Frank's term, *lumpen*-bourgeoisie. But continuity into and through post-colonial Korea, it did not form: of the top fifty chaebôl in Korea today, only three or so had founders who accumulated wealth under the Japanese: Samyang, the Tusan Group, Samsung, and perhaps Lucky-Goldstar.[79]

The colonial period may not have passed on accumulated wealth and Schumpeterian entrepreneurial talent to posterity, but it did pass on something else that remained critically important, right up to this day: Korean entrepreneurs who, with or without a sovereign state, were forced to learn that collaboration with political authority was the essential prerequisite for business survival and expansion. They were essentially "political capitalists." Little wonder, then, that the popular acceptance of big business in Korea has always neatly dovetailed that of the regime in power. Then as now, politics, and not innovative drive, has always been considered the umbilical cord nurturing big business in Korea.

If detachment of monied might from political power were to be taken as a valuable goal in itself—as in the liberal paradigm—Japanese colonial rule was a bad augury for the future. There were

differences, however, in benefits that could be accrued by businessmen through their connection with political power; whereas entrepreneurs looked covetously at the colonial authority for extension of
business subsidies and loan allocations *within clearly circumscribed
limits,* businessmen in the 1945–1960 period rushed to the state as
if it were a grand jackpot. In some ways, it was.

The first prize was Japanese vested enterprises, entrusted first to
the American Office of the Property Custodian and later to the state.
Estimated at 85 percent of the national wealth, and including 3,551
operating plants and firms, land, infrastructure, and inventories, its
gradual auction through 1957 proved to be the greatest bargain in
history; small-time businessmen who cultivated government connections could now claim ownership of large factories, with inflation
taking care of the cost.[80] According to one account,

> Japanese investment in industries on the eve of the Liberation
> amounted to 94 percent of the total. . . . Select individuals who
> received vested enterprises did so at minimal cost. Take an ex-
> ample of one textile plant valued at 3 billion won in 1947. It was
> later appraised down to 700 million won, and then auctioned off
> at 360 million won: a mere one eighth of the original price and a
> half of the re-appraised price. Payments were to be in annual
> installments stretching fifteen years in accordance to the Law
> Governing Disposal of Vested Properties. In those fifteen years,
> however, the price jumped 300 times, and so the factory was a
> give-away. Payments were annual . . . but only fools paid debt on
> time: it was always rescheduled, and then finally, the intervening
> war was an excuse never to pay.[81] [Author's Translation]

Government jurisdiction also led to windfall profits in the following: noncompetitive allocation of import quotas and licenses; access
to bank loans, aid funds, and material; noncompetitive award of
government and U.S. military contracts for reconstruction activities.
Select examples might illustrate the mechanism.

A scandal involving tungsten, well publicized and long remem-
bered, is an example in the abuse of import license and foreign
exchange allocation: $3 million from government exports of tung-
sten were distributed to a group of entrepreneurs holding licenses to
import grain and fertilizers, entrepreneurs who reaped huge profits
through the vastly overvalued exchange rate and monopoly sales,
even after paying back the government handsomely for the initial
loan and other favors bestowed.[82]

State-mediated lending in hyperinflationary conditions (the
wholesale price index jumped 7,000 percent from 1947 to 1954)

constitutes another subsidy, which should need no elaboration, only a simple calibration: a man borrowing 400 million won in 1947 on three-year repayment terms would have seen the principal shrink down to a mere one-fourth in May of 1950, and if payment of principal and interest were rescheduled beyond initial maturity, say to 1954, the principal would have shrank to 54,000 won. If the loan were for factory construction through ICA project aid, profits would include lucrative exchange rate differentials; ICA would require of the prospective factory builder only some 15 percent to 20 percent of equity, which could be financed by borrowing a small sum from a commercial bank, and then putting it on collateral deposit in the Industrial Bank, in return for a much larger loan of long term and low interest. Such a loan would then be converted into U.S. dollars through official exchange rates, to finance construction.

On the production side, raw materials were purchased with KRIK aid at the official exchange rate, and profit was further assured through monopoly practice. In a nutshell, this is how Yi Pyŏng-ch'ŏl of Samsung, one of Korea's richest men, is said to have built his fortune in the 1950s.[83] Before this time, he had owned a small rice mill, some real estate, and a trading concern, all concentrated in Taegu; in the 1950s, he owned huge sugar (Cheil Chedang) and textile (Cheil Mojik) factories through the mechanisms described above, and by the end of the 1950s, was known as a formidable chaebôl leader. Not surprisingly, Yi was later accused of having contributed 64 million won to the Liberal Party coffer.

Procuring noncompetitive contracts from the government and the U.S. military was the forte of Chông Chu-yông of Hyundai. A young proprietor of an automobile repair shop, his eldorado years began in wartime Pusan where his brother, a graduate of Aoyama Gakuin in Tokyo and fluent in English, wrested contracts to build army barracks and airport runways for Americans; the brothers were to repeat the same in Vietnam and Thailand.

But, perhaps nobody benefited from intimacy with the state and the U.S. military more than Hanjin, otherwise known as the Korean Air Group. The basic asset of Cho Chung-hun in 1945 was one used truck and some command of English, which turned out to go a long way and quickly; during the Korean War, his planes crisscrossed the peninsula with American military supplies. By 1956, he contracted to supply transportation for the U.S. Eighth Army at $70,000, a meager sum by today's standards but a fortune at the time; the receipts grew in succeeding years to $100,000 in 1957, $300,000 in 1958, $1 million in 1959, and $2.28 million by 1960. In 1961, the

U.S. Air Force rewarded Cho for his services by disposing—at fire sale prices—eighty surplus buses, which he turned into the first "Express" buses running the Seoul-Inch'on route. But, all this was only prelude for the story behind the U.S. role in the growth of this Korean chaebôl; the Fortuna in the waiting was the Vietnam War.[84]

All of the above—the disposition of state properties through noncompetitive means, access to loans in a hyperinflationary milieu, import quotas and licenses, procurement of noncompetitive government contracts—are the stuff of what Ann Krueger might call "the political economy of the rent-seeking society," with all its deleterious and suboptimal effects.[85] But, one might add that the dynamics of the Korean political economy were such that economic efficiency lost in rent-seeking was recovered in the political realm, with the state and business sustaining each other like Siamese twins, buttressed by the police and a huge bureaucracy.

But all good things must come to an end, and the Gordian knot was cut by the very power that had given Korea so much aid and that ballooned an artificial middle class through that same aid: the United States.[86] Americans finally abandoned the policies of the Mutual Security Act, and demanded a wrenching stabilization program as a precondition for aid.

1957: History in the Gear of Change

In the existing history of Korean economy, the year 1957 is just a little blip on the radar screen, a year that began a stabilization program, but otherwise innocuous. In truth, though, 1957 marked something vastly more important than run-of-the-mill stabilization; it inaugurated in Washington an era of foreign aid that sought its foundation in a holistic theory of development, of modernization, and not just security contingencies. The momentous happening that year was the instituting of the Development Loan Fund (DLF), which signaled among other things the resolve to switch from grants-in-aid to productive loans, and away from putting out brush fires toward concentration on the developing world.

This had profound implications for Korea. Korea was the most outstanding *negative* example in the minds of the architects and supporters of the DLF, and when they thought about a new direction in aid, it was invariably in terms of avoiding the Korean type of quagmire: a situation whereby America was beefing up the military and the bureaucracy in Korea, pouring money into industrialization schemes that made a mockery of America's goals in the East Asian region, and yet hapless to change course, handcuffed as it was.[87] But, if the strongest American advice had not been effective with Rhee, how was it that America could switch gears so rapidly away from the Mutual Security Program aid in 1957, displacing emphasis on the military with the economic?

The answer is that the new direction in foreign aid presented development not as a virtue in itself but as the most expedient means to the political ends of the cold war. This idea, soon to find perfect patronage in the Kennedy brothers (in face, the older one launched the opening salvo of development cooperation in 1958 with the Kennedy-Cooper resolution), had numerous advocates at the Center for International Studies at MIT.[88] People like C. D. Jackson and Nelson Rockefeller saw to it that the ideas of W. W. Rostow and Max Milliken got into the "official think-stream" of the administration.[89] Rostow's developmentalism caught Rockefeller's attention because it was really a cost-benefit analysis of the Cold War, of making Russia and China scream economically so that they would give up their military expansionism. In East Asia, it meant this; for Peking:

> Frustrate its efforts at geographical expansion whether undertaken by soft means or hard; outrace its economic efforts in India, Burma, etc; put Japan firmly on its feet within the Free World; and then the latent forces for radical change in Peking will win, aided by the fact that the Long March veterans will then be out of the picture. . . . *It requires that [at] the key points of competition— notably the arms race and Asian economic growth—we throw our full weight in resources and technical know-how into the scales and make the enemy break his back in the effort to stay in the race.*[90] [Italics mine]

Such economic strategies of managing the Cold War had been percolating since 1955 if not earlier, but they finally got a boost when Dulles threw his weight behind them in 1957.[91] The timing was fortuitous: America faced at the end of the 1950s deteriorating balance of payments, which by 1958 translated into current account deficits of $4 billion, and rapidly rising federal deficits.[92] In that context, the Mutual Security Program got panned in 1957, with the Fairless Committee—the President's Citizen Advisers on the Mutual Security Act—recommending greater emphasis on private initiative and capital in development, separation of military and economic aid, and most importantly, replacing grants with development loans.[93] The Johnston Report, issued in the same year, seconded the recommendations made by the Fairless Committee, while placing a new emphasis on Rostovian long-term economic development as a major objective in foreign economic policy, thus adumbrating the new era about to begin.[94] ICA was bitterly opposed to separating military and economic aid, as well as replacing grants with loans to a substantial degree, thus clinging to the old, indulgent days of the Mutual Security Act.[95] But the ICA opposition was brushed aside (in fact, ICA was itself soon dismantled), and a modest loan program— the Development Loan Fund (DLF)—was instituted as a pilot project to open the new era of foreign aid. It was immediately applied, among other places, to Korea.

The influence of Rostovian ideas on Korea may be gleaned from the NSC documents on U.S. policy toward Korea in 1957 (even if the full impact was not felt until 1960.) The principal document called for reducing ROK military forces by at least four active divisions at the time, and lowering American financial contributions to Korea while concentrating on training technical and professional personnel, restoring ties with Japan, and most immediately, "adopting and implementing sound economic and fiscal policies, taking an increasingly greater responsibilities for improving fiscal management."[96] In other words, Rhee's political economy was to be no more.

The goad to improve Korea's fiscal management took the form of a wrenching stabilization program (1957–1960). Formulated and executed by the Combined Economic Board where the American voice was preponderant, it was an all-out attack on incontinent government spending, but it also retarded new investment. No net monetary expansion was allowed for 1957 and the first half of 1958, to be followed by a small increase thereafter; a ceiling was imposed on the government deficit; and commercial banks were required to receive an approval with the Monetary Board of BOK, now under scrutiny and direction of the Combined Economic Board, for loans exceeding 10 million won. The program succeeded in dampening hyperinflation, partly thanks to bumper crops in 1957 and 1958 that sharply reduced grain prices. However, in a manner reminiscent of the notorious Chilean deflationary program of the same period by the Klein-Saks mission,[97] the economy entered into a long recessionary oblivion. The expected spurt in investment from the private sector never came, unemployment soared, GNP growth plummeted. Chileans at least had the global "money doctors" to blame for the butchered job, but Rhee had none, for stabilization was Washington's prerogative.

Were this prolonged recession and the regime demise that came in the midst of it related? At the very minimum, it would seem reasonable to postulate that economic downturn, if not an outright crisis, is always a contributing factor in regime breakdown. But, something else had to slide downward beside the GNP growth rate before one saw the writing on the wall: decline in aid as a *historically irreversible* trend. Because if it could be reversed, Rhee would have bent all his considerable manipulative skills to doing so. But it was not to be. Aid dropped from the all time high of $382,893,000 in 1957 (that year's extraordinarily high figure was to absorb deflationary shock) to $321,271,000 in 1958; then came a shocking $100 million cut in 1959, slashing the aid figure down to $222,204 million.

The Rhee system, in short, was now in deep trouble. Its survival was predicated on his skills as a bargainer, his virtuoso bluffing, his ability to wrest resources away from a pliant America. But the U.S. was less indulgent as the 1950s turned into the 1960s, aid reduction being the Sword of Damocles not simply hanging over the health of the economy, but Rhee's political system as well.

4

In the East Asian Cauldron: Korea Takes Off

*H*UMAN HISTORY is like paleontology, Marx once said; for a long time even the best intelligences fail to see what is before their very noses, and then all of a sudden everything becomes obvious. The best intelligences in the literature on development have taken as their turning point the 1964–1965 fluorescence of export-led growth in the ROK.[1] But 1960 was the real turning point, both in Seoul and Washington, with 1957 and the launching of the DLF as the adumbration of what was to come. Rhee's downfall was also the demise of his conception of state and economy, and of his vestigial Hermit-Kingdom ideas about import-substituting industrialization, making Korea another Japan while keeping the real Japan at bay, all of it succored by an indulgent America. In Washington, the Eisenhower era of big military budgets and support for the Rhee type anticommunism gave way to the developmental energy and dynamism of a new generation of American internationalists and their developmental Svengali, W. W. Rostow.[2]

The early 1960s connote the apotheosis of American power, so it was fitting that Rostow should bring forth an economic development theory seeking to explain to the rest of the world how America reached this pinnacle. It was just as deterministic, if not more so, as that of Marx—both in its Rostovian incarnation and in the more generic modernization theory framework—something relevant and revelatory for the study of Korean economy. Korea shows that ideas have consequences. As Keynes once noted, not without some prescience about his own impact, "the ideas of economists and political philosophers, both when they are right and when they are wrong, are more powerful than is commonly understood . . . practical men who believe themselves to be quite exempt from any intellectual influences are usually slaves of some defunct economist."[3] But Rostow was not one to wait for ideas to work their way into the zeitgeist. The diffusion of ideas in the 1960s was not so subtle and unconscious: proselytizing often involved bludgeoning, with plenty of *pan y palo.*

The thrust of the new aid policy was that Korea would have to "take off" on a sustained basis, led by one or more manufacturing sectors, financed by a more effective mobilization of Korean domestic savings, with the shortfall made up not by the United States alone but by Japan as well. Cementing ties between the two Far Eastern allies was critical against the backdrop of the Southeast Asian war and DeGaulle's recognition of China. Korea's piqued press would call this "economic assistance on the cheap, packed with advice"[4]—and it did possess a frugal quality, the determination that aid would be used judiciously, and with maximum political-economic externalities.

During this decade Korea would indeed take off, in the Rostovian sense, inundating the world market with textile goods, taking wing again in the "flying geese pattern" that Akamatsu described in the 1930s.[5] It would also wrest away what one pundit called "a Texas-sized gratitude" from Johnson for partaking in the Vietnam War.[6] This last quality relaxed the no-nonsense tenor of aid policies; Korea the mendicant was now Korea the well-armed beacon of the Free World, not like Japan which pansied about on a "free ride." In these halcyon days of U.S.-Korean relations, even democracy seemed to be a dream not forever deferred: two direct presidential elections occurred, in reasonably open conditions. Korea was going to "have it all."

The Turning Point

The contour of "development cooperation," when applied to East Asia, displayed three broad strokes. The first was of course the much celebrated insistence on the primacy of economic development, both in rhetoric and in realty. Secondly, whereas in Latin America development was now seen by liberal America as an antidote for popular mobilization—a breakwater against the spread of Cuban style revolution—in East Asia a decade of the Mutual Security Act had done its job buttressing internal security (at least in the Northern corner of Asia). Hence, aid could become developmental and economizing at once. But, thirdly, there was still Southeast Asia, America's new and old problem; not only was there a specter of conflagration throughout the region but Socialist China's rapid economic progress was feared to have a Circe-like effect on its impoverished southern neighbors.[7] Here, "development cooperation" had to be regional in scope, what William F. Bundy called an "Asian solution to Asia's problems."[8] This meant, for example, that Japan had to find a way somehow to share the burden of Asian development. But each of these aspects had important application to Korea.

Seoul in 1960 was the site of the largest U.S. aid operation, providing a quarter of the Korean GNP in military and economic assistance combined, and was also one of the first places where the old assumptions of the Mutual Security Act were reviewed and tossed away. No sooner had the electoral tally come in for Kennedy's victory than the National Security Council forged—presumably with the participation of the transition team—a new Korea policy (NSC 6018) that really wiped the plate clean of the past.

The policy document hammered on political and social development, and trailblazed such codewords as "democratic institutions," "inclusive politics," "free world ideals," and "constructive labor policies" as America's major objectives in Korea. (It read like an undergraduate textbook on comparative politics, or more precisely, modernization theory.) Much of this was explicable, of course, in the context of the student uprising that hounded Rhee to Hawaii, but the document is still remarkable because Americans now opined that democracy was both possible and that it mattered in Korea; this presaged the American armtwisting of Park Chung Hee, maker of the 1961 coup, to don mufti and hold an election in 1963.

The U.S. notion in the 1950s had been to get Koreans to sell rice and seaweed to the Japanese and in turn become a receptacle for Japanese industrial goods: this, mostly to help Japan's recovery (which

Rhee refused)—and not because "export-led growth" was an economic virtue in itself. By 1960, all of that changed. NSC 6018 stressed the exigent need to dismantle the foreign exchange system—the lynchpin of Korea's import substitution industrialization—and "to stimulate domestic production for export and domestic use": in other words, export-led growth. Just as Rhee had insisted on ISI to exact more aid, Americans would now press the export agenda on Koreans, thus giving them less aid, and stalling the terrific drain on America's resources. This required reforms of bureaucracy and fiscal policies, so the Americans would supply generous *technical* and economic aid to bring the reforms to fruition. Other ways to buttress the new economic orientation were to normalize relations with Japan, and to reduce military expenditures so as to release greater resources for economic development.[9]

These policies, set forth in November of 1960, received intense scrutiny as the test case in the new global and holistic approach to development. Robert Komer, a former member of Directorate of Intelligence and Office of National Estimates at the CIA (1947–1960), and now senior staff member at the National Security Council, was one of the earliest advocates of the new development approach to Korea. In his memorandum to Rostow, he argued that while the U.S. priority remained a viable South Korea "before it crumbles like Vietnam may," military assistance was being squandered to maintain "huge ROK forces far beyond the likely need." The obstacle to the substantial American troop reduction that he wanted, he said, was the American military establishment—yet the key to Korean growth was to "rob the military Peter to pay the civilian Paul."[10] At another time, Komer wrote to Rostow: "in my opinion, one of the basic reasons why we have accomplished so little in Korea since 1953 has been our predominantly military focus. We have spent more money on MAP 1953–1960 than on domestic economy." Komer directly challenged the military's favorite theme, played before Congressional appropriations committees: "I would argue that the possibility of local aggression [in Korea] is less than almost any place else around the bloc periphery."[11]

In March 1961, Rostow sent to Komer a paper written by Hugh Farley, an ICA officer until recently in charge of the Technical Assistance Program in Korea: it was a damning report on the Korean prospect for development, arguing that the Korean problem was an "endemic oriental problem with hundreds of years of history" that cannot be changed "overnight."[12] But, Komer rather thought that a swift change was possible, even in Korea.

In a memo to Rostow and the Director of Central Intelligence, titled "Action in Korea," Komer outlined themes that would later emerge in the more detailed Presidential Task Force reports that prescribed American actions to bring forth economic reforms in Korea.[13] Actually, he set an agenda for Korea policy over the next decade, and it was striking in its emphasis on economic, and not military, priorities, which presaged the Guam Doctrine of the Nixon years.

The ROK is saddled with the staggering task of supporting a far larger military establishment that it is really able to support, or is needed. . . . Underlying ills and needs are economic . . . the major thrust of U.S. effort over the next decade must be:

1. Substantial cutback in ROK military establishment, with the diversion of U.S. funds thus released to *crash economic development.*

2. Build of ROK economy, stressing public sector, *creation of light labor-intensive industry, and full utilization of main ROK resource—people.*

3. *Much more vigorous, imaginative U.S. action in directing and supervising ROK economic development.* . . . *Closer and more active instruction and supervision of ROK government, but also more attribution to ROK government of their benefits.*

[Granting of SOFA agreement to ROK so that] we can buy public acceptance that our greater involvement in ROK economic direction will acquire. . . . *Sharply reduce political role in ROK of the U.S. military and its spokesmen; make U.S. ambassador indisputes [sic] spokesman of U.S. policy in Korea.*[14] [Italics mine.]

This is a remarkable and prescient document. Few thought that "crash economic development" could occur in a country either written off as a reprobate or seen traducing for a decade the "best economic advice." But it was from this sort of general perspective that a whole cluster of policies for transforming Korea's economy were formulated, and with lightening speed: instituting of a national development plan, reforms in budget and accounting procedures and tax collection, and rationalizing interest rates.[15] We might reconstruct Komer's diagnosis by turning to Walt Rostow's work, *"The Stages of Economic Growth,* and to his vaunted work "takeoff."[16]

A "takeoff," roughly defined as the ability to sustain a productive investment of 10 percent or more of the national income, is said to require four essential prerequisites, which Korea either possessed or could easily acquire in 1961. First and foremost were technological prerequisites. Rostow was a technological determinist, and even if he were not aware of the history of colonial industrialization, it did not escape him that Korea with its enormously well-educated populace had an unusual capacity (for a Third World country) to absorb technology. Second was the emergence of one or more leading sectors in manufacturing. Here, given Korea's factor endowment, it was obvious that it would have to be in textile and other labor-intensive products. The third precondition was finance: initially, an ability to mobilize domestic savings productively and, subsequently, a structure which permits a high marginal rate of savings. A sweeping fiscal and financial reform would do the trick, which aid-donor America was in an exceptionally good shape to implement. So, in 1961 there was the "Dillon Package," which sought to institute a realistic exchange rate in Korea. In 1963, the A.I.D. withheld supporting assistance for nine months until the Korean junta effected tax reforms to reduce the size of its budget deficit, and in 1964, forced a whopping 50 percent devaluation in Korean currency by holding up the PL480 agreement.[17]

It was the final requisite that was most problematic, and that the Americans had to deal with first: the existence or quick emergence of a political leadership which could exploit the potential effect of a takeoff and give a sustained character to growth. Here, the efficacy of the Chang Myôn regime (1960–1961) was quite suspect. A secret memorandum prepared by the Director of Central Intelligence homed in on just this last point, reporting that the Chang Myôn government "bears responsibilities for the absence of significant political or economic advances," and is "politically unstable so that internal crisis or threat of crisis will be the norm."[18] Field officers in Korea concurred. In March of 1961, Hugh Farley wrote that "the Republic of Korea is a sick society," with "endemic Oriental problems of graft, corruption, and fraud." While the "two power groups were students and intellectuals on the one hand and the United States on the other," he continued, "the government has not even discovered how to enlist United States assistance in the right way,"[19] a tragic and ironic twist for Chang Myôn, long a myrmidon of American lords. The American ambassador reported to the State Department that Chang's extreme subservience to the United States was hurting his credibility, and in April, Assistant Secretary of State McConaughy also cabled Dean Rusk a diatribe against the feckless leadership in Seoul.[20]

When the colorless Chang Myôn passed from the scene in May, a multi-hued junta made the Americans by turns confused, wary, and then approving.[21] At first, they thought Park Chung Hee was a communist, then a miscreant, then a nationalist, but finally and most happily, a nation-builder.[22] Within three months of the coup d'etat, Samuel Berger, the new ambassador to Korea, enthusiastically reported to Rusk that "the Supreme Command and cabinet moving on all fronts [sic], especially economic, with lightning speed, and by and large in the right direction." The atmosphere was "one of deadly earnest to get the job done," and Park Chung Hee was a man with "a sure sense of power, a fine sense of timing, a common sense, unideological approach":[23] in short, here was the perfect epaulet for a leadership poised before takeoff. That this was an emergency junta which had demolished the American-sponsored 1948 constitution mattered not.

For Ambassador Sam Berger, a labor economist by training (and respected by McGeorge Bundy as "understanding economics better than most ambassadors"),[24] the problem with the junta was not a shortage of economic goals, but a heartwarming excess of them; for every economic idea Americans entertained for Korea, Park ricocheted with an ampler plan of action. "This genuine revolution from the top," Berger reported to Rusk, "was breathlessly implementing across the board the much talked about reforms of the past: banking and credit policy, tax, foreign trade, increased public works for the unemployed, agriculture, education, public administration, and welfare."[25] It turned out to be an exaggeration, but that is not the point: Berger thought Rostow's fourth prerequisite for the developmental embarkation had arrived just in the nick of time, in the unlikely person of peasant-born General Park.

The First Five Year Plan, Berger thought, was less promising— notable less for its feasibility than for its nobility of intent. Its projected goal of 7.1 percent annual GNP growth appeared unrealistic, given the 4.5 percent average rate in the years 1953–1960; also questionable were the projected rates of domestic savings to GNP, which were 19 percent for 1961 and 24 percent for 1966, when it had only been 13 percent in 1960.[26] (ICA projections for the 1960s had East Asia growing at the rate of 4 percent a year, trailing behind Latin America, the Near East, and South Asia.[27]) Not even the key American cheerleaders of Korean development, in other words, could gauge the true scope of the nation's potential—a pattern that would recur time and again. Nonetheless, Berger and Killen, the director of the now more vigorous USAID Korea, appealed to their government for greater aid, to boost the junta.[28]

U.S. aid still came mostly in grants, but there were some loans.

TABLE 4.1. Total Economic Aid Received, by Source: 1961–1965 ($ million)

	1961	1962	1963	1964	1965
Nonproject supporting assistance	113.6	126.6	102.7	72.8	79.2
Project assistance	29.8	21.7	13.0	5.5	4.3
PL 480 sales	32.6	36.1	62.7	94.7	54.4
PL 480 Title II and III	10.2	24.0	21.8	27.6	28.5
Development loans	3.2	10.5	20.0	4.5	2.6
Total	192.8	245.5	252.3	164.8	176.9

SOURCE: Krueger, *The Developmental Role of the Foreign Sector and Aid*, p. 113.

The first loan was received prior to 1959 and had been less than 1 percent of aid, a total of $1.3 million through the Development Loan Fund. As can be seen in table 4.1, loans increased from the early years of the 1960s, but were still miniscule in comparison to grant assistance. The peak year for aid was, as we know from table 3.1 in the previous chapter, 1957 at $383 million, and then the volume of aid dropped precipitously, reaching the nadir in 1961. Table 4.1 indicates that the volume of economic aid picked up in 1962, to the 1959 level, stayed there for a couple of years, then dropped again in 1964.

From 1964 onward, it was clear that America meant to uphold the principle of development assistance through advice, loans, and help from the private sector, international agencies, and Japanese "burden sharing"—i.e., aid on the cheap. This tendency was not at all idiosyncratic to Korea, reflecting a general trend in the U.S. policy: the 1965 budget request for foreign assistance (military and economic combined) was the lowest in sixteen years, and this despite Vietnam and an expanded Latin American program.[29] Table 4.2 provides a quick glance at the decline in foreign aid. One might note that 1958 was the first year when economic aid outstripped military.

TABLE 4.2. U.S. Foreign Assistance

	1954	1958	1960	1964
Military	3,230	1,340	1,300	1,000
Economic	1,301	1,428	1,925	2,000

Reforms and Dependency

The political economy of a mendicant state is zero-sum. Maximum extraction of grant-in-aid requires a display of abject helplessness thus to mock the idea of self-help. The Korean savings ratio in 1960 is a case in point, summarizing in a nutshell the adverse effects of aid-dependence. Private savings achieved the grand total of 1.6 percent of GNP, and government savings showed constant deficits, reflecting a very limited tax extraction. The effective tax burden rate of 9.9 percent to GNP was low even by the weak standard of other LDCs. Investment remained the turf of grants-in-aid, which financed 78 percent of the total. Rhee explained this dismal record of domestic savings as merely a reflection of the nation's abject poverty (which was of course true to a great extent), and sought to break the vicious cycle of low income, low savings, low investment, low growth by injecting more aid. Americans had a different diagnosis, and so did the military junta that came to power in 1961. [Henceforth, the military leadership in 1961–1963 will be referred to as the junta.]

To Americans, it all looked like a gigantic policy failure that could be traced to the lack of Korean resolve in raising tax revenue and savings to finance investment. Accordingly, the first step in solving this development bottleneck was to remake the tax structure and to mobilize savings through a financial reform that would establish proper market channels and offer attractive yields on financial assets. This was to be combined with a realistic valuation of the currency to promote exports.

The junta came around to acknowledging the merits of those arguments, if only because there really was no choice in the face of dwindling U.S. aid. Over time, financial reform—with a truckload of salt, it was sometimes called financial liberalization—was instituted. It would be profoundly misleading, however, to think of the junta leadership as liberal in its economic orientation. These were men of peasant origin and harbored, like ultranationalist Japanese officers in the 1930s, a peasants' suspicion of the wealthy. When they thought of capitalism, they thought of a conspiracy of the rich; when they entertained the notion of economic development, they thought of a rich nation and a strong army, and wartime Japan came to their minds; and when they awakened to the need for domestic resource mobilization, they badgered the rich and forced citizens, through campaigns and edicts, to salt away chunks of their salaries. Joseph Schumpeter knew this type, and he called them mercantilists.

They did not analyse at all. They had no conception of any but the most obvious relations between economic phenomena. Living at a time when nations braced themselves to match their fighting power, they impulsively resented imports of unnecessary luxuries—that does not imply considered rejection of Adam Smith's grand commonplace that consumption is the 'sole end and purpose of all production.' They looked at the antics of exchange rates and attributed them to the machinations of speculators. . . . They felt it was nice for a nation as well as for individuals to have money—without thinking any more about it. They were staunch nationalists—and the foreigner, of course, was an object of aversion and distrust. They were . . . naively critical of business and of the doings of merchants.[30]

The Korean monetary reform—the first big economic reform that the junta enacted without Americans being privy to it—offers a pristine glance at neo-mercantilism in action. If money was not finding its way into banks and investment, the junta reasoned, it must be under rich men's mattresses. Hence, the hunt for potential savings started with a sweeping currency reform. An abrupt change in currency denomination made ten old *hwan* into one new *won*, and a freeze was placed on all bank deposits. Conversion was limited to 500 new won, equal to less than four dollars, which was to meet current living expenses. Citizens were required to register all cash, checks, and money orders, and attempts were made to direct the "surplus" funds into a new Industrial Development Corporation that would finance industrial activities. But the hunt turned up amazingly little idle money, which was not too surprising; the Korean money supply had been only but 12 percent of GNP. Instead, the reform precipitated the very inflationary behavior it sought to prevent, a shift from holding money to hoarding goods. Business came to a virtual standstill, confidence in government and financial institutions plummeted, and a recession resulting from dislocation of the market mechanism was protracted beyond expectations.

Americans were horrified by this specter, especially since the policy measures that fed it eventuated in the absence of prior consultation or notification to the U.S. government.[31] Never before, starting in 1945, did Koreans enact such sweeping economic reform without American approval. Faced with a severe rebuke from the Americans, the chagrined junta soon terminated freezing the bank accounts.[32]

Something more than pique and concern over the efficacy of the reform was at issue. Korean leaders had touted their currency reform as a Korean counterpart of the ignition phase of the Miracle on the Rhine—another Operation Bird Dog, which General Clay and Joseph Dodge spent two years preparing as a stunning act aimed at liberalizing the German economy and making the price mechanism an effective means of allocating resources. As Ludwig Erhard described it for Germany, hundreds of decrees for regulating economic behavior went "into the wastebasket in one fell swoop."[33] In contrast, the Korean version of the German currency reform was not only highly confiscatory but sought the opposite or market liberalization: greater control over the economy and the business community.[34]

Around the same time that currency reform was promulgated, an anticorruption campaign rounded up the richest men in Korea, now stamped as profiteers with "illicit fortunes." Profiteers under arrest were defined as shortly follows, and it so happened that most prominent businessmen qualified. "Illicit profiteers" were those who during the period of July 1, 1953, to May 15, 1961, had:

1. Illicitly earned profits totaling more than 100 million hwan by either purchasing or renting publicly owned properties

2. Obtained loans or purchases of more than $100,000 worth of government or bank owned foreign exchange

3. Provided political funds of more than 50 million hwan in return for bank loans

4. Earned profits of more than 200 million hwan in the process of contracting or bidding for public works or commodity trade in an illegal way

5. Earned profits of more than 200 million hwan by monopolizing the purchase or allocation of foreign exchange

6. Avoided taxes of more than 200 million hwan

7. Illegally transferred their wealth abroad[35]

In other words, it was a crime to have indulged in the political economy of the Rhee era.

Populism of this sort, the junta soon found out, was inherently unstable, a political waste. This was hardly a "left" program. The junta possessed from the beginning a visceral dislike of all shades of leftism, and never purported to mobilize workers and/or peasants onto a redistributary warpath. What it coveted instead was power and then economic development—à la Japan, not, say, Mao's China. Why, then, alienate the business sector? Who, if not businessmen, would finance the governing party, regime consolidation, and growth? Did not the prewar Japanese ultranationalists, too, ultimately embrace the zaibatsu? Amid alarming recession caused by this empty bravado—needless in retrospect because even the populace, let along the United States and the business sector, remained surprisingly reticent and unimpressed about such populist measures—the junta swung to the other direction. From then on, the state would still be interventionary and regulatory: but not against business.

General Park summoned the ten major business leaders and struck a deal with them. In exchange for exempting businessmen from criminal prosecution and respecting their properties whether ill or well gotten, business "paid" fines levied on them by establishing industrial firms and then donating shares to the government. In retrospect, this deal had the quality of an historical compromise; in any case, it occasioned the launching of "Korea Inc." Henceforth, state and big business would share the same destiny: prosper or perish.

For all the sound and fury of the 1961–1963 reforms, the most durable and significant was the reorganization of the banking sector. It illustrates, more than anything else, the Korean state's proclivity toward interventionism in development, an example of what Alfred Stepan might call "organic statism" for Latin nations.[36] The banking sector was the only exception to the guarantee of nonconfiscation that the state had promised to businessmen. In fact, all commercial banks were swiftly nationalized, and all financial intermediaries were quickly lined up under the direction of the Ministry of Finance. The raison d'être of the banks became that of seconding and executing national macroeconomic goals, not profit-mongering through lucrative money lending. Along with the nationalization came a full revival of the specialized banking system that had developed during the colonial era. Agricultural credit institutions were strengthened, a bank specializing in commerce and small industry was founded, and the capital and functions of the Korean Development Bank were now enlarged to enable borrowing from abroad and the guaranteeing of foreign loans obtained by domestic enterprises. The last point, state guarantee of foreign loans, was to have a great impact in the nation's financial history. This, coupled with a series of reform measures (in 1964–1966) that displayed to potential lenders both developmental resolve and continence in Korea's domestic financial policies, opened the floodgates to foreign credit that financed rapid growth. But that, in turn, occurred in a radically altered regional environment.

Japan-Korea Normalization, the Vietnam War, and the Reintegration of East Asia

Even as American aid declined in the early 1960s, two things intruded to give Koreans a break: the rapprochement with Japan, and the Vietnam War. The latter was a true deus ex machina, bringing with it enhanced U.S. military assistance that allowed the Korean government to release scarce resources for economic development, and to make of Korea, in William Bundy's terms, "a touchstone and partial model for later hopes and plans in South Vietnam."[37] Thus, to understand Korean development, one has also to grasp how security issues played into it. U.S. military assistance to Korea in 1965, when Korean troops were dispatched, accounted for 7.2 percent of GNP, whereas the ratio for the previous year had been 4.9 percent. This war also bestowed windfall payments for troops, procurement, and various other civilian contracts. Most of the economic literature either denies, neglects, or eschews as too sensitive the issues of the Japan connection and the Vietnam War in Korean development.[38] But Japan and Vietnam were a large part of the much-touted tale of Korea's world-beating economic growth. So long as security issues remain segregated from studies of economic growth, any speculation of whether or not the "East Asian pattern" can be duplicated in the rest of the Third World must remain incomplete, if not fruitless.

Korean rapprochement with Japan was on the American agenda dating back to the late 1940s. Under Rhee, imports from Japan had to balance the amount of export, which severely limited the extent of trade. There was, of course, a sub rosa realm of economic activity, such as pirating and smuggling, time-honored practices between two neighbors. But in the 1950s, governmental negotiations to effect realistic levels of trade and to restore diplomatic relations were exercises in futility. Rhee refused any figure lower than $2 billion as reparations from Japan, and even the malleable Chang Myôn thought that $1.25 billion was the rock bottom price. The Japanese, for bargaining purpose, filibustered to the effect that it was they who needed compensation for properties left behind in Korea. When Park Chung Hee, a former lieutenant in the Kwantung Army, became the chief of state in 1961, all of that changed: Ikeda, Japan's Prime Minister, assured Rusk that with Park in charge, normalization would only be a matter of time.[39]

By 1963, imports from Japan had leaped to $162 million, 30 percent of total imports to Korea, and four times the level under Rhee. If aid imports were excluded, the figure was tantamount to 70 percent of total imports. Financially, Japan advanced $40 million in short-term credit to Korea in 1962, and $18 million for grain purchases in the same year, $37.4 million in long-term supplier's credit in 1963, as well as an unrevealed sum provided through their U.S. subsidiaries. By 1963, Korean debt to Japan stood at $130 million, and its exports to Japan only 16 percent of its imports.[40] The Korean leadership thus needed quick normalization in order to cover the trade deficit and debt, not to mention paving the road for further financial inflow from Japan to fuel the Five Year Plan. Korea was hooked to Japan.

The Japanese capture of influence, not to mention the market, in Korea produced some of the most awful and sordid scandals in Korea's economic history, so much so that even Americans, the invisible hands behind Normalization, at one point wondered if the only thing that the military regime in Korea cared about was bucks from Japan.[41] (This fear was reinforced later in CIA information revealing that Japanese firms provided two-thirds of the Korean ruling party's 1961–1965 budget, six firms having paid a total of $66 million, with individual contributions ranging from $1 million to $20 million.[42]) Nonetheless, Americans pressed on to get the Normalization, now an economic fait accompli, all signed and ratified.

That final hurdle, however, was not as easy to jump as some thought. Dean Rusk, for instance, could not figure out why Korea and Japan could not simply and amicably conclude the deal, but in Seoul a sea of demonstrators vowed to oppose unto death any attempt at restoring relations with—and become economically dependent upon—Japan.[43] Negotiations stalled, and by the summer of 1964, American patience was running short not only with the negotiating parties but with their own mediators, Ambassadors Winthrop Brown in Seoul and Edwin Reischauer in Tokyo. McGeorge Bundy exhorted Reischauer to remember that President Johnson considered the ROK-Japan settlement and normalization of relations "top priority."[44] This got the American Embassy in Tokyo moving, and it soon came up with a stream of proposals to give Park Chung Hee the "necessary backbone" to conclude the deal, including a package of economic incentives, *open* partisanship with the governing party on the issue, and even threats to the Korean opposition that "if [they] caused Park's fall on this issue, it would jeopardize continued U.S. support for Korea."[45] Almost simultaneously, Americans were pressuring Taiwan to deepen ties with Japan.[46]

Business interests in Japan, or what some called the "reconstructed zaibatsu," had a stake here; Korea's property claims could be settled by granting suppliers' credit, which meant restoration of a market for Japanese goods.[47] In fact, even before the relationship between Japan and Korea was restored, Japanese zaibatsu groups, especially those with prewar connections to Korea, were conducting project identification and feasibility studies in Korea. Once the projects were identified—and this often happened before the Korean government made the request—*Keidanren* would make policy recommendations to the Japanese government, which might take them into consideration in directing the Official Development Assistance (ODA) loans.

Nippon Koei, for instance, had thick ties dating back to colonial days, when Kubota Yukata ran power companies in Korea—the Chosen Denryoku Kabushiki Kaisha (Chosen Power Company) and the Chosen Manshu Oryokko Suiyoku Hatsuden Kabushiki Kaisha (The Yalu Hydroelectric Power Company)—and it was one of the first Japanese zaibatsu to make project identifications before the Japan-Korea relationship was restored. Predictably, these were in power generation. With the settlement of claims, Nippon Koei won the contract for the construction of the Soyang'gang Dam, which was financed through the reparations money; it also made a successful tender for a multipurpose dam for which the Japanese made loans in 1974. Another example of an early identification leading to the reparations claim-financed capital construction was the Seoul subway system, undertaken by the Nissho Trading Company. Later, Mitsubishi Trading, Marubeni Trading, and Hitachi would all get in on the act of selling various parts of the subway system to Koreans.[48]

To the outraged public in Korea all this looked like neocolonialism, and when all is said and done, there was some truth to that. But the military regime bulldozed through all opposition and the normalization treaty was finally concluded in 1965. The final reparation figure was substantially lower than that sought by previous regimes: Korea was to receive from Japan $300 million in grants, $200 million in government loans, and $300 million in commercial credit. But the total—at $800 million—was no small sum for a country whose entire exports in 1964 amounted to $200 million.

Yet, in retrospect the amount of reparations (Japan still refused to call it that, preferring the expression "grant") would seem less significant than the uses to which these new financial resources were put. Notwithstanding the provision in the 1965 settlement that $300 million in grants were to be paid out at a rate of $3 million each year for ten years and were to be utilized exclusively for agricultural development and importation of industrial materials—a curious déjà vu of the initial phase of colonialism described in chapter 2—Koreans had in mind more the pattern of the 1930s and the 1940s. If Koreans insisted on using the money for industrial development, then the Japanese wanted it to be for light industries, like textiles and household electronic goods.[49] But, the money quickly found its way into other types of industrial investment, and made possible, inter alia, Park's fervent dream of a steel complex. (Foreign countries had refused to be part of what appeared to be a white elephant, and the World Bank and the U.S. EXIM reneged, on the advice of the U.S.O.M., on an earlier pledge to help Koreans build a steel complex. Therefore, Park used the reparations money to build Póhang Steel.)

The remaining $200 million in government loans, borrowed at a 3.5 percent interest rate and repayable over twenty years after a seven-year grace period, was invested for social infrastructure including power plants, railroads, irrigation networks, and communication facilities. $300 million in commercial loans went into financing plant exports from Japan, such as power facilities, textile production machinery, and transportation equipment. In other words, the Japan-Korea rapprochement might have been a neocolonial arrangement, but it was not ruled by an inexorable logic of underdevelopment.

By 1966 Japanese capital accounted for a good half of total foreign loans to Korea, triggering an investment spree. But the loans were also dispensed with ruthless efficiency in the form of "suppliers' credit," prefiguring at the outset two tendencies that would mark the Korean economy for the next twenty years: increasing imports, hence deteriorating balance of payments vis-à-vis Japan, and an economy hooked on external financing to cover trade deficits. In this manner Korea came back, two decades after World War II, to join the Japanese orbit—although one that now allowed a significant degree of development. Without either the huzzahs or the brouhahas that marked programs for regional economic integration in Latin America and Europe, what silently eventuated was the investiture of a dual and complementary hegemony of Japan and America in Asia, an incipient "Pacific Rim."

The character of this dual hegemony is explained by its relatively unique origins. Economic assistance to Asia in the 1940s at first reflected the war victors' zeal to protect the old and new spheres of influence: the French in Indochina, the Dutch in Indonesia, Britain in Burma and Malaya, the United States in Japan, Korea, and the Philippines. Aimed at averting economic and political disasters, the assistance was sporadic and short term. This colonial mosaic was replaced in the 1950s by an America that picked up the tab for everyone, to combat insurgent nationalism in the region and to counteract material assistance coming from the communist bloc.

In the early 1960s, however, Japanese capital began making inroads, starting with Thailand and Malaysia, then coming heavily into neighboring countries by the end of the decade. Much of this was prompted by the slackening of trade with Southeast Asia and the Far East in the late 1950s—caused by the U.S. reduction in MAP and aid procurement offshore—which necessitated that Japan do something to prop up these economies to absorb Japanese exports, as they used to do in the days of the East Asian Co-Prosperity Sphere. Japan, in the classic fashion of a late developer, had traded in the past mostly with less developed nations,[50] with 71 percent of its total exports absorbed by the LDCs in 1934–1936; but this dropped to 66 percent in 1953, and to 45.5 percent by 1962. To reverse the tide and increase exports to other East Asian countries, the Japanese way was to recruit American help and to disburse reparations money so that capital goods could be procured from Japan.

In the late 1950s, the daily Japanese staple was to plead with the United States to mediate and ease the trading difficulties Japan faced, such as protectionism with the formation of the EEC, refusal of Korea and Burma to make reparations settlements at terms set by Japan, and even competition from China in the Southeast Asia. The Japanese, for instance, enlisted American help in beating Chinese cotton textile competition, first through the Commodity Credit Corporation credit program, and later through the American PL 480 agreements under which the Japanese secured contracts for the processing of cotton for Southeast Asian countries, especially for Burma and Indonesia.[51] But it was really in the 1960s that the Japanese exported capital to other parts of East Asia in order to make up for dwindling United States offshore procurement and thus Japanese exports, and to become the leader, as Walt Rostow had urged, in Asian regional development.[52]

Succored by a favorable balance of payments position, Japanese capital outflow leaped to $557 million in 1968 from the previous $275 million; and there was no longer much fuss over capital exports, the Bank of Japan having granted automatic approval. If the 1950s and early 1960s saw the migration of Japanese manufacturing industries to Latin America, mostly to circumvent import substitution policies in that continent, Japanese industries in the late 1960s now spilt over to more immediate surroundings in search of cheap labor and lower manufacturing cost.[53] Nearly half of total capital outflow from Japan to developing countries by 1970 was in Korea (17.3 percent), the Philippines (8.7 percent), Indonesia (7.4 percent), Taiwan (7.3 percent), and Thailand (5.5 percent). This coincided with and complemented a decline in the U.S. financial resource outflow to the region—a 20 percent drop in 1969 from the previous year, for instance—that reflected both the Vietnam fiasco and disillusionment with foreign economic aid activities. Of the Japanese total, however, only $436 million was what could properly be termed "development assistance," such as grants, loans, and contributions to multilateral organizations; the remaining $827 million consisted of private investment and lending, and government and private export suppliers' credit.[54]

Precisely because of the preponderant role of private capital, coupled with the demure, low-profile attitude of the Japanese government, scholars have often failed to note the very existence of this regional integration. This oversight is not incidental to academic parochialism; rather, it is testimony to Japanese efficacy in forging a postwar modus vivendi in that part of the world where the past looms large and Japanese money was both coveted and resented. Thus, for instance, even the most visible and official symbol of regional integration, the Asian Development Bank, escaped the attention of those international relations experts who were otherwise wont to uncover political rationale behind economic relations. Stephen Krasner argued that regional banks were essentially political phenomena, but saw the Asian Development Bank as a curious anomaly, an organization entirely concerned with profit-making and not with regional integration.[55]

From the beginning, however, the Asian Development Bank was a political institution, concerned with regional integration—or reintegration, as the case may be—that could provide a united front against communism, and simultaneously, a market for Japan. The idea of an Asian regional bank was not new in the 1960s, nor did it spring from Asian initiatives, as the American leadership so painstakingly tried to pretend.[56] Economic regionalism had germinated in the American mind a good decade before the bank was actually founded, primarily as a way (as some correctly surmised) of "establishing . . . [sic] the Japanese co-prosperity sphere by peaceful means," and "to help Japan delay, as long as possible, from re-establishing its old relations with mainland China."[57] But it really took Vietnam to turn this glint in the American eye into a reality.

Vietnam was a black hole that sucked in nearly all the energy in the Johnson administration, and so it is not surprising that ideas on

Asia and Asian development perforce had to relate to America's war effort. (President Johnson's Johns Hopkins speech was really a case in point.) Unlike the European instance, East Asian reintegration could not be attacked frontally: Walt Rostow, then head of the Policy Planning Council at the State Department (1961–1966) and an expert on European economic integration, knew this very well.[58] Rostow's first task at the State Department was to explore the possibilities of intensified regional economic cooperation in East Asia, but the prospect of East Asian reintegration really awaited the outcome of the confrontation in Southeast Asia and the question of relative power in Asia of China and the United States. In the meantime, integration had to be piecemeal, which meant the settlement of the Japan-Korean relationship first, coaxing Japan to make greater commitments in Asia, and coping with and dampening nationalist fervors in Southeast Asia where possible—first through ad hoc, bilateral measures, but ultimately through multilateral and regional measures. That meant the establishment of the Asian Development Bank.[59]

Ideas for an Asian bank had also teemed in the Japanese imagination. Prime Minister Kishi advanced in 1957 a plan for Southeast Asian development that included a regional bank as an Asian edition of the World Bank. His successor, Ikeda Hayato (1960–1964), proffered a common market for Asia, as part of his proposal for the "three pillar approach" to international politics. The brains behind reconstituting the postwar economic order in East Asia are said to have been Ohashi Kaoru, a shadowy figure on the fringes of the Japanese financial community, and Watanabe Takeshi, a former employee of the World Bank, who went on to become the first president of the Asian Development Bank.[60] When the Vietnam War escalated, the Japanese desire to augment the market in Asia finally merged with American concern for the security and cohesion of noncommunist Southeast Asia, thus kicking off the regional bank for Asia.

The Asian Development Bank was, in the words of Joseph Burr, the U.S. under-secretary of the treasury and the American delegate to the final negotiation for the ADB, "a crucially important instrument of U.S. policy in a highly explosive area in the world." The stake was even higher for Japan. Southeast Asia, declared the deputy governor of the Bank of Japan, was Japan's "own back yard," akin to what Latin America was to the United States. To garner greater control of the ADB, then, Japan made ruthless use of bilateral aid programs to influence other Asian countries during the final negotiation in Manila.[61]

What Japan eventually obtained from the region—and this did not conflict with the profit-maximizing principle—was a vertical integration, and the pattern of ADB loans strongly reflects it. From 1966 to 1972, 61 percent of all ADB loans went to the six strongest developing members: Korea, Taiwan, Singapore, Hong Kong, Thailand, and Malaysia, with Korea claiming the largest share. In 1968–1973, the roster was about the same, with Korea again on top, taking up 17.9 percent of the total ADB loan. The top recipients of the ADB loans were those with the highest GNP per capita in the area *and* the highest growth rates. The countries in South Asia, that is, India, Nepal, Pakistan, Afganistan, and Sri Lanka were neglected, almost as if they did not qualify as Asian. Of the cumulative $926 million loaned out by the ADB through 1972, 31 percent was recorded as having gone to nonsoutheast Asia, but two-thirds of that amount went to Korea. In 1972, 60 percent of regular ADB loans went to Southeast Asia, with nearly all the remainder taken up by Korea. And nearly all ADB funds were for immediate use in industries and infrastructure, not social projects like education.[62] Not so insignificantly, the East Asian countries receiving most ADB loans also happened to be destination countries for Japanese private investment. In 1972 Korea, for instance, received Japanese private investments in the amount of $146 million; Indonesia, Singapore, Thailand, Malaysia, and the Philippines received respectively $119 million, $42 million, $30 million, $13 million, and $10 million.[63]

Vertical integration did not place an inordinate burden on Japan because regional hegemony was shared, in complementary fashion, by Japan and America. Here is the nub of the difference between the ADB and, say, the Inter-American Development Bank. A negative correlation between per capita U.S. assistance and ADB allocation indicates that the American hegemonic role would rest essentially on regionwide security, and under that umbrella, Japan would expand its market—carving out in the process a developmental hierarchy of preference amongst nations in the region. The advantages of this type of dual hegemony became clear to noncommunist Asian countries when the war in Vietnam escalated.

Assessing the economic impact of war—any war—is particularly difficult because the indirect effects of war are often greater than the immediate ones of, say, procurement of war supplies. Japan, for instance, was the largest single beneficiary in absolute terms of the Vietnam War, more than any other noncommunist Asian nation, but even the sharp rise in war-related triangular (Japan–United States–Vietnam) and bilateral (Japan–Vietnam) trade was miniscule compared to the indirect one of gaining access to the American and other Asian markets that were expanding by leaps and bounds in the war-induced boom. The same applied to Korea. Given, however, that the war-related multiplier effect is nearly impossible to assess, we will focus on some immediate economic effects of the War on Korea.

Korea sent to Vietnam 47,872 troops in the first year alone, and a total of more than 300,000 by the time the war was over; this was more men per capita than any nation in the world, including the United States[64]—something rarely mentioned, and even more rarely studied. The total cost to the United States of equipping and paying for these men was "peanuts compared to what it would be for a comparable number of Americans," but those "peanuts" went a long way to finance Korea's takeoff, and also to indulge Park Chung Hee into solidifying his dictatorial grip.[65] The Brown Memorandum, dated March 4, 1966, is the governing document—and an astonishing one —laying out arrangements for American utilization of Korean forces, which the Pentagon was to coordinate with AID. Although the two had always worked closely together, the link between economic development and war-induced profits was never made so lucid as in the memorandum. Quoted here is the economic portion of the compact governing the Vietnam dispatch:

B. ECONOMIC ASSISTANCE

1. To release additional won to the Korean budget equal to all of the net additional costs of the deployment of these extra forces and of mobilizing and maintaining in Korea the activated reserve division and brigade and support elements.

2. To suspend the MAP transfer program for as long as there are substantial Republic of Korea forces, i.e., at least two divisions in the Republic of Vietnam with offshore procurement in Korea in the United States fiscal year 1967 of items suspended in fiscal year 1966 plus those on the fiscal year 1967 list.[66]

3. (a) to procure in Korea insofar as practicable requirements supplies, services and equipment for Republic of Korea forces in the Republic of Vietnam and to direct to Korea selected types of procurement for United States and Republic of Vietnam forces in the Republic of Vietnam. . . .

(b) to procure in Korea, in competition only with United States suppliers, as much as Korea can provide in time and at a reasonable price of a substantial amount of goods being purchased by the Agency for International Development (A.I.D.) for use in its project programs for rural construction, pacification, relief, logistics and so forth, in the Republic of Vietnam.

(c) to the extent permitted by the Republic of Vietnam, to provide Korean contractors expanded opportunities to participate in construction projects undertaken by the United States government and by American contractors in the Republic of Vietnam and to provide other services, including employment of skilled Korean civilians in the Republic of Vietnam.

4. To increase technical assistance to the Republic of Korea in the general field of export promotion.

5. To provide, in addition to the $150 million A.I.D. loans already committed to the Republic of Korea in May, 1965, additional A.I.D. loans to support economic development of the Republic of Korea as suitable projects are developed under the same spirit and considerations which apply to the $150 million commitment.

6. If justified by performance under the 1966 Stabilization Program, to provide $15 million of Program Loans in 1966, which can be used for the support of exports to the Republic of Vietnam and other development needs.[67]

American payments to Korea directly under the provisions of the Brown Memorandum from fiscal year 1965 to 1970 are said to have been more than one billion dollars.[68] In a study that compares the economic impact of the Vietnam War on various Asian countries, one economist assumed correctly that the rapid increase in U.S. military expenditures abroad after 1964 (as appears in the U.S. bal-

TABLE 4.3. Shares of U.S. Defense Expenditure and Korean Exports to Vietnam in Gross Domestic Product

	Total Revenue (defense expenditures & exports to Vietnam)	GDP at Current Price ($ million)	Revenue-GDP Ratio (percent)	Incremental Revenue-GDP Ratio (percent)
1962–63	96.5	3,192.3	3.02	
1964–65	104.6	2,826.6	3.70	−2.21
1966–67	209.2	4,163.4	5.02	7.82
1968	306.6	5,500.0	5.57	7.29
1969	372.9	6,597.4	5.65	6.93

SOURCE: Naya, "The Vietnam War and Some Aspects of Its Economic Impact on Asian Countries," p. 49.

ance of payment) was directly related to the Vietnam War, and divided the incremental increase by each nation's GDP. According to such tabulation, Singapore got the greatest benefit, a whopping 42.82 percent of its GDP in 1965, and declining thereafter. Korea, Taiwan, and Thailand came after. While Japan showed the largest earning through the war, the ratio was not impressive relative to its huge GDP. As shown in table 4.3, the Korean ratio ran minus 2.21 percent for 1964–1965, and then plus 7.82 percent for 1966–1967, 7.29 percent for 1968, and 6.93 percent in 1969.[69]

Korea's export to Vietnam, 3.5 percent of the country's total, was only a tiny fraction of its export to the United States. (The figure for exports to Vietnam is underestimated, however, since it appears without including those financed by U.S. economic and military assistance.) The statistical insignificance rapidly disappears when the nature of export commodities are reviewed. Unlike Japan and Hong Kong, whose exports to Vietnam consisted of items they were exporting to other nations, Korea—and to a lesser extent, Taiwan— began shipping new industrial products. Whereas Korean exports to America and Japan remained labor intensive goods such as textile and plastic goods, wigs, plywood, etc., Vietnam absorbed a stunning 94.29 percent in the total Korean steel export, 51.75 percent in

TABLE 4.4. The Commodity Composition of Exports to Vietnam and Total Exports and the Share of Exports to Vietnam

	Commodity Composition of Exports		Exports to Vietnam as Percent of Total
Description	Vietnam	Total	
Total percent	100.00	100.00	
Subtotal percent	87.27	18.60	
I-O 2 Other agric.	5.19	13.55	1.31
8 Beverages	1.70	0.13	44.20
16 Printing & publishing	1.50	0.16	32.84
20 Other chemical products	0.53	0.04	40.87
26 Steel products	45.87	1.66	94.29
29 Nonelectrical machinery	15.53	1.30	40.77
31 Transportation equipment	9.50	0.63	51.75
24 Glass, clay, stone	3.91	0.40	32.98
27 Nonferrous metals	13.54	0.73	16.53

SOURCE: Naya, "Vietnam War and Some Aspects of Its Impact on Asian Countries," p. 43.

transportation equipments, 40.77 percent in nonelectric machinery, and 40.87 percent in "other" chemical exports. Admittedly, production of the above industrial goods was more import-inducing than other export items—induced imports for export to Vietnam being 40.7 percent as versus 11.4 percent for "normal" exports. But the greater learning effect that the Vietnam War provided cannot be denied. The commodities listed in table 4.4, accounting for only 18.60 percent of Korea's total export, were sources of 87.27 percent of exports to Vietnam.

While commercial exports to Vietnam formed an insignificant fraction of Korea's foreign exchange earning in the late 1960s, such was decidedly not the case with construction and services (see table 4.5). In fact, Vietnam marked the coming of age for some of Korea's largest conglomerates. The first international contracts ever granted to Hyundai (today, one of the world's 50 largest corporations), were from the U.S. government for projects in Southeast Asia: the Pattani-Narathiwat Highway in Thailand, dredging work in Vietnam, and the like. In the service sector, the Korean Airlines Group (Hanjin) received a major boost by exploiting an old link with the U.S. army dating back to the Korean War when it was a supply agent. In Vietnam, Hanjin signed a contract for $7.9 million for supplying

TABLE 4.5. Korean Earnings from Vietnam, 1966–1968
(in $ million)

Types of Earnings	1966	1967	1968
Commercial exports	$ 13.8	$ 7.3	$ 5.6
Military goods sales	9.9	14.5	30.8
Construction and service contracts	12.3	43.5	58.4
Remittances			
Civilian	9.7	40.6	38.4
Military	13.2	30.0	34.4
Others	0	8.8	4.6
Total	$ 58.9	$144.7	$172.2
Total receipts from exports of goods and services plus private transfers	$558.0	$744.8	$993.0
Vietnam earnings as percent of total	10.6	19.4	17.3

SOURCE: Cole and Lyman, *Korean Development*, p. 135.

transportation for the U.S. Air Force, using trucks imported from Japan and the United States, sea transportation with barges from Hong Kong, and managed on behalf of the U.S. Army the complete operation of the strategic port, Qui Nhon.[70]

Thus, the Vietnam War was not only a cornucopia of huge invisible earnings and immense U.S. assistance, but an incubator of new industries before testing the fires of international competition. The phenomenon whereby a foreign market is turned into a laboratory for infant industries is, in other words, often political and, therefore, foreign to the assumptions underlying neoclassical trade theories. Nonetheless, it is one of the ways in which a mercantilist state engineers a movement upward in the industrial product cycle. It is important to grasp the context in which this occurred, a matrix of global security and regional integration managed by the United States and including a dynamic, expanding economy such as Japan. These essentially political advantages lead to a learning effect, as well as to a market that can be created and exploited. Just how fully such an opportunity may be seized will depend, of course, on the type of leadership in the dependent country.

THE POLITICS OF GROWTH. Economic growth is now widely considered a virtue in itself. But economic development as an all-consuming national passion has not been a universal aspiration, whether in Korea or elsewhere. Broadly speaking, it is an intensely modern phenomenon, and within that rubric, it was a temporary global artifact of the Development Decade known as the 1960s; Korea just happened to be positioned and motivated to exploit this external milieu better than most. The United States touted the virtues of development as a legitimizing formula for Pax Americana, and in the epidemic of coups d'ètat that spread from the late 1950s, progress and economic growth became a routine agenda. If the Korean particularity added a certain urgency to this general trend, it was because the Achilles heel of any military regime—the mandate to rule—was even more exposed in Korea than in others.

Unlike Japan, the Korean variant of Confucianism long held the Man on Horseback in supercilious contempt and equated the ascendence of praetorians with national degeneration. Added to this was American success in seducing the Korean imagination with the idea of liberal democracy. The military had to reckon with this, and with those students and citizens still restless and confident of their mobilized power after the 1960 tour de force in ousting Rhee. For the military, then, the most immediate prerequisite of power was to sublimate the pent-up energy of a highly literate populace before it erupted again in political turmoil: hence, a high-pitched economic development.

Legitimacy is, moreover, a matter of creating and reinforcing politically expedient myths. For economic growth to substitute for legitimacy, it has to be transmogrified into a symbol that appeals to some collective primordial sentiment—such as, for instance, nationalism. That symbol in Korea was a number: a talismanic double-digit GNP growth figure that was the Korean score in the race to catch up with Japan and also to surpass the DPRK's economic performance. It walked in the place of the exhilarating utopian slogan that every revolution requires, and if we were to see the industrial spurt of the 1960s as a miniature "capitalist revolution," it was all too fitting that the promise should come in some aggregate numerical, and not substantive, terms.

This number- and goal-orientation in national economic conduct muffled concerns over social justice and equitable distribution of wealth; these were "historically immature," or dismissed as academic squabbling over balanced growth. With steep growth in GNP as a political agenda, the target GNP growth rate became an uncompromising goal in the economic planning process and could only fluctuate in the limited range of, say, 7 percent to 11 percent GNP growth per annum. The Korean manner of determining the overall rate of growth was roughly like this: the same as the past growth rate if the latter had been high, and a precipitous increase if it had been unfavorable.[71] Inputs were extemporized to meet the output growth target; investment as a portion of the GNP was so hefty and rigid as to impart the impression that financing feasibility was always an afterthought for Koreans. This developmental chutzpah became, by 1970, a cause of serious concern for officials of international economic agencies, as the Korean debt service ratio reached a dangerous level.[72] But Korean "recklessness" was not an artifact of the late 1960s; from the early 1960s on, Americans spotted what they considered an excessive investment zeal on the part of the military leadership.

The type and level of investment the junta coveted—iron and steel projects, an industrial complex in Ulsan as a "symbol of national political commitment [sic] of the military junta,"[73]—worried Americans who thought that the future debt-servicing would surely translate into an American aid burden. Hence, the Americans pressed for caution and stability: reduction in investment programs and growth targets in the First Five-Year Plan (1962–1966, henceforth

FFYP), balanced budgets (1964), greater tax collection (1963), interest rate increases to garner more household savings (1965).

The severe downward revision of the FFYP in 1964 that the Americans forced was a lesson, however, that taught neither humility nor caution to Koreans. If anything, this intervention proved to be utterly needless, confirming to the Korean leaders the correctness of their original confidence, for the annual average GNP growth for the FFYP ended up being over 10 percent, almost twice the revised estimate. Investment, which had been tempered down to 13 percent of the GNP in 1962, also leaped high to an historically unprecedented 26.7 percent by 1968. This was primarily a function of spectacular export performance, and also of a set of fortuitous circumstances, viz., the Vietnam War and the inflow of Japanese capital. Nonetheless, the ROK government began to eschew American advice from that point on. Drafting of the Second FYP incorporated greater participation of the Korean Economic Planning Board, and the Third FYP was nearly an autochthonous product.

The growing rift between the American economic mission and the increasingly confident Korean policy makers may be gleaned from the following vignette. (It also revealed the modus operandi of the dependent state, which had to cloak its disagreement in terms palatable to the hegemon.) The end of the FFYP in 1966 found the Korean leadership inebriated with success and confidence, and they thought it outrageous that the bean counters at the U.S. aid mission were still balking at Korean schemes for economic expansion. The best way to rebut these Americans, Koreans figured, was to use the argument of none other than Rostow, the head of Policy Planning at the State Department and thus boss to the mission directors at the USAID. According to the complaints that Joel Bernstein, the director of the aid mission to Korea, filed to Rostow:

> You are being quoted as saying that conventional economists always underestimate demand for the products needed in a growing economy, that Korea should not worry about overcapacity because demand is always underestimated, that estimates of requirements should be made in the ordinary way and then everything should be doubled, and that economic development is too serious a matter to leave to economists who do not understand it adequately.[74]

Bernstein also told Rostow that Koreans, with their "damn the torpedoes" attitude, had not yet learned the principle of marginal utility: Rostow's "good advice [was] being given to the wrong patient." He urged Rostow to write the Korean leadership, and caution them about inflation.[75] Rostow did write Chang Ki-yông, the head of the Economic Planning Board and the Deputy Prime Minister, but the tone was tepid: it is possible that he thought the Koreans were rather in the right.[76]

At any rate, Koreans were getting better at planning (Korean style); they knew how to set targets: The remaining problem was where the money would come from for this developmental ambition; they found it through foreign loans, as we will see, but first let us consider the usual means: MNC direct investment.

MOBILIZING CAPITAL FOR GROWTH: FOREIGN DIRECT INVESTMENT. Nationalist concern, it has been argued, prompts many Third World nations to eschew direct investment, preferring instead an indirect one via loans. That is partly true and goes some of the way to explain Korea's policy of selective foreign investment inducement in the 1970s. But the relative absence in Korea of foreign direct investment can be traced to more obvious reasons; being a resource-poor country —no bananas for the United Fruit Company, no tin, no oil—Korea seemingly had little to offer the MNCs. Besides, MNCs are less than omniscient about global investment possibilities, preferring instead a historically known entity, such as Latin America (or in Asia, the Philippines). Domestic political instability and, combined with it, the precarious peace with North Korea dismayed potential investors.[77]

Koreans, for their part, did what they could to break the reticence of the MNCs. The Foreign Capital Inducement Law, passed in 1966, stipulated no minimum requirement for Korean participation in equity capital; provision for governmental assumption of management responsibilities in the event that any foreign-financed firm threatened default; limitation of governmental guarantee so that debt-service liabilities from them could not exceed 9 percent of annual foreign-exchange receipts (thereby ensuring the worth of the guarantee); and an increased tax exemption and tax holidays for foreign firms and investors. But even this law ended up whetting the appetites of commercial lenders, not of investors.

Japanese investors, however, were exceptions to the rule. They knew Korea in ways that the Westerners did not, knew that Korean export of labor-intensive goods was not only a theoretical possibility deriving from factor endowment but a historically proven fact from the 1920s. And, there was a grander design at work here, a dictate of the Japanese plan for industrial restructuring: Japan needed to relocate declining industries to nearby countries.[78] Korea, especially the Masan Free Export Zone (MAFEZ), was to be one of the receptacles.

Masan—and Korea's southeast, which hugs the city—was, in the mind of some Japanese, more an extension of the Japanese industrial powerhouse than it was Korean. Yatsugi Kazuo, a member of the Japanese delegation to the ROK-Japan Cooperation Committee and Permanent Director of the National Policy Research Society, advanced the "Yatsugi Plan" for "an Asian EEC," which would be launched by creating a "cooperative economic sphere" linking Korea's Namhae industrial region south of Pohang with Japan's Chugoku industrial region, stretching from Tottori and Yamaguchi in southern Honshu to a part of Oita in northern Kyushu.[79]

With the Normalization Treaty in effect, Japan and Korea swiftly formalized plans for MAFEZ, from construction and infrastructure to administration. Business operations in MAFEZ bypassed Korean central government. MAFEZ became a "one-stop shop" involving one authority within the zone, with no regulation over performance or domestic procurement of inputs, and enjoying complete tax exemption for the first five years. Even so, in the peak year in 1974, exports from MAFEZ remained only 4 percent of the total Korean exports.[80] As can be seen from table 4.6, foreign direct investment was, in comparison to loans, small, not even 5 percent of loans until 1969. In 1970, foreign direct investment climbed up to match almost 15 percent of the borrowing, and 11 percent in 1971. But loans really remained the main recourse for mobilizing foreign capital.

FINANCIAL REFORM AND THE ACCUMULATION OF DEBT. Rapid growth, as we saw, was the political agenda from the early 1960s on. But a serious bottleneck still remained to play havoc with the ambition of rapid growth: the Korean inability to attract foreign invest-

TABLE 4.6. Net Borrowing, Direct Investment, and Export Earnings, 1966–1971 (in $ million)

	Net Borrowing (1)	Direct Investment (2)	Total (3)	Exports (4)	Capital Flows/Export (3)/(4)
1966	218.2	2.2	220.4	250.3	.88
1967	419.8	19.9	439.7	320.2	1.37
1968	533.2	24.2	557.4	455.4	1.22
1969	499.2	28.2	527.4	622.5	.85
1970	420.0	61.4	481.4	835.2	.58
1971	395.3	45.2	440.5	1067.6	.41

ment, and most seriously, its failure to boost domestic savings. Therefore, the first task of the Third Republic, inaugurated in 1963, was a series of reforms, of which the most significant and controversial was a financial—more precisely, an interest-rate—reform.

Financial reform was of course not new to Korea. From the early 1950s, Americans had pressured Koreans to accept Bloomfield's recommendation on banking, which assumed and recommended a system of checks and balances in decision making. But it was only in 1957, when American advisers tightened the screws, that the first step toward liberalization (privatizing the banking sector) was taken. Unfortunately this was accompanied by the most nefarious consequences: the takeover of banks by a few chaebôl, with none of the benefits of financial liberalization, such as an increase in financial stocks as a precondition and companion of economic growth. This experience of bank privatization—to be terminated in three years— would dog, for the next few decades, proponents of financial liberalization, and provided the strongest historical and social defense for the government control of finance.

As the military junta scrapped this very modest step toward financial liberalization that took place in the late 1950s and renationalized the banking sector, the Americans assumed a wait-and-see attitude, partly because Korea was in a political maelstrom and partly because patience was a necessary virtue in steering the junta to hold elections in 1963. But once the Third Republic was politically ensconced, USAID launched a massive assault to liberalize the trade regime and financial sector, in what Anne Krueger called "the most dramatic and vivid change in any developing country since World War II."[81] The thrust of these reforms was to promote exports and create greater reliance on international prices.

Experts were shipped off to forge a new order in the Korean smithy: Edward Shaw, John Gurley, and Hugh Patrick to aid in developing financial institutions; Irma Adelman to advise on conceptual approaches to planning and planning models; Richard A. Musgrave for tax and fiscal policy; Peggy Musgrave for foreign trade policy; Edward Hollader and Edgar McVoy on manpower planning; and Allan Strout also on planning models.[82] The reforms started with the unification of exchange rates, followed in 1964 by a devaluation, the benchmark of export-led growth strategy, then import liberalization (however selective), establishment of an export incentive system via exemptions in a myriad of duties (domestic commodity tax, business activity tax, income tax), increased wasteage allowances, and of course credit subsidies, which constituted in 1964 more than one-fifth of the total export subsidy. These reforms are written about elsewhere and in such detail that it is redundant to go over them here.[83] What is relevant to us is the financial reform that happened in 1965, as part and parcel of the package of liberalization.

In truth, the 1965 financial reform was a very simple measure to enact: interest rates were hiked to mobilize domestic savings. Interest rates on time deposits jumped from 15 percent to 30 percent overnight, not much below the curb rate, and interest on some types of loans to 26–30 percent. At the source of this quantum leap upward in financial price was a theory of economic development that placed central emphasis on finance. Unlike both Keynesian and monetarist theories, which assumed *perfect* capital markets with a single governing interest rate or a term structure of interest rates, Edward Shaw—and later, Ronald McKinnon—argued that a unified capital market should not be treated as a given: rather, it was to be the goal and the very definition of economic development.[84] High interest rates, it was hoped, would augment total supply of financial resources not only through increased savings but through luring capital out of inferior investment in fragmented, uninstitutional markets; high costs of capital would also ensure efficiency in allocation as inefficient investments are curtailed. While American advisers of liberalization—Hugh Patrick, Edward Shaw, and John Gurley—had advocated a more comprehensive program, interest rate increases in time deposits and the establishment of the BOK stabilization account were the only major changes accepted by the government.

For a while, at least, it appeared that the reform achieved its intent: in three months, the level of time and savings deposits increased by 50 percent and grew at a compound annual rate of nearly 100 percent over the next four years. Between the end of 1965 and the end of 1969, time and savings deposits rose from 3.9 to 21.0 percent of GNP, and M2 leaped from 12.7 percent of GNP to 32.7 percent. The increase in the real money stock was even greater: in 1969, M2/WPI was seven times what it had been in 1964. Understandably, the reform was heralded as a veritable coup in boosting domestic savings, a spurt in investment, output, and employment in Korea.[85]

Others remained skeptical because the reform was only half-done. There was an obvious, glaring problem of selectivity in the interest rates that were affected: demand deposits were left out of consideration by the government, and increases in loan rates were selective, leaving out export, agricultural, and many other categories of investment loans (although they were rediscounted at lower rates at the BOK to ensure the profitability of banks). But it was in the late 1960s, as Korea began accumulating staggering amounts of debt, that the gravest reservations about the reform surfaced.

Detractors of the reform charged that the debt crisis—which, by the beginning of the 1970s, reached a foreign debt/GNP ratio of 30 percent up from 2.3 percent a decade earlier—stemmed directly from this financial reform, and further, that something was gravely wrong with the theoretical assumptions behind the reform: to wit, the reform assumed a closed model which was not only irrelevant but detrimental to conducting economic affairs in an open economy like Korea, where firms could borrow from abroad to increase their stock of capital. If there were a positive discrepancy between domestic and international interest rates, other things being equal, Korea would be inundated with foreign capital, and increases in financial holding would occur without reduction in consumption. In fact, this was what happened.

As can be seen from table 4.7, the foreign rate of interest (LIBOR)

TABLE 4.7. Cost of Foreign Capital (annual average—percent)

	1966–70	1971–75	1976–80
Domestic lending rates[a]	24.4	17.0	18.0
(Curb Market Interest Rate)	(54.2)	(40.1)	(41.3)
Foreign interest rate[b]	6.4	7.9	11.5
Foreign inflation rate (GNP Deflator)[c]	4.7	8.3	6.0
Exchange rate depreciation[d]	5.1	7.8	5.5
GDP deflator, Korea[e]	14.6	19.8	20.7
Real foreign exchange rate (2-3)	1.7	−0.4	5.5
Interest rate differential between home and foreign markets (1-2-4)	12.9	1.3	1.0
Real private cost of borrowing abroad (2 + 4 − 5)	−3.1	−4.1	−3.7

SOURCE: Bank of Korea, *Monthly Bulletin*, various issues, as cited by Yung Chul Park, 1985.

[a] Discounts on bills of Deposit Money Banks.

[b] LIBOR (90 days).

[c] Average of Japan and the United States.

[d] BOK standard concentration rate (three-year moving average).

[e] Three-year moving average.

in the 1966 to 1970 period (when the reform was in effect), adjusted for an exchange rate change, was lower than the rate paid on domestic borrowing by 12.9 percentage points. This was an incredible gap, particularly in comparison to the figures for 1971–1975 and 1976–1980 (when the reform was dropped), which stood at 1.3 and 1.0 percentage points, respectively. Not surprisingly, foreign debt skyrocketed during the period of the interest rate reform. Table 4.8 shows that foreign borrowing almost doubled in 1966, and continued to snowball through the end of the decade. Korea's debt service, which stood at 5.2 percent of exports in 1966 was, by 1971, 28.16 percent of exports in 1971.

A flabbergasted Korean economist charged that the interest rate reform, instead of bringing about "financial deepening," opened a floodgate for foreign capital. As Cho Sun saw it, the reform not only created dependency on foreign resources, but bifurcated industrial structure and put heavy pressure on banking sector.

The high interest rate policy provided strong incentives to borrow foreign capital, and made Korean economy dependent on external debt. The difference between domestic rates and foreign rates, 30 percent and 10 percent respectively, made foreign borrowing profitable. Investment increased rapidly as enormous amount of commercial loans flowed in from outside. . . . Korea's *chaebôl* came to depend on foreign loans to finance their investment . . . [But] to control credit expansion, the government resorted to suppressing loans to small and medium industries that were not beneficiaries of foreign loans. The result was a dualism in Korean industrial

TABLE 4.8. External Debt and Debt Service

Year	Total Foreign Debt (U.S. $ million)	Total Debt as % of GNP	Debt Service as % of Exports
1963	157	4.06	2.30
1964	177	5.29	4.17
1965	206	6.81	8.00
1966	392	10.26	5.20
1967	645	13.62	10.15
1968	1,199	20.07	9.47
1969	1,800	24.07	13.68
1970	2,245	25.48	28.34
1971	2,922	30.06	28.16

SOURCE: Bank of Korea and Economic Planning Board.

structure. . . . High interest rates on the rapidly rising time and savings deposits also put an inordinate burden on banks, not to mention the problem of bad loans to (foreign loan receiving) insolvent firms.[86] [Author's Translation]

This explosive growth in foreign debts and the bankruptcy of large firms receiving the loans was finally dealt with through draconian steps, to be discussed in the next section. But the measures taken were inconceivable in a democratic polity. The solution to the financial problem, touted as the savior of big business, heralded the dissolution of the 1960s political system. The measures arrived simultaneous with the inauguration of a bureaucratic authoritarian regime in 1972, and we will argue that this was not mere happenstance.

The Politics of Debt and the Rise of Bureaucratic Authoritarianism in Korea

We have argued that Korea's sustained growth is best understood as issuing from a fortuitous collocation of dynamism on three levels: global, regional, and national. This ensemble generated resources for Korean development in the form of war-related baksheesh and foreign capital, but a back-and-forth dialectic also worked here, a process that increasingly fed corruption, secrecy, and centralization in the decision-making process, thereby nourishing the existing tendency toward authoritarianism in Korea.

Almost all literature on regime-change in Korea points to domestic sources of authoritarianism, either citing "tradition" in the body politic or Linzian "breakdown of democratic regimes."[87] When the literature touches upon external factors—which is rare—the a priori assumption is that the Korean authoritarian phenomenon happened *in spite of* foreign prodding and not *because of* it, a stark contrast from what some theorists are wont to argue for Latin America. And the assumption is justifiable, at least for the early 1960s. The American prerogative then was to steer the junta to the ballot box, and to that end, Kennedy even withheld $25 million in economic aid to Korea—this, amid famine and drought.

But when we trace the movement of foreign capital, particularly Japanese commercial loans, a different picture emerges: tight and surreptitious relations between the Korean leadership and Japanese big business, sealed with prewar ties and lubricated with bribery, subverting and bypassing what there was of democratic process in the Korea of the 1960s. This was dubbed a relationship of *yuchaku*, a harmony of interest among the Liberal Democratic Party, the Park regime, Japanese big business, and Korean conglomerates as scalawags.[88] Yuchaku—connoting thick political ties—was a direct offshoot of the mode of Japanese capital inflow to Korea: the Japanese MNCs' concentration on the sale of plants through commercial loans rather than production for domestic consumption. Where the Japanese invested in Korea, it was in the form of subcontracting, for exports only. Thus, the modus operandi of the Japanese MNCs in Korea was radically different from that of the American MNCs in Latin America. This capital influx from Japan did not require an understanding of the Korean market, but only the existence of fluid nonmarket channels—political connections and direct bribery.

The Japan connection was particularly noisome from the beginning, exposing the proclivity of the Young Turks to go to any length to draw resources for state-building: duty-free imports from Japan of pinball machines, Datsun automobiles for resale at windfall prices, a "turn-key" hotel-casino (even the poker chips came from Japan)—all to finance the launching of the KCIA. There were allegations, too, of a secret concord with Japan prior to negotiations for diplomatic rapprochement, bargaining down the price of reparations in return for a Japanese donation of $20 million to finance the new ruling party in Korea (among other things).[89] According to the secret report prepared by the CIA in 1966, Japanese picked up the tab for launching the governing party (Democratic Republican Party—DRP for short) in Korea.

> Japanese firms reportedly provided two-thirds of the party's 1961–1965 budget, six firms having paid the $66 million total, with individual contributions ranging from $1 million to $20 million. According to the strongman [sic] Kim Chong-pil, newly renamed to the DRP chairmanship he held before his "exile" 21 months ago, the party needs up to $26 million for the 1967 presidential campaign. . . . Kim [also received] payments for promoting the Korea-Japan negotiations, and payments by various Japanese firms for granting monopolies in Korea.[90]

But for all this, it was really the institution of sovereign risk that became the major conduit of political funds in the era of debt-led growth. The reasons stem from the choice of development strategy and financial policies in the late 1960s. The termination of ISI as an industrialization strategy also meant an end to the political contributions that derived from import licensing and the allocation of U.S. dollars, grossly undervalued at official exchange. Revenues from granting access to cheap bank credits also dwindled because the financial reform of 1965 had raised interest rates on domestic loans. Now, low cost foreign capital, approved and guaranteed by the government, became the most coveted prize for business, which was more than willing to deposit the "commission" for foreign loans in party coffers. Other and less significant sources of political contribution included quid pro quos for granting low-interest Industrial Bank of Korea loans and for procurement of government sponsored projects.

It is not easy to find out the value of the said "commission." The press in Korea speculated that it hovered around 10–15 percent of foreign loans, with one scholar putting it at as high as 20 percent.[91] If we use a very conservative estimate of, say, 5 percent, the commission from guaranteed foreign loans in the three-year period from 1963 to 1966, which totalled $800 million, would have yielded $40 million.[92] If the precise amount of foreign loan commissions remained a matter of speculation, their overall importance in political campaign was an open secret. One powerful figure in the governing party admitted that "businessmen who had received more than $10 million in foreign loans expressed considerable sông-i (gratitude)," meaning "political contribution." Another politician bragged: "If some businessmen in the past did not comprehend the resolve for modernization of the ruling party, they do now. They understand who they owe their wealth to. . . . For the party, it is more convenient to collect big from a few than to collect small from hundreds."[93] "Big" usually meant contributions over $100,000; names such as Lucky-Goldstar, Hyundai Construction, Samsung, and Ssangyong figured prominently in the list of such contributors.[94]

Some politicians, rather than relying on the kindness of strange businessmen, resorted to a more "direct" financing: they got foreign loans themselves. The three largest recipients of loans, for instance, were firms owned by the governing party politicians and/or their siblings: Ssangyong, whose founder Kim Sông-kon was an influential assemblyman, was a recipient of more than $100 million in foreign loans in the late 1960s; Lucky-Goldstar received $62 million in loans; and Korea Explosives received $67 million.[95]

Thus, one might say that a massive influx of foreign capital in the late 1960s financed half of the nation's total investment, and tumbling after it was an avalanche of a particular kind of corruption that presented the regime with electoral victories and impressive influence over the nation's business. The press did considerable muckraking over this, panning the government for its connection with large foreign loan recipients like the infamous Hanguk Fertilizer Company, which was caught smuggling, and Saenara Motors, which was found importing virtually everything—down to the last bolt—from Toyota. The opposition also bitterly complained of the heavy-handedness with which the ruling party financed its campaign.

Corruption is a relative concept, however, and a certain forgiving quality—or inurement—inheres in the body politic if corruption occurs in conjunction with economic growth, and if the fruits of such growth are relatively fairly distributed. This certainly was the situation in the late 1960s, so much so that the military regime could win, hands down, the election in 1967. Seen from that year, the prospect of continuing the 1960s arrangement seemed excellent—an electoral machine greased with a foreign loan lagniappe, delivering to the electorate fruits of economic growth, and thereby muffling dissenting grumbles. Then something happened, with awesome velocity: the first debt crisis in Korean history. The cozy 1960s political economy fell of its own weight. When it rose again, Korea was in the grip of a bona fide bureaucratic authoritarian regime.

The strain was palpable in 1969 when the government took over management of thirty firms, all foreign loan recipients, which had gone belly-up; another ninety such enterprises were found to be on the brink of bankruptcy. By 1971, the number of bankruptcies of enterprises receiving foreign loans climbed to a record two hundred, and the total external debt pushed over the $3 billion mark, its ratio to the GNP now cresting 30 percent.

The situation was almost overdetermined from the beginning—the problem of an unbalanced economy obsessed with exports, which sustained big businesses with impossible debt-equity ratios through export subsidies and unreasonable fiscal and financial policies. According to the report of the Insolvent Firms Settlement Team, the average ratio of net worth to total assets in the thirty bankrupt enterprises was a stunning 1.1 percent.[96] The culprits were widely thought to be the interest rate gap between domestic and foreign loans, and a corporate tax structure which made interest payments on business borrowings tax deductible. Added to that was the massive increase in money circulation—8.4 percent a month—at the time of the 1969 referendum and 1971 election, an increase which subverted the government's own stabilization policies.[97] The state was stiff-armed by, in the parlance of social sciences, the electoral business cycle. The IMF stepped in to break the impasse.

The IMF imposed a set of tough stabilization policies, the first such ever to be imposed on Korea by the IMF. The package was unlike the later ones in that it did not follow in the wake of an external shock, and it did not involve further expansion of foreign capital inflow. Rather, it issued in the absence of international disturbances (like the oil shock), and reflected a serious concern over internal financial management. The IMF argued that there was a fundamental distortion in the Korean payment regime. The Korean government relied on expanded export subsidies, rather than currency depreciation, to bridge the gap between external and internal price movement, and so the won became increasingly overvalued. The order of the day, then, was a devaluation of the currency, abandonment of export subsidies and import restrictions, as well as a temporary ceiling on the influx of foreign loans.

The Korean government viewed these demands as outrageous, thwarting the Second FYP and jeopardizing rapid growth. But the pressure was intense: Americans made the consideration of additional PL480 and development loan funding conditional on Korean acquiescence to the IMF demands. To allay Korean fears, the United States said it would take the "responsibility" for the consequences.[98] Koreans then swallowed the IMF pill, save for the demand to end export subsidies; the incentive system was, after all, the pillar of the government's export-led growth strategy, and its abandonment at the time of export slowdown and financial squeeze would have been a lethal blow to exporters.

The IMF urged the Korean government to issue, in a standby agreement, a letter of intent to limit foreign capital to one- to three-year loans. Consequently, the growth of foreign debt slowed to 25 percent and 30 percent in 1970 and 1971, and investment plunged; export growth rates fell, too, down from 36 percent in 1968–1969 to only 27 percent in 1970–1971. A sharp contraction in monetary expansion dropped the growth rate of M2 from 61 percent in 1969 to 27 percent in 1970. Finally, the growth rate of GNP also decreased, from 13.8 percent in 1969 to 7.6 percent in 1970.

The next measure was devaluation: a whopping 18 percent in 1971, followed by another 7 percent a year later. This was bitterly resented by businessmen, including exporters, who considered the sharp rise in the won cost of debt financing ill-timed, adding insult to injury. Domestic banks could not provide relief. In spite of a large reduction in bank reserve requirements in 1971, banks still groaned under nonperforming loans and were unable to help firms finance the increased foreign loan repayment. Business turned to the last available resort: the curb market with its hefty price and short maturity on loans. When businesses could not pay back the curb, they capsized.

Business was in an uproar. The Federation of Korean Industrialists, the nation's most powerful interest group representing big business, clamored that *something* be done fast: something short of declaring national bankruptcy to the world, something besides another contraction and stabilization, but still something to bail them all out. In fact, never before in the history of Korea had business demanded something of this magnitude from the government, in unison, and in imperious certainty that it was the duty of the state to bail them out as a group. And never before did it happen that business could confront with such anger and hubris the mighty economic bureaucracies. What had happened?

Two explanation may be given, one of which has to do with the makeup of "Korea Inc.," a particular form of capitalist state that traces its postwar origins to the 1961 compromise discussed earlier in the chapter. The truth is that, although the political economy of the 1950s was predicated on the state and business being Siamese twins, it was really the farcical "punishment" of illicit accumulators that revealed the real steering mechanisms of Korea Inc.: the state has its hand on the tiller but business provides the motive force. The state is strong in that it can—and does—give and take life away from individual firms; but it is also constrained by virtue of being a capitalist state whose survival is contingent on the health and contentment of the business class.

The lesson to members of the business community was clear; united they would stand, divided they would fall—by the hand of the state. In crisis, then, the capitalists of Korea united. In 1971, the head of the Federation of Korean Industrialists specifically requested President Park to freeze the curb, transfer outstanding curb loans to official financial intermediaries, reduce corporate tax, and then slash interest rates. When met with a pregnant silence from President Park, big business went for the state's jugular: the state should either do as it is told, or slash the government budget in half—in other words, no tax. Business was on the warpath.[99]

Another explanation has to be sought in the vastly expanded realm of political action that the hurly-burly of regime change opened up for business. The pace of change at the turn of the decade was brisk: in 1969, the controversial referendum for a third presidential term signaled the end of the semi-competitive electoral system. This was followed in 1971 by Korea's last real presidential election, then an emergency decree (in January 1972), then a state of siege, and finally the inauguration of a bureaucratic authoritarian regime in October of the same year. Troubles that surfaced ranged from student and labor unrest, tax revolt, civil disobedience-cum-strike by the judicial branch, sabotage by the medical doctors, and revolts of slum dwellers. Table 4.9 reveals the extent of labor unrest in 1971. In sharp contrast to the remainder of the decade, reported cases of disputes totaled 1,656—a level which would not be obtained again until 1980. All of these became simultaneously protests *and* pretext for instituting a bona fide authoritarian regime in Korea.

The crisis triggered by these desperate and scattered acts of violence reached its height with the revelation of rampant disobedience within the ruling party and, amazingly, in the military. The intraparty discord stemmed from the attempt to emulate the structure of Japan's Liberal Democratic Party, which eventuated in the development of factions centered around four "bosses," some of whom were strongly in favor of passing the mantle to Kim Chong-pil, and therefore against the continuing rule of Park. As for the military, the first sign that something was amiss came amid a bizzare mutiny of twenty green berets in the summer of 1971, demanding an end to Park's dialogue with North Korea.

Thus, the tableau at the turn of the decade was that of a crisis from below *and* incoherence at the top, which made it far from certain that a bureaucratic authoritarian system was in the cards. In that confusing moment, business was the pivotal force that finally tipped the balance in favor of a full-fledged authoritarianism. This momentous outcome issued neither from a conspiratorial compact nor the usual political quid pro quo. Rather, it emanated from the

TABLE 4.9. Labor Disputes, 1971–1979

Issues	1971	1972	1973	1974	1975	1977	1979
Wage	1,014	171	100	361	74	66	67
Labor conditions	137	59	81	41	14	9	—
Unfair dismissals	182	38	63	51	10	4	6
Unfair employer practice	96	41	95	46	19	6	3
Others	227	37	28	156	16	11	29
Total	1,656	346	367	666	123	96	105

SOURCES: Compiled from *Nodong Yônmaeng Saôp Pogo* [Report of the Federation of Korean Trade Unions] for 1971–1974, and the Ministry of Labor for 1975–1979.

logical impossibility of a liberal political order to satisfy the imperious demands of business: first, to be bailed out of financial crisis, and second, to shift the burden onto someone else—a hapless stratum in society, who happened to be the small savers.

The bailout dropped like a bombshell in August of 1971: an immediate moratorium on all payment of corporate debt owed to the private, domestic financial market—the curb. The crushing burden of interest repayment on foreign loans was thus shifted to the small investors who had followed their entrepreneurial instincts and put their savings in the curb market that yielded higher interest on financial assets than banks. The curb had long been a part of the dualistic financial system in Korea, and had proved flexible, pervasive, and resilient. While outside the rule of law, it was tolerated, if not implicitly encouraged, by financial authorities in Korea, because the curb was the *only* source from which households, as well as some businesses, could obtain loans. During phases of tight monetary policy—as, for instance, in the 1969–1972 period—the curb became a major source of funds to large corporations as well.

The size of curb is difficult to measure. In 1969, it was said to have been 82 percent of M1, equal to some 30 percent of total outstanding bank loans including that from Korean Development Bank. Of this total, an estimated 79.1 percent was ploughed into corporations, 14.3 percent to farms, and the remaining 6.3 percent taken up by urban households.[100] When, following the moratorium, all curb debtors and creditors were ordered to register with the government, the amount totaled about one-third of the outstanding bank loans. Still, this is probably an underestimation, since many creditors decided for various reasons that a loan write-off was preferable to exposure to the authorities. Who, exactly, were these creditors?

A total of 209,896 persons were registered as creditors, of which 70 percent were small lenders with assets in the market below 1 million won (with the official exchange rate in 1971 at 346.1 won to a dollar, this equalled $2,889); in other words, they were not the "big loan sharks" the government dubbed them. They were ordinary citizens: female factory workers saving for marriage, parents preparing their children's college tuitions, would-be homeowners, senior citizens wanting higher yields on their retirement funds, maids and shoeshine boys scrimping for a better future.[101] Many were blithely ignorant of where their money went, trusting benign judgments of acquaintances who served as intermediaries or those curb brokers who were deemed reputable. When the government finally revealed the original sources of the money that had been fed into some 40,700 debtor enterprises, many creditors, stunned and incredulous, disputed the verity of such information; some had not even known that such enterprises existed, let alone made loans to them.[102]

The moratorium was to last for three years, after which all curb funds had to be turned into five-year loans at the maximum annual interest of 18 percent. The government said its action would promote price stability. The curb had handled more than 30 percent of corporate financing, at a monthly interest rate of 2 percent for large corporations of high credit standing, 3 to 4 percent for smaller and lesser-known ones. Interest financing in the manufacturing sector came to 9.4 percent of net sales—thus contributing, the government argued, to a cost-push inflationary spiral. The governor of the Bank of Korea asserted that the moratorium would open an era of low inflation, 3 percent annual.[103] That prediction was never fulfilled.

The August decree on business bail-out also meant the end of the high interest era (1965–1972), and a lapse into financial repression, which would last through the entire 1970s: negative real interest rates and state-directed credit allocation. The time-deposit rate was now lowered from 17.4 percent to 12.6 percent, and as table 4.10 shows, the rate on loans up to one year dropped from 19 percent to 15.5 percent. The rate on curb, payable after the end of the moratorium, was half of what it was before.

Korean business was thus resuscitated overnight. But old problems remained—in fact, they became exacerbated. One was the problem of the highly leveraged corporate financial structure; in an inflationary and negative real interest milieu that followed, and per-

TABLE 4.10. The Measures Contained in the August 3rd Decree

	Realignment of Private Loans	Special Banking Measure	Reduction of Bank Interest	Total
Amount of affected loans	2,445	1,933	all bank loans	
Interest rate reduction	36.0% to 16.2%	15.5% to 8.0%	19.0% 15.5%	
Amount in interest relieved (per year)	483	165	380	1,028

SOURCE: Bank of Korea, *Report on the August 3rd Decree*, p. 83.

sisted throughout the 1970s, it of course became far more sensible to rely on indirect financing. The only silver lining here could have been a reduced appetite for foreign credit, now that interest rate differentials between domestic and foreign loans were significantly reduced in comparison to the 1966–1970 period. Still, thanks to inflation, the real private cost of foreign loans remained negative. (Table 4.7 provides a bird's-eye view.)

Another problem that the decree professed to eradicate, once and for all, was the curb market. But, a unified financial system with negative real return to financial capital was an oxymoron. In fact, notwithstanding bullying by the government, the curb market sprang up again, mushrooming throughout the 1970s. Then, why did the government insist on this illogicality?

The explanations ordinarily given by economists have to do with the efficacy of the state's fiscal and monetary policies: to recover tax revenues lost in the gigantic curb market, and to gain control over the flow of money. But, this is merely a classic illustration of a catch-22: to effect a particular type of industrial development and political control, the state wanted financial repression, and thus bifurcation of the financial market; but such bifurcation begets a vast market uncontrolled by the state. Was the Korean state mired in a loop of catch-22s? Perhaps not.

Regardless of the philippics against the curb, the state was perhaps not too unhappy about it. The curb is, after all, the flexible part of a symbiosis, regulated and unregulated, that forms the financial system in Korea. Furthermore, it is the part vulnerable, precisely because it is not regulated, to a raid by the state. It is a critical component in industrial financing, a lifeline for firms; at the same time, it cushions business and the regime by dying conveniently in time of financial crunch (and returning to life when times are better). To ensure the political and economic usefulness of the curb through this life and death cycle, in economic expansion and crisis, the state had to enforce illegality of the curb. The function of the curb was such that if it had not existed, an authoritarian state would have had to create it.

Conclusion

In the 1960s, Korea made a major transition. For economists, this transition was the turn *outward*, around 1964–1965; for political scientists, the 1961 coup d'etat and the installation of a reformist leadership was the turning point. In truth, the 1960s saw a more fundamental and broad transition than that: a resurgence of a state that was iron-fisted at home and, therefore, capable of restructuring domestic economy and supporting sustained growth. We focused on this phenomenon from three different angles—global, state, and class. Looked at this way, we found that the "transition" was perhaps about ten years in the making.

The prognostications of Korean development were first made in 1960, if not in 1957–1958, in the minds of internationalist economic policy makers in Washington. Such dating and such a cast of characters may seem odd, and make little sense to those to whom Korea is the universe, but that is how it was. We place Korea squarely in the context of the "global opportunity structure" of the 1960s, lest we err in thinking that the Korean "miracle" was sui generis.

It took another five years before one knew for sure that the regime was harnessing a powerful state, one capable of exploiting the opportunities available to a parvenue like Korea. This was not only owing to the legacy of Japan and Rhee. Rather, we see again a back-and-forth dialectic between international and domestic realms. Japan as a regional surrogate of America bolstered the military government by financing its politics and its industries; and America, grateful for Korean camaraderie in Vietnam, indulged and supported Park. Thus, the tableau in the mid-1960s showed the military in Korea as state-builders par excellence, invincible: it succeeded in erecting not only a formidable state apparatus with enormous repressive power, but it also whipped civilian politicians at the ballot box—a feat never to be repeated after the early 1970s.

In the critical years 1969–1972, Korean capitalists first had a show of strength, threatening a collective tax boycott to break the back of the regime should the state fail to devise some form of financial rescue package (in this case, a debt write-off.) They were no longer the subservient bureaucratic capitalists living off their "rents" in the economic maze of ISI, or the bourgeoisie of the 18th Brumaire, prostrate before the rifle butt, exchanging political rights for the right to make money. Rather, Korean business at the end of the 1960s was increasingly confident and politically savvy, and if it struck a Faustian bargain with Park in 1972, it was by choice, not through fear of rifle butts: business *chose* to remain in the economic grip of the state.

Thus, by the end of the 1960s, the three indispensable conditions for development could be found in Korea: a global economic structure that accomodated and welcomed an upstart, a developmental state that could exploit its external conditions and harness its grip on domestic sectors, and finally a hardworking and increasingly confident bourgeoisie. This was a formidable mosaic for economic growth; for democracy, however, it was none too auspicious.

For the military regime, the pull toward full-fledged authoritarianism was strong, and for the chaebôl, an authoritarian solution was welcome as long as the state remained their industrial financier and strong-armed the working class. And the hegemonic structure in East Asia was no breakwater against bureaucratic authoritarianism in Korea—it was unlike the dual hegemonic structure in Southern Europe, where liberal democracies of Western Europe showed massive hostility toward the southern pariahs, and ultimately contributed to their fall.[104] The truth of this general observation appears particularly self-evident as we recall the circumstances at the turn of the decade: the sordid tie between the ruling parties of Korea and Japan and the zaibatsu, and the inauguration of Richard Nixon, who was interested in blocking Korean textile imports, but not dictatorship.

Thus, while the cold war alliance was not the *cause* of authoritarianism in Korea, it provided the space in which authoritarianism could inhere. But, once in motion, Park's authoritarianism moved to the beat of a different drum. It was the beat of nationalism.

5

The Search for Autonomy: The Big Push

Economic backwardness, rapid industrialization, ruthless exercise of dictatorial power, and the danger of war have become inextricably intertwined

Alexander Gershenkron

We cannot let our vigilance down at the reemergence of Big Power politics. Just as an individual must protect himself, so a nation must consider security and survival as indispensable. When a nation's survival is at stake, politics, economy, culture, everything should be organized and mobilized for that single purpose.

Park Chung Hee

A MENISCUS is a physical curiosity: convex under one kind of pressure, it reverts to concave under another. The Korean economy is an industrial curiosity: outward-leaning in the 1960s, it abruptly retreated under the changed circumstances of the 1970s. Internally, politics was dead and deadly, a recrudescence of the colonial war years that saw a thorough extirpation of liberal vestiges. In industrial policy, the emphasis on exports still remained, but otherwise the look was inward toward self-sufficiency: accelerating import-substitution; an emphasis on heavy, chemical, and defense industries at the expense of light industries; money and credit that heeded, more than ever before, the siren call of the state and not of the market; and finally, a massive popular mobilization to reduce the urban/rural gap—a potpourri of rural self-help and basic needs.

Why did this happen? Many explanations may be advanced, but the most important was the profound shift in hegemonic policy, and its adverse effects on Korean security. In the days of the Vietnam War when Korean soldiers substituted for Americans for a pittance, Park Chung Hee was the patron, and Johnson guaranteed Korean security lock, stock, and barrel, and told him so. But the new world according to Nixon was an unfriendly and minatory one, where God only helped those who helped themselves: the Nixon Doctrine wrote off Indochina, and shoved off, through protectionism, economic parvenues like Korea. No longer could refuge be found in the indulgence of Mutual Security and the exuberance of the Development Decade. Park put it like this:

> Looking back at the days of the Cold War, we find that the question of national security was much simpler and easier then. Among the nations within the free world, a broad relationship of credibility and fraternity existed. In time of emergency, friends could be counted upon. Not so any more.[1]

In what were perceived to be the waning days of the Pax Americana, the first provision for survival was to purge all uncertainties from both the body politic and industry: elimination of electoral uncertainties and replacement of a self-regulating market by a regulated market. With the steering mechanisms thus made predictable, the nation then veered toward the Big Push: massive investments in steel, shipping, machine-building, metals, and chemicals. The ambition was to turn Korea, in the span of one decade, from the final processor of export goods to one of the world's major exporters of steel, ships, and other producer goods. The development of basic industries also held the promise of a vibrant defense industry, thus to end the reliance on American largess in weaponry and various attendant political inconveniences.

The Big Push had an economic rationale in backward linkages and benefits of externalities, but nothing attested more eloquently to the logic of the Korean variant than President Park's simple equation: steel is national power *(Ch'ŏl ŭn kunggyŏk)*. This is what Stalin had said before, and also what the Japanese militarists in the 1930s meant when they equated steel with rice. Thus, steel was a metaphor for self-reliance and national security, and the push for heavy industrialization was a way of fortifying the frontier.

If this illiberal politics-cum-forced march of heavy industrialization appears idiosyncratic to Korea, a typically Korean overkill perhaps, it was a paradigmatic national reaction to a larger crisis, the malfunctioning of the global system. In a brilliant exegesis of market society, Karl Polanyi pointed to three historic state responses to the collapse of "nineteenth-century civilization": fascism, which, however barbaric, was an attempt at severance from and destruction of the existing order; the New Deal with its very real possibilities for national capitalism; and the Stalinist "socialism in one country." In all three, states attempted to protect their societies from the vagaries of the international market by looking inward, and repudiating, in varying degrees, the principles of laissez-faire.[2]

The analogy between these inward solutions and the Korea of the 1970s has its glaring limits. Whereas the sustainability of fascist autarky was predicated upon, first, the existence of a national industrial base, and then upon aggression into, and acquisition of, markets abroad, Korea was unable perhaps even to defend itself, let alone launch an aggressive foreign policy. That, as it turned out, was what ultimately squelched, in scarcely a decade, the Korean aspiration for national capitalism: the lack of resources to go it alone.

The situation was really not unlike that of Russia at the end of the nineteenth century.[3] Money for industries had to be gotten through greater exports, and heavy industries had to be established and sustained through furious borrowing abroad. By 1978–1979, moreover, the future of defense-related and heavy industries, in which so much had been invested, seemed as parlous as ever; and the light industries, faithful earners of foreign exchange that had suffered from the state's benign neglect in the 1970s, were now badly threatened by global competition, rising wages, and U.S. protectionism. Finally, it would take massive riots—triggered, not accidentally, by protests of workers at a shut down textile plant—to reverse the gear of economic policy and to end Park's reign of terror.

In the 1980s, with "economic liberalization" as its new shibboleth, the recent past is now seen as a negative example, something to undo, never repeat. But, notwithstanding all the excess and terror, we will argue that the belabored economics of the 1970s laid the foundation for a maturer industrial structure. This chapter examines the rationale for, and progress of, industrial transformation in the 1970s. How such efforts were funded—a study of financial policy— we hold for the next chapter, along with the consequences of such policy on social formation.

Reassessing Security: Korea in the Nixon Era and After

The Korean economic boom in the late 1960s was a splurge on borrowed time. As American fortunes turned for the worse in Vietnam at the close of the decade, Korea braced for hard times and a new set of tasks ahead: how to bargain with America so as to prevent the turning-off of the economic and military aid spigot that the Korean and Vietnam Wars had kept open, and how to handle, short of sabotaging, the predictable eventuality of U.S. troop reduction in Korea. But what the Korean leadership failed to anticipate—and the same could be said for all American allies—was just how systematic and imperious the devolution of the U.S. global burden was to be.

The trigger for the change in the ground rules of Pax Americana was the deterioration in the U.S. balance of payments. The payments deficit had been a source of some concern, academic and otherwise, from 1958 on, when the drain on U.S. gold stock first became apparent. To defend the dollar and rectify the deficit, Americans had entertained a variety of solutions: minor adjustments in the Atlantic Alliance, capital controls program, the Interest Equalization Tax shortly after the Tonkin Gulf incident, voluntary restraints on banking and corporate transfers of funds abroad in 1965, and finally, in 1968, making the voluntary restraints mandatory.

But it took Richard Nixon to come up with a drastic but antinomic solution to the deficit problem: on the one hand, an aggressive containment of the deficit by attacking some of its root causes (dollar outflows, especially for U.S. troops abroad, and more broadly, the costs of maintaining an empire, and private merchandise trade) and declaring, on the other hand, that the U.S. deficit was not really a problem, and if it were, it was not so much an American problem as a problem for the rest of the world. That is, foreigners would have to adjust their interest and exchange rates or else face some sort of global financial catastrophe. The shorthand way of putting it is to say that the Bretton Woods system came to an end.

Just about every aspect of Nixon's global design affected Korea:

the Nixon Doctrine reduced the payments deficit via cuts in military spending abroad, and sharing the imperial burden with regional economic powers (in this case, Japan); the import surcharge and rising protectionism rectified the U.S. trade deficit, caused in part by Korean imports; and floating rates, followed by dollar devaluations, threw Korean planning off kilter.[4] It was these issues, along with the 1973 oil shock, that help us understand the external challenges to which the belabored economics of the 1970s was a response.

THE NIXON DOCTRINE. Nixon's electoral year was a particularly trying one for Korea. In 1968, Korea still had two divisions in Vietnam, and just as the war in Indochina was escalating, so was North Korean guerrilla infiltration into the South, possibly in coordination with the Tet Offensive designed to demolish the American position in Vietnam. Of some 629 guerrilla-related incidents reported for 1968 alone, the most noteworthy was a North Korean commando attack on the presidential residence that claimed some 100 casualties and was a near miss on Park's life. But, American hackles were raised only when an American spyship was captured by the North Koreans in the same year. Park must have deeply resented all the Pueblo-related brouhaha and the subsequent U.S. negotiations with North Korea, which placed the latter in the international limelight.[5] Warned of South Korean expendability in the American scheme, Park let it be known that Korea would have to "go it alone" to defend itself if Americans were reluctant to do the job.

"If the United States does nothing to keep Korea from becoming another Vietnam," declared Pak Chung-gyu, the chairman of the Foreign Affairs Committee of the National Assembly and a confidant of the President, "we have no recourse but to carry out the duty of national defense by ourselves alone." He suggested that U.S. passivity in the Pueblo crisis warranted an end to American operational control of the Korean armed forces. President Park also told the U.S. ambassador that there was "a limit to our patience and self-restraint."[6] In the event, Cyrus Vance was flown over to Seoul to placate the leadership, but the decision, as Mao might put it, to "stand on two legs" was already set in motion.

Park called for an armed militia of 2.5 million men, with units even in the smallest villages. To comply with the presidential decree that the men be armed with Korean-made weapons, the Economic Planning Board announced a joint-venture with an American company to produce small arms and ammunitions; the Ministry of Finance financed the ammunitions factory with a portion of $60 million commercial loans being obtained from Chase Manhattan Bank and First National City Bank.[7] Here was the beginning pitch for defense industries.

Notwithstanding heightened vigilance, North Korean infiltration increased in frequency and in discomfitting mimicry of the Vietcong's subversion strategies in South Vietnam in the late 1950s. Then, in what Henry Kissinger called the first major crisis in the Nixon administration, North Korea downed an unarmed American reconnaisance plane, the EC-121, in the Sea of Japan in early 1969. Despite Kissinger's urging that several North Korean airfields be bombed in retaliation, Nixon, on the advice of Laird, refrained from a tit-for-tat with the North. Kissinger was to complain later that the handling of EC-121 incident was "weak, indecisive, disorganized," that "it showed major flaws in the [U.S.] decision making—[The administration] made no strategic assessment; no strong leadership; no significant political move; lacked both machinery and conception; made no demands that North Korea could either accept or reject."[8] This was one more incident that failed to inspire Korean confidence in America, and an adumbration of still greater conflicts in store for United States-Korean relations.

Nixon's new foreign policy design, first unveiled to the Congress in early 1970, revealed a switch from what was hitherto known as a two-and-a-half war strategy, to a one-and-a-half one. The former had meant initial defense of Western Europe against Soviet attack *and* a sustained defense against an all-out Chinese attack on Southeast Asia or Korea, plus meeting a contingency elsewhere. In the new strategy, the second category was simply dropped. This revision was a logical, if belated, response to the Sino-Soviet split, to the fact that a third of the Soviet and one-half of the Chinese military forces were now stacked on the Sino-Soviet frontier. If the Sino-Soviet bloc were no more, there was no reason—beyond bureaucratic pork-barreling —to fund military programs based on an old Cold War assumption.

The first place, besides Indochina, where the axe of the Nixon Doctrine fell was Korea. During the Johnson presidency, the National Security Council had recommended reducing U.S. troop commitment to Korea in five or more years depending on the Korean pace of military modernization, but the Nixon administration accelerated the withdrawal out of budgetary pressure: some 20,000 American soldiers were removed from Korea by the middle of 1971, with the rest to be phased out in the next five years. Seoul had little say in the decision, having lost its trump card once the United States had determined upon Vietnam disengagement.[9]

Foreign investor/lender confidence in Korea plummetted—no light matter for a country that financed more than a quarter of its total imports with foreign credits in 1969. In the investor panic bred by the Nixon Doctrine, only the Chile of Salvador Allende jostled with Korea for the dubious distinction of topping the list of countries covered by the Overseas Private Investment Corporation. Korea in the early 1970s was such an investment risk that 10 percent of the world's total in political risk insurance covered through the OPIC since 1969 was issued for U.S. investors in Korea.[10]

Koreans demanded compensation for the U.S. troop withdrawal. In a tense eight-hour negotiation during Spiro Agnew's visit to Korea in August 1970, Park presented the Vice President with a detailed list of Korea's military needs, and reportedly asked for $3 billion over five years for military modernization.[11] But Park only got half a loaf ($1.5 billion), and the disbursement was painfully slow: the Pentagon juggled its bookkeeping, diverting the Korea appropriations to Phnom Penh and Saigon.[12]

The Nixon Doctrine was not supposed to be an exercise in self-help as much as in group-help—that is, the Americans would retain essential hegemonic rights while relegating some duties to regional powers such as, say, the Shah's Iran or Japan. The notion of Japan as the regional leader was hardly novel, having been integral to America's postwar Asia policy. This time around, however, Americans tried to put teeth into the old design, publicly suggesting at one point that the Japanese conventional forces might have to "fill a regional vacuum" in East Asia as American forces withdrew from Korea.[13] Japan would assume a bigger responsibility for regional security, giving, for example, greater economic aid to Korea so that the latter could release its scarce resources to defend the DMZ, and by extension, the Japan archipelago.

Just before the Nixon-Sato Communiqué, Japan provided a large package of economic and technical assistance to Korea for building the P'ohang integrated steel mill, something Koreans had been desirous of, and thwarted in acquiring, since 1961. The Japanese government justified this action on security, and not economic, grounds. The Koreans received $73.7 million in loans from the Japanese government, $50 million in deferred payment credits from Japan's EXIM Bank, technical assistance from the Nippon Steel and Nihon Kokan Corporation, and an additional $59 million a year later for building ancillary plants for P'ohang. *The Mainichi News* remarked that the bilateral collaboration on P'ohang smacked of the Greater East Asian Co-Prosperity Sphere.[14]

Rather than Co-Prosperity, however, the neighbors more often indulged in mutual hostility. The catapulting of China onto the world scene so immediately captured Japanese attention and whetted their commercial appetite that the political and economic community, harkening to "The Four Principles of Chou En-lai" that barred China from trading with nations offering technical aid to South Korea, suddenly appeared reluctant to do business with Korea.[15] This was reflected in the fast dwindling of the Japanese participation in the Korea-Japan Economic Cooperative Conference. Of the 48 Japanese companies that showed up at the first meeting, only 29 made a reappearance for the third meeting of July 1971, and merely 17 in March 1972.[16] This appeared to be a deplorable bit of perfidy to the Korean eyes, and helps to explain the anti-Japanese campaigns and outbursts of the 1970s.

Things hardly improved when the Korean CIA abducted Kim Dae Jung, the prominent Korean dissident, from a hotel in Tokyo, which placed Japan in an awkward position of having to challenge (for the first time since Normalization) the conduct of the Korean government—a sort of moral diplomacy by default. This cooled off the *yuchaku*, with the Korean government fanning, if not organizing, anti-Japanese street demonstrations. To reduce dependence on Japan, the Economic Planning Board began planning the substitution of Korean products for Japanese imports.

The Nixon Doctrine terminated an epoch of rank clientelism whereby Korea was, from 1950–1972, one of the world's largest recipients of American military assistance; the burden of defense was partially transferred to Japan in the form of greater economic aid to Korea but without overall improvement in the Japan-Korean relations; and all this forced Korea to search for autonomy in the world system.

TEXTILE WARS. U.S. protectionism, like the troop withdrawal, was not completely unexpected. Korean leadership knew that Richard Nixon was indebted to the cotton growers and textile interests in the South, and also that he had to do something about the balance of payments deficit. Hence, an advisory committee was set up in 1968 to recommend policies in anticipation of protectionist measures—a year before the first request for voluntary curtailment in textile exports. But U.S. trade protectionism still seemed odd—in fact, a bit unreal to Koreans.

It must be Japan, the Korean leadership reasoned, that America was really after; *nobody* could be serious about trade threats from

Korea, since Korean exports accounted for a picayune 0.6 percent of total American textile consumption in 1970. So insignificant in the American context, this figure was very significant to Korea: equivalent to 15 percent of all Korean exports in 1970.

Koreans believed, deep down, that America would eventually make an exception for Korea: unlike Japan, Korea was in perpetual trade deficit vis-à-vis the United States, hardly deserving of protectionist thrashing. Second, textiles were still Korea's leading sector in 1970, with a projected 100 percent export growth in the next four-year period; a percentage clamp based on the past export figures would have a devastating effect on Korea (unlike say, Hong Kong, Taiwan, and Japan where textiles was a mature, if not already declining, industry and thus past the rapid growth phase). Third, since Korean textiles constituted one-third of total Korean manufacturing, 38 percent of total exports and employed 32 percent of the manufacturing population, United States protectionism would threaten not just the textiles industry, but the entire Korean economy.[17]

Textile negotiations became heated and prolonged. The American side, led by David Kennedy, proved every bit as intransigent as its negotiating partner: every time Koreans resorted to the "special relationship" argument, Americans ricocheted: yes, there was a "special relationship," but one in which Korea had a duty to be a good sport and help America out by being a model for other textile exporting nations.[18] An infuriated Park concluded that the textile negotiations was an American pretext for breaking the friendship between the two countries.[19]

In September 1971, Nixon threatened a unilateral institution of quotas, and the issue was finally resolved. Korea capitulated at gunpoint, with almost nothing to show for the knock-down drag-out fight—the longest of those put up by all four East Asian textile-exporting countries. The settlement satisfied virtually every U.S. demand, putting a clamp of 7.5 percent annual increase for synthetics exports over the next five-year period and additional restrictions for twelve items with high U.S. market shares, with a 5 percent figure for carryover allowables thrown in as a sweetener.

To soften the blow to Korea's foreign exchange situation, America offered $100 million in concessional loans and $275 million in food during the period of voluntary textile export restraint. What depressed Koreans was not a foreign exchange loss here and now, but the frustrating structural weakness of their trading position: Korean textiles were too easily substitutable in America; they lacked the privilege in America that American agriculture did in Korea.[20] In the remainder of the 1970s, five more bitter trade conflicts ensued over textiles and shoes, each with an outcome more severe than the preceding one.[21]

Some adversities can be turned into opportunities, however, and trade barriers may be one such example, a blessing in disguise for those nations adversely affected.[22] Both the reality and the anticipation of protectionism can jolt a nation out of the complacency of churning out the same product until the available productivity gains are fully exploited, and reap the long-run rewards and benefits of industrial upscaling.

THE OIL SHOCK. The quadrupling of petroleum prices was a disaster for all energy-short nations in the early 1970s. In Korea, it wreaked economic havoc and gave an existential shock to a nation totally bereft of oil. There was a security angle to this, as well.

The problem was that North Korea had plenty of energy reserves, a point Seoul had chosen to ignore as long as the oil flow was cheap and plentiful. While the South depended on oil for 60 percent of all its energy consumption, North Korea possessed great hydroelectric and fossile fuel reserves (greater in per capita terms than France); in hydroelectric reserves alone, North Korea was estimated to have 8 million kilowatts, owing to its excellent geomorphological condition. By comparison, hydroelectricity in South Korea was, on the eve of the first oil shock, a pitiful 1.4 percent of total energy. As if to compound the problem, Pyôngyang was also on better terms with the Arabs, with pilots stationed in Egypt, and missile technicians in Syria. Seoul, mimicking the United States, was pro-Israel.[23]

The management of this crisis gradually crystallized in three forms. Coal and nuclear energy were to substitute, to the greatest extent possible, for oil; secondly, Korea's Middle East policy, like Japan's, switched from pro-Israel to pro-Arab. Seoul called on Israel to withdraw from the Arab territories captured in 1967 or during the October War and to respect the legitimate claims of the Palestinians, and dispatched a trade delegation to the Middle East to negotiate direct imports of crude oil from Saudi Arabia and Kuwait. Some observers, noting Kissinger's conspicuous failure to influence foreign policy in Tokyo and Seoul, thought the occasion a watershed in United States-Korean relations.

The third adjustment was economic, and notable for its extraordinary boldness in comparison to, say, the "gold standard" approach of Taiwan, a country which the oil crisis placed in predicament similar to Korea. (Rather than devalue, lest it increase the cost of oil imports, Taiwan maintained a fixed exchange rate of its currency against the dollar and made a balance of payments adjustment primarily through domestic deflation and restrained growth of imports.[24]

The Korean response was fully to absorb oil price increases (accounting for a 62 percent rise in imports in 1974), and then finance the current account deficit—at $2.2 billion in 1974–1975 from $0.5 billion in 1972–1973—by depleting foreign reserve holdings and borrowing abroad. Korea's total foreign debt shot up by 42 percent. Investment climbed to a historical high of 32 percent of the GNP in 1974, from 26 percent in 1973, expansion in domestic credit hit over the 40 percent level, and in 1974, Seoul's Wholesale Price Index went above 42 percent. The hope was that better export performance would somehow get Korea out of this hole (which it eventually did).

Why did Korea gamble like this? The program of the "Big Push," the economic backbone and symbolism of the *yushin* system,[25] was already in place by 1973, and could not be dismantled—or, at least, the leadership did not wish to do so. Rather than curtail investments in basic and defense-related industries, Seoul simply bulldozed ahead on its course of expansion, slashing its currency to push exports, and amassing debts to finance the imports needed to sustain production and investment. Instead of alternatives to petroleum, they recycled petrodollars.

Thus, even the energy crisis did not deter—and in fact exaggerated—Korean political resolve to promote the Third Five-Year Plan with its themes of greater economic self-sufficiency and industrial deepening. This resolve only got stronger with the fourth FYP, when the talk about economic autonomy grew increasingly cantankerous. The reason for accelerating the tempo of self-sufficiency had a great deal to do with the further erosion in the United States-Korean relationship, occasioned by Jimmy Carter's hostility toward human rights abuses in Korea, and the latter's propitiatory bribing of the American Congress ("Koreagate"), which eventually backfired.

Heavy Industrialization in the 1970s

In 1973, six industries—steel, chemical, metal, machine-building, ship-building, and electronics—were officially targetted for rapid growth, as objects of intense government scrutiny and development. It is fascinating to find that the architects and executers of the heavy industrialization program were not the technocrats of the Economic

Planning Board, as might be expected, but a coterie headed by a political appointee at the Presidential Palace—the First Economic Secretary to the President, the man responsible for "inventing" and carrying through the August 3 Decree (discussed in chapter 4).

The raison d'être for this team of economic cowboys (called the Corps for the Planning and Management of Heavy and Chemical Industries) was the speedy formulation and execution, unfettered by bureaucracy, of policies relating to investments in heavy industries.[26] The Economic Secretariat at the Presidential Palace became firmly ensconced as a critical—if not the most critical—economic decision-making body in the Republic, bypassing and sometimes dictating to the Economic Planning Board and the Ministry of Finance.

The project of the corps was not etched on a tabula rasa. The broad features for the Heavy and Chemical Industrialization Plan had already been limned and target industries selected as far back as July 1970, when Korea had to come up with an economic plan for the hefty loan it was requesting of Japan. This original plan went nowhere because Japan refused to consider, from the outset, the possibility of helping the Korean shipping industry—lest it boomerang against Japan—and proceeded to veto the plans regarding special steel and machine-building, as well.[27] But if this exercise did not generate cash for Korea, it did bequeath a set of ideas, soon to become a blueprint for the 1970s.

The first conspicuous feature in the Heavy and Chemical Industrialization Plan was its ambition to create one large industrial complex with "state of the art" production facilities for each target industry; hence, the Yôsu-Yôchôn complex for petrochemicals, Ch'angwôn for Machine-building, P'ohang for steel, Okpo for shipbuilding, the Kumi Complex for electronics, and finally, Onsan for nonferrous metal industry. This was done in the easiest and fastest way that an authoritarian regime knows: the state would procure these industrial bases from farmers, bulldoze the land, install infrastructure (roads, harbors, water and electricity, etc.), and force-draft relevant industries with fiscal/financial sweeteners and exemptions on commodity and customs taxes on imported capital goods.

Once ensconced in these complexes, the enterprises were the first to receive available foreign capital (and the last to pay it back), with low interest to boot; first to receive financial help from the government when purchasing raw materials and machinery; first to be directed through administrative guidance; and first to receive discounts on freight rates, harbor use fees, water, electricity and gas costs. Heavy and chemical industries, like gadarene swine, swiftly waddled into these complexes.

The projected economies of scale of the Plan were truly breathtaking: the production of producer goods had to substitute for imports *and* simultaneously (or with as little lag as possible) to be good for export. The tight sequencing of stages in ISI, as found in Latin America, telescoped in Korea, a condensation that entailed great risk: if lucky, Korea might blaze the trail of the "late" industrializers (as versus "late-late industrializers" of Latin American ilk),[28] but if markets for new exports could not be found, then enormous waste, idle capacity, unemployment, and serious financial problems would follow.

To place Korean heavy industrialization in perspective, it is worth recalling the following propositions on "late" industrialization, enunciated by Alexander Gerschenkron:

1. The more backward a country's economy, the more likely was its industrialization to start discontinuously as a sudden great spurt proceeding at a relatively high rate of growth of manufacturing output.

2. The more backward a country's economy, the more pronounced was the stress on bigness of both plants and enterprise.

3. The more backward a country's economy, the greater was the stress upon producer's goods as against consumer's goods.

4. The more backward a country's economy, the heavier was the pressure upon the levels of consumption of the population.

5. The more backward a country's economy, the greater was the part played by special institutional factors designed to increase the supply of capital to the nascent industries and, in addition, to provide them with less decentralized and better informed entrepreneurial guidance; the more backward the country, the more pronounced was the coerciveness and comprehensiveness of those factors.

6. The more backward a country, the less likely was its agriculture to play any active role by offering to the growing industries the advantages of an expanding industrial market based in turn on the rising productivity of agricultural labor.[29]

The gestalt of Korean industrialization in the 1970s fit that of "late" industrialization in all six tendencies: a marked contrast to the economies of Latin America, where historically only the last two propositions have found resonance. But, if the idiosyncratic tendencies of the 1970s—"a sudden great spurt," emphasis on producers' goods, concern with economies of scale—fit economic rules rather than exceptions, the political culture that interacted with and fueled the Big Push was also redolent of Gerschenkron's historic examples.

The Heavy and Chemical Industrialization Plan was an offshoot and reflection of a political obsession, and the new developmental discourse was a measure of this grand resolve: every new plant had to be one of the *best* and the *largest* in the world and boasted of as such, the quickest ever built, or the most efficient ever operated, almost as if the program jostled for a place in the Guinness Book of World Records. This is the political culture of late development: intense competitiveness vis-à-vis the outside, a collective sense of precariousness at home.

In principle, the projected capital would come from within, primarily through a National Investment Fund garnered from pension funds and issuance of national investment bonds. As for external capital, the priority rested with foreign loans over direct investment or joint ventures. Should the direct participation of foreigners be unavoidable—due to, say, the need for stable supply of raw materials as well as advanced technologies, development of international markets, and supplements of necessary investment capitals unproduceable in Korea—the maximum foreign share would have to be kept under 50 percent.

This crusade for heavy industrialization was not without its detractors, the most important ones being international economic development agencies, such as the IMF and the IBRD. The IBRD country report for Korea expressed, early in 1974, "grave reservations about the practicability of many of the export goals set for individual heavy industries," and questioned the wisdom of underestimating the continuing export potentials of light manufacturing goods. The IBRD mission strongly urged Koreans to reconsider their priorities.[30]

The textile industry, the World Bank believed, must remain the most important industry for Korea: it still employed 30 percent of manufacturing employment, churning out 39 percent of total exports and 22 percent of the value added, and could be neglected only at great peril to national employment and foreign exchange earnings. Thus, the World Bank recommended a greater expansion program and infusion of funds to the textile sector—$2.7 billion in capital equipment, through 1980, for instance—but worried (correctly) that the Korean government was not likely to heed their advice on this issue.

Korea ought also to dampen its appetite for investments in heavy industries, especially in steel and shipping. The Korean shipbuilding plan appeared to the World Bank as a reckless and fantastic leap into the global produce cycle: Koreans, taking into account the probable decline through the late 1970s of shipbuilding in Japan, Sweden, and Germany, anticipated capturing nearly 80 percent of the growth in world shipping trade between 1972–1980 and over 100 percent between 1972–1985. "Even in Japan, which now accounts for over half of world production in ships," went the World Bank protest, "the growth of shipbuilding industries was not historically as rapid as the planned rate expansion in Korea."[31]

In steel production, Koreans wanted to bring onstream nearly 10 million tons of additional capacity within a short time and expected to export, notwithstanding sharp acceleration in domestic consumption, a good one-third of its total steel output by 1981. The World Bank Mission cautioned that since steel plants were extremely capital-intensive and Korea had to rely almost entirely on imported iron ore and coal, the net benefits for the balance of payments were likely to be limited for some time, not to mention the high risk of a large-scale venture into a new export field.

Predictably, this Korean plan—and others throughout the rest of the 1970s—also showed a great proclivity to downplay the problems of financing: the government did not seem to think that its projection of the marginal savings rate for 1972–1981 at 30 percent was problematic, even when the record of the past decade only averaged around 26 percent.

Notwithstanding foreign misgivings, the Heavy and Chemical Industrialization Plan coasted along (even hovered above) the basic 1973 projection, and was completed before the end of the decade. Just as the World Bank feared, Koreans achieved their goals by claiming a disproportionate share of resources for heavy industries and shoving aside small and medium industries. This was by design, not accident: the guiding principle of the heavy industrialization scheme had always been the achievement of scale economies through exporting and by participation of the handpicked few, monopoly conglomerates. Regardless of World Bank boilerplate, Big was Beautiful in Korea.

The share of heavy industries in manufacturing output rose from

39.7 percent in 1972 to 54.9 percent in 1979. Exports of heavy manufactures, which had claimed 13.7 percent of total exports in 1971, rose threefold to 37.7 percent by 1979. Correspondingly, the share of light industries in total manufacturing output had stood at 60.3 percent in 1972, but dropped to 45.1 percent in 1979; the importance of light-industrial commodity exports also dropped from 86.3 percent to 62.3 percent by 1979.[32]

Between 1976 and 1980, $4.66 billion of foreign loans, accounting for 80 percent of total loans absorbed by the manufacturing sector and 30 percent of total foreign loans, would be pumped into heavy and chemical industries.[33] Since a large part of foreign lending was earmarked for augmenting infrastructure facilities, the actual infusion of foreign resources into the heavy and chemical industries was much greater than indicated by the amount of fixed investment in these industries. Let us now turn to the progress of each of the five target industries.

Five Pillars of Wizardry

IRON AND STEEL. The history of iron and steel in Korea dates back to 1918, when Nippon Steel, in responses to the British and American steel exports restriction of 1915, set up a branch at Yômlip'o. Equipped with two blast furnaces, the plant had production capacity of 50,000 metric tons of crude steel a year. But until 1930, the growth of the steel industry remained fairly modest. When Japan prepared for aggression abroad, however, all of that changed.

Steel factories sprouted around many iron ore mines scattered around North Korea, in Sôngjin, Chôngjin, Hûngnam, and, in the center of the Peninsula, in Inchôn, Pupyông, Chinnamp'o, and Samchôk.[34] There was an explosive growth in 1944, when a sizable portion of Japan's steel industry, escaping the Allied bombing, migrated to Korea. In that year, production in Korea reached over 556,000 metric tons in crude steel, although of course the destination of the output was across the Strait of Japan.[35]

A decade later, after territorial division usurped most of the steel industry and a civil war destroyed what little remained, South Korea could count on only two plants in Samchôk and Inchôn—the latter badly damaged—scrap iron left over from the war, and the United Nations facilities to satisfy portions of domestic demand for steel. As late as 1962, Rhee's efforts notwithstanding, only 141,000 tons of rolled products came off the mills in 1962, necessitating steel imports of 179,000 tons to meet demand. Production technology was also primitive, steel bars still accounting for 51 percent of the total production of rolled products.

When Park seized power, he seemed obsessed with an integrated steel mill—both as the symbol, and reality, of national prowess. In the short run, he envisioned a steel industry like the one the Japanese implanted all over Korea and Manchuria (although the junta settled for 300,000 tons of rolled steel as a part of the First FYP, slightly over half the level achieved in 1944), but in the long run, he wanted something that might be considered the best in the world. But kicking off a steel industry was not easy at all. The junta's attempt to solicit foreign money and support for a Korean version of Pittsburgh or Manchester began with the ill-fated Van Fleet mission in 1962, and continued for several unfruitful years.[36] The consensus of international development officials was that the steel complex the junta desired was sure to turn into a white elephant, as Korea's domestic demand for steel was not likely to explode. An integrated steel mill came about only after eight years of waiting and searching for money, and when it did occur, it was with capital from Japan, offered to Korea almost as a quid pro quo for Nixon's troop withdrawal.

The economic benefits to Japan of aiding the Korean steel industry were immediate and probably outweighed the possible problem of a "boomerang" against Japan's interests.[37] A case in point was Japanese plant exports: during the 1976 Third Expansion of P'ohang, one Japanese manufacturer was already expecting a steel plant order of about Y100 billion, and another for a Y30 billion deal for port facilities at P'ohang.[38]

Park's wish was fulfilled posthumously: Korea's integrated steel mill is today one of the world's most efficient and profitable, rapidly capturing a sizable market share in crude steel in the United States and Japan.[39] When the P'ohang Steel Mill started operating in 1973, for the first time Korea had an integrated complex that churned out iron, steel, and rolled products all at once and provided a yearly output of 1 million tons of crude steel; then a 2.6 million ton annual output by 1976 when the second expansion of P'ohang was complete; then 5.5 million tons by 1978, 8.5 million by 1981, and so on. Between 1972 and 1982, Korea's annual overall steelmaking capacity multiplied fourteenfold, and the steel-rolling capacity went up sevenfold. This impressive performance was matched by the corresponding government commitment: 40 percent of all loans to the heavy industrialization sector in the period between 1975–1982 went to steel.[40] Even today, P'ohang remains the only heavy industry project still owned and managed by the state.

An integrated steel mill like P'ohang connoted a resolve for industrial deepening, to bend backward in one stroke to produce a vast array of input materials for rolled steel: steel ingots, billets, slabs, hot coils, and even pig iron.[41] This deepening has been quite successful: taking the production capacity for rolled steel products in 1976 as the unit of reference (1.00), production capacities for pig iron and steel were 0.420 and 0.725 respectively, and the rate vastly improved thereafter.

This success, of course, required constantly expanding demand for iron and steel, generated by a rapidly growing economy. The state carefully nurtured steel-consuming (construction and metal) and machine (general, transport, and electrical) industries which grew the fastest among all manufacturing sectors, emerging as predominant export industries by the end of the 1970s. Steel's big success was just a part of the mosaic that formed the Big Push.

SHIPBUILDING. Shipbuilding guzzles thick steel plates, therefore it is likely to grow big with the steel industry. In Europe, shipbuilding trailed after steel and naval expansion.[42] The remarkable fact about the Korean example, however, is that massive development in shipbuilding was carefully and simultaneously calibrated with that in steel, to take advantage of external economies.

By 1975, 80 percent of all thick steel plates that P'ohang produced was going to shipbuilding. Shipbuilding industry dependence on imported thick steel plates was 100 percent before 1966, down to 60.2 percent in 1969, 25.1 percent in 1972, and 26.9 percent in 1976. The magnitude of demand for steel can be better appreciated when we

TABLE 5.1. Iron- and Steel-Making Capacity

	Iron-Making Capacity (rolling capacity = 1)	Steel-Making Capacity
1957	0.251	0.304
1960	0.131	0.393
1969	0.143	0.533
1973	0.226	0.427
1976	0.420	0.725

SOURCE: Toshio Watanabe, "Heavy and Chemical Industrialization and Economic Development in the Republic of Korea," p. 391.

examine the phenomenal growth of shipbuilding, which had accounted for the meager 4.3 percent of the total Korean exports in 1976, but it is now the world's second largest after Japan. This massive growth was, in turn, a boon to 200 other types of metal, machineries, chemicals, and electronic goods.

The history of shipbuilding in Korea, notwithstanding its recent entry to the world, is far from puerile. Koreans were skilled shipbuilders from time immemorial, a fate thrust upon them by geography, and they passed on shipmaking know-how to Japan. They were the first in the world to construct fleets of ships cast in metal, deployed at the end of the sixteenth century to push back Hideyoshi's invading armies. But this brilliant performance had no curtain call until another Japanese invasion, three centuries later, put shipbuilding on the move again.

Japanese built the first modern shipyard in Korea, with a capacity of 10,000 g/t (and 15,000 g/t in repair), which, when renamed Taehan Shipbuilding, remained the largest shipyard in Korea until 1974. In 1945, the annual shipbuilding capacity in Korea was up to 30,000 g/t a year; in the south, a total of 56 large and small shipyards accounted for the annual capacity of 19,000 g/t in shipbuilding and 383,000 g/t in repairing. After 1953, shipbuilding was a reconstruction priority, but start-up costs were too high and state help too little for the impecunious small shipbuilders, and progress was slow in coming.

In the First FYP, the junta gave shipbuilding a bigger push: establishing a support fund that compensated for price differentials from foreign vessels, a special interest rate of 5 percent per annum for shipmaking (payable in 15 years), substitution of government guaranteed loans for mortgages, tariff exemption of raw materials for shipbuilding, and most importantly, the resuscitation and expansion of Taehan Shipbuilding Corporation which received nearly 1 billion won. But the result at the conclusion of the Plan was anticlimatic, with only 84.5 percent of the production goals met (a low figure for a Korean FYP), because a good half of the funds earmarked for shipbuilding had been siphoned off into production of fertilizer, cement, and electricity.[43]

Shipbuilding fared better in the late 1960s, when a series of measures sought to facilitate financing of shipmakers. Thus, by 1971, the increase in shipbuilding capacity reached five times that of a decade prior, and the jump in actual production was ninefold.[44] The number of enterprises also leaped to 140 shipbuilders, but only 2 of them could produce steel ships over 1,000 tons, whereas more than half were still hammering on wood to put together vessels.[45]

The breakthrough, as with other basic industries, came in 1973. Park vowed in his New Year address that Korea would become, in the 1980s, a major exporter of ships. The short-run goal was to expand production capacity to 2.6 million g/t by 1976, a fourteenfold jump in four years, to be made possible by the addition of two world-class shipyards. Marching to the beat of the government drum, Hyundai Shipbuilding came into being in 1974, followed by Daewoo at Okpo and Korea Tacoma; and the pace at which these enterprises moved was a match for their government, for the first container vessel rolled off the Hyundai shipyard exactly thirty months after the ground was broken.[46]

The achievement was impressive: the rate of dependence on ship imports (imports over domestic production plus imports) had been 82.4 percent in 1972, but, in four years, the rate dropped to 36.9 percent in 1976; simultaneously, the rate of dependence on exports increased from 1.0 percent in 1972 to 58 percent in 1976. Again, there was a little time lag between import-substitution and export expansion, and the expanding total demand consistently pulled forward domestic production.

Pushing shipbuilding took considerable courage. The World Bank was skeptical about Korea's resolve to be a world-class shipbuilder, and the Japanese did not make it easier when they refused to fund it. Where did the Korean government get its confidence to push shipbuilding so massively? One of the answers was that Korea had found in Japan's shipbuilding industry a cynosure.

Some observers noted that the Korean strategy to promote shipbuilding was very simply a carbon copy of Japan's.[47] Broadly, two ideas stood out; one was the notion of deep state involvement, through fiscal, financial, and managerial means so as to maximize economic, diplomatic, and defense effects. The state would intervene, match, and mediate between the industry's customers and suppliers, select transportation companies and ocean liners, and even determine for the shipbuilders the type of ship and the length of time required to build it. Another ploy was the notion of "systemized" shipbuilding, whereby a coterie of small and medium-sized shipbuilders and other subcontractors would coexist with, and supply parts to, large shipbuilders. It turned out that Korea was more successful in emulating the first policy than the second.[48]

Shipbuilders relied on three sources of financing: equity equal to a minimum of 8 to 10 percent of the vessel price; government loans through the National Investment Fund and the Industrial Bank Fund for Planned Shipbuilding, at a 9 percent rate (below inflation), payable in 9 years, and which would account for 50 percent of the vessel price; and, finally, foreign loans which made up the remaining 40 percent of assets, payable in 5 years after a 2-year grace period. The government also exempted ship manufacturers from sales tax, petroleum tax, VAT, textile tax, and any tariff on imported raw materials.

Such munificent support soon bred trouble, as many rushed into shipbuilding to reap financial benefits and then accumulated ruinous amounts of debt, which the banking system was not able to write off.[49] But, all in all, the industry proved its mettle as it surmounted the global slump of the early 1980s, despite the sneers of economic pundits, and then proceeded to capture more than 20 percent of all new orders in the world market.[50]

CHEMICAL INDUSTRY. Chemicals also sprinted forward in 1973, with the idiosyncratic promise to become "one of the best in the world." It was an industry both appropriate and inappropriate to Korea. Given the politics of the time and Park Chung Hee's touting of national autonomy, its development was inevitable in that it is the preeminent industry of "self-reliance," substituting synthetics for naturally occurring substances. It would supply synthetic fibers and textiles to the nation's most dominant industry, textiles. But, in another sense, it was an inappropriate industry for Korea to emphasize: too capital-intensive, its employment effect was minimal. Chemical production in the twenty-one years between 1955 and 1976 jumped a stunning 179.6-fold, and the increase in value-added was 296.7-fold, whereas the number of employees rose merely 11.7 times.[51]

It was inappropriate, and also incongruous. At a time when foreign loans, and not foreign investment, were the favored form of foreign capital inflow, chemicals was an industry that could not do without foreign equity participation and technical assistance. Not a single fertilizer plant, not a single petrochemical complex, was a product solely of Korean capital and know-how. All seven fertilizer plants that were built by the end of the 1970s were either foreign creations or joint ventures, and the roster had names like McGraw Hydrocarbon, Tennessee Valley Authority, the Swift Consortium, Gulf, Mitsui, Bechtel, and Agrico. In petrochemicals, the Ulsan Petrochemical complex was in partnership with Gulf as early as 1964, and the Yôchôn Complex in 1976 was with Honam Ethylene (partly owned by Mitsui). By 1978, foreign investment in chemicals and petroleum refining accounted for almost 40 percent of the value of the entire stock of foreign investment.[52]

Yet, by no stretch of the imagination could this industry be called a boon to foreign investors; in fact, it was the arena of one of the most vituperous and well-publicized conflicts between the MNCs and the local industry/host government, the conflict between Dow Chemical and its Korean partner—an illustration showing that, contrary to the neodependency argument about the state mediating between local and foreign capital *for* the benefit of the latter, the host government can and does utilize foreign investors for its own political-economic goals, often with little regard for foreigners' profit. The trouble started when Dow priced chloride it was providing to its Korean partner at higher than market value, so as to transfer profits from the Korea venture to an upstream plant owned exclusively by Dow. Koreans balked and threatened to import their raw materials from elsewhere. Because the Korean state supported the action of the Korean partners, Dow pulled out in a huff in 1982, suddenly alleging that it was impossible to do business with a military dictatorship.[53]

The chemical industry in Korea was built on practically nothing, unlike other industries that had some vested enterprises to start from. Korean dependence on imports of fertilizers from 1955–1961 was an amazing 100 percent, a fact that appears almost antic when one recalls that in the 1930s Hûngnam (in North Korea) housed the second largest fertilizer plant in the world. The Korean War left only two very small fertilizer plants intact, both of which ceased to operate by 1955; construction of the Ch'ungju fertilizer plant began in 1957, but was not completed until 1961. Hence, Korea produced no chemical fertilizers from 1955 to 1961.[54] The loss through ravages of time and politics had been truly complete.

When the First FYP was started in 1961, the government lavished immediate attention on fertilizer production, granting it nearly a third of the investment in manufacturing, which was in turn a sizable 34 percent of the total investment. Five new plants were brought on-stream by 1967, ridding the nation of an albatross in foreign exchange. By the end of the 1970s, Korea would be completely self-sufficient in fertilizer production and was exporting one million tons of chemical fertilizer a year, bringing in $38 million in revenue.

With the Second FYP (1967–1971), the emphasis gradually shifted to petrochemical production, although the phenomenal growth in the chemical industry for the period (at 41.8 percent per annum) was mostly the result of the two fertilizer plants that began operation in 1967. By the Third FYP, which imbricates the period of the Big Push, petrochemicals were the major thrust behind the 40.9 percent annual growth in the chemical industry. There are roughly three processes to the production of petrochemical goods. First, basic materials such as ethylene, propylene, benzene, and butadiene are produced by distilling and cracking petroleum; next, secondary materials are produced, such as low-density polyethylene, high-density polyethylene, polypropylene, acrylonitrile monomen, and caprolactum, by polymerizing or combining the basic materials; the third and final process is the production (using secondary materials) of synthetic resins, synthetic fibers, and synthetic rubber.

The birth of the Korean petrochemical industry came in 1973. In that year, Ulsan Petrochemical Complex turned on its naphtha-cracking facility (in addition to the BTX factory in operation since 1970) and seven affiliated plants, which would spew out such secondary materials as low-density polyethylene, VCM, methanol, polyprophylene, polystyrene, and acrylonitrile. The Yôch'ôn Complex, opening in 1976 with help from Mitsui, added one more naphtha-cracking and fifteen other factories for secondary processing. By the end of the 1970s, the total naphtha-cracking capacity was expected at an annual 900,000 m/t.[55]

The 1973 output in the petrochemical industry increased almost by twentyfold over that in 1968; and in 1978, it was 92 times that of a decade prior.[56] As in shipping and steel, progress occurred through extremely rapid compression; for instance, import dependence of synthetic fibers, which was 94 percent in 1966, plunged to less than 10 percent by 1975, while the degree of export dependence shot up to 75 percent by 1973: in synthetic resin—another important petrochemical product in Korea, along with synthetic fibers and textile— the rate of import dependence dropped from 90.8 percent in 1966 to 28 percent a decade later.[57]

The pressure for backward linkage, bred by the near completion of import substitution in final petrochemical products was met rather unevenly as can be seen in table 5.2: import substitution for PVC was almost complete even by the end of the 1960s, whereas domestic production of DMT/TPA and ethylene glycol was not off the ground by 1978. In other intermediate inputs for synthetic resin and fiber, import dependence was reduced by about half.

Thus, the Korean pattern of importing intermediate materials for synthetic fibers and resins was undone in the 1970s, a trend that accelerated in the 1980s, although the rate of progress in import substitution tended to be buried in the faster growth in domestic consumption of petrochemical products.

MACHINE-BUILDING. The Ch'angwôn Machine-building Industrial Complex was, like P'ohang, an obsession of Park Chung Hee. It was here, in this huge hollow hugged by Masan Harbor and as far away from the DMZ as economically feasible, that the defense/machine industries found a home, industries essential to any serious, autonomous heavy industrialization. The plan for Ch'angwôn had predicted an investment of $1 billion by 1981, construction of 104 factories, and an annual output worth $1.5 billion. Big manufacturers immediately moved into the complex, led by Taehan Heavy Machineries, Daewoo Heavy Industries, Lucky-Gold Star, Hyosông Heavy Industries, Korea Bearing, etc. Hyundai and Samsung followed, daunting others by erecting plants of mammoth scale. When the project was finished, Ch'angwôn along with other industrial complexes formed a sprawling industrial belt in the southern part of Korea.

Ch'angwôn was controversial from the word go; its detractors were many and varied, from populist elements who took umbrage at government intimacy with big business, to penny-pinching pundits who argued that national resources were dreadfully misallocated on unreasonably large, unaccountably expensive and very inefficient enterprises. (The detractors were proven right, it seemed, in the

TABLE 5.2. Import Dependence of Intermediate Petrochemical Products (percentage)

Synthetic Resins:	1968	1973	1975	1978
Low-density polyethylene	100	27.8	15.2	60.7
High-density polyethylene	100	100	94.1	45.4
PVC	5.1	2.7	11.4	4.4
Polyprophylene	100	14.2	8.0	42.5
Polystyrene	60.6	12.9	24.2	26.4
Synthetic Fibers:	1971	1973	1975	1978
Caprolactum	100	100	79.6	59.9
Acrylonitrile monomer	100	16.0	59.7	62.8
DMT/TPA	100	100	100	100
Ethylene glycol	100	100	100	100

SOURCE: Compiled from *Hanguk sôkyu hwahak kongôp hyôphoe* [Association of Petrochemical Industries] *Yearbook*.

crisis of 1979–1980, when many plants were abandoned half-built, or if completed, lay idle or barely operated in a negative-growth economy that failed to generate sufficient demand for Ch'angwôn's widgets. The capacity utilization rates for manufacturing were 83.4 percent, 77.5 percent, and 69.5 percent for the three years from 1978 to 1980, whereas capacity utilization for transport equipment was 40.4 percent, 38.8 percent, and 41.9 percent for the same period.[58] The critics of the Ch'angwôn idea still had to concede that the Korean machine-building industry at the start of the 1970s had been stymied, and that it had needed a push.[59] One gauge of the problem was the deterioration in the rate of import substitution, or to put it differently, a slower growth in the production of machinery relative to domestic demand; in general machinery, import dependence in 1963 was 60.3 percent, growing to 68.3 percent in 1970, and then jumping to a remarkable 86.1 percent in 1970; in electrical machinery, import dependence was 50.5 percent in 1970, rising to 62.9 percent a year later.[60]

The 1973 Long-Term Plan for Promotion of the Machine-Building Industry, in which Ch'angwôn and "Koreanization" were the novel features, sought to satisfy domestic demand with domestic products to the greatest extent possible, and at the same time to increase exports of machinery. To reduce imports of turn-key plants, and thereby also improve the balance of payments, the state now required projects costing over $1 million in foreign loans to clear their imports list with the government: nothing domestically substitutable was to be imported. The Plan specifically targetted for "Koreanization" forty-three industries that produced 123 items and vowed to support them with the greatest administrative flexibility and devotion.[61]

The result was spectacular. Through the Third FYP, the growth rate in machine building was 35.3 percent per annum, twice as great as the rate achieved in the Second FYP. And the new rate was far ahead of the overall growth in manufacturing which stood at 20.2 percent.

The centerpiece of this spurt in machine building was the automobile industry which, to produce vehicles, requires no fewer than 2500 parts, mostly sophisticated manufactured components (Automobile production is a central force in any heavy industrialization effort, consuming substantial quantities of steel, aluminum, glass, rubber, etc., not to mention other spillover effects such as the industry's creation of demand for extensive distribution and service networks.) By 1977, the domestic component in passenger cars came to

90 percent, 87 percent in buses, and 65–80 percent in trucks. This was a far cry from the 1950s, when the automobile industry was synonymous with assembling primitive types of jeeps, with parts smuggled out to the U.S. military,[62] or from the mid-1960s when Shinjin Motor Company was assembling Toyotas under a Korean name, Saenara.[63]

How was such a rapid transition possible, from parts-assembling under foreign auspices to domestic manufacturing?[64] The first and obvious answer is the vigor of state action: once the decision to nurture the automotive industry as the leading export sector in the 1980s was reached, the state exercised stringent controls through the Domestic Content Program, which meant localization, after 1974, of functional items such as engines, transmissions, and axles.[65]

Another and less obvious answer is the colonial legacy: Japan had bequeathed to Koreans the essential know-how for parts manufacturing. During the war years, the Japanese produced some automobile parts in Korea and transferred them to Manchuria and Northern China: piston rings were manufactured at the Chosôn Iron Company in Taejôn, springs at the Kuksan Automobiles Company in Pupyông, bodies at Kyôngsông Body Company in Seoul, bearings at the Chosôn Bearings Company at Pup'yông, etc.[66] Repair and maintenance shops also proliferated, some of which were owned and operated by Toyota, Isuzu, or Nissan. Korea supplied parts to Manchuria and Northern China, and was a market for finished cars produced in Japan.

Thus, unlike Latin America where production of parts was dependent on primary firms (usually MNCs), Korea experienced substantial development of ancillary firms prior to, and independent of, primary firms. It was relatively easy for Korea, therefore, to move

TABLE 5.3. Rate of Growth in Machine Building
Industry (percentage)

Years	Growth Rate (machinery)	GNP Growth	Growth Rate (manufacturing)
1960–1966	21.3	7.2	12.6
1967–1971	17.5	10.5	21.0
1972–1976	35.3	11.0	20.2

SOURCE: Chunghwahak kongôp ch'ujin wiwônhoe kihoekdan [The Corps for Planning and Promotion of Heavy and Chemical Industries].

from parts assembling to domestic production of cars. By the end of the 1970s, almost all cars on the streets of Seoul were manufactured, parts and as a whole, in Korea. And today, three Korean automobile companies export upwards of 700,000 vehicles a year, the lion's share to the United States.[67]

ELECTRONICS. The literature on comparative economic history is generally concerned with the *pace* or *sequence* of industrialization, and there is little disagreement over which industries have been associated with various phases of industrialization. Thus, we find that textiles appear in economic history textbooks as the leading sector for incipient industrialization; iron, coal mining, metallurgy, and railroad building form the early phase of second industrialization; and electrical engineering, internal combustion motors, automobiles, and chemicals characterize the latter phase of the second stage of industrialization.

One industry in the twentieth century, however, disrupts and rearranges the classic pattern: electronics. The electronics industry is really a *deus ex machina* for the upstarts of the late twentieth century—like Taiwan and Korea—because it so neatly fills the lacuna between the light and heavy phases of industrialization. It is a bridge between the two phases, and offers the best advantages while avoiding the worst pitfalls of a lead-off industry such as textiles. Like textiles, it is labor intensive, with a low start-up cost, easy-to-plagiarize technologies, and small-scale factories—in other words, it is an ideal industry for a country on the ramparts of "takeoff" to emphasize. It also brings in much-needed foreign exchange. Yet, unlike textiles, the electronics industry is directly concatenated with all sorts of heavy industries, especially the defense industry. Whereas the historical role of textiles in development was an indirect one of generating surplus capital that could be invested in heavy industries (and later was concatenated with chemical industry through chemical dye and synthetic textiles), electronics could now do what textiles has done *plus* technologically and economically (through greater value-added and lower production cost) aid in the development of other industries.[68]

Little wonder, then, that the electronics industry was seized upon, during the First FYP, as Korea's "strategic export industry," along with textiles. But much of the hoopla at the time was based more on theoretical possibilities than on plausibilities: in 1965, value-added in electronics was a mere 0.4 percent of the GNP, 2.6 percent of total manufacturing, and a pathetic 1 percent of exports; the first television had not even been assembled, and the first transistor radios were pieced together only in 1959.[69] In ten years, the picture was radically altered, with the policy makers once again proving right in their wild optimism: between 1965 and 1976, the value-added in electronics quadrupled, claiming 4 percent of GNP and 11.3 percent of total manufacturing; the annual rate of growth in production averaged 53.2 percent in the same period. And the weight of electronics in exports took a quantum leap, from 1 percent to 13.4 percent by 1976.

This last phenomenon, the more than thirteenfold rise in exports, was due to "international subcontracting," a form of manufacturing most often associated with the electronics industries in Taiwan and Korea. The success of this arrangement cannot be understood apart from a fortuitous collocation of different factors in the East Asian regional economy: the Japanese utilization of cheap and competent labor across the Straits of Japan.

International subcontracting began in a big way in Korea with the Normalization Treaty, and with the designation of the electronics industry as one of the mainstays of exports. The first array of foreigners had been Americans, but the Japanese soon eclipsed the American presence, and by the peak years of 1972–1973, "international" subcontracting was mostly subcontracting on Japanese orders. The importance of subcontracting for the electronics industry as well as for the Korean balance of payments may be gleaned from the fact that by 1968, joint-venture or FDI firms claimed an amazing 80 percent of total electronical exports. This disproportionate share of foreign subcontracting firms in exports declined over time as domestic firms quickly got in on the act during the export boom; yet, as late as 1977, a whopping 60 percent of electronics exports was still handled by foreign firms.[70]

So long as international subcontracting brought in a sizable portion of foreign exchange and was not damaging the domestic electronics industry (which was not sizable by the end of the 1960s), the ROK government had every reason to encourage greater foreign participation. Accordingly, the decrees designed to stimulate the electronics industry showed conspicuous favoritism toward foreign enterprises: tax exemptions and reductions, generous expatriation policy, and a guarantee of labor peace by outlawing any form of labor agitation in the foreign-owned enterprises.[71]

Once the electronics industry got moving, thanks to the Japanese and others, the government adopted a more comprehensive measure to "rationalize" the industry—to create a complementary relationship between international subcontracting and domestic firms. At the beginning of the 1970s, the state concentrated the industry in one huge complex to facilitate communications and technological transfer: the Kumi Electronics Complex, situated along the Seoul-Pusan Expressway, was singled out as the guts of the "$10 Billion-in-Exports-by-1980 Drive," and the Ministry of Commerce ensured its success through a package of incentives and palliatives for the domestic and foreign companies finding new domiciles in Kumi— permission for the foreigners to retain 100 percent ownership, exemption of tariffs on imported raw materials, exemption of corporate and income taxes for five years, and for the next three years following, a 50 percent tax reduction. In lobbying for the Kumi relocation, the Ministry of Commerce targetted some 500 Japanese electronics and related firms and touted to them—through brochures, audio-visual means, and see-for-yourself invitations—the virtues of docile, skilled, and cheap labor in Korea. The success of this campaign and the subsequent influx of Japanese capital was critical in meeting (actually surpassing) the goal of $2.5 billion in electronics exports by 1980.[72]

Thus, the Korean electronics industry was the result of cross-pollination. But the industry was spared the worst effects of MNC penetration—permanent economic apartheid in the form of a dual economy. A shift took place in the pattern of subcontracting: large *domestic* enterprises replaced the foreigners in subcontracting to small domestic firms. In this sense, Korea may be deemed a show-case for apologists of the MNCs, exhibiting as it does the alleged munificent effects of direct foreign investment on the domestic economy: foreign provision of sorely needed capital, the employment effect, the demonstration effect, and positive contribution to the balance of payments.

In one critical aspect, however, the Korean experience with the MNCs in electronics resembled the experiences of other Third World countries: transfer of technology was painfully slow. The more Korea exported electronic goods, the more it had to import the part-components, a predictable consequence of subcontracting in the "manufacturing product cycle." Whereas the export dependence of the electronics industry grew from 49.6 percent in 1970 to 63 percent in 1977, the import dependence remained at a plateau, at 61.8 percent in 1970, and then dropping only very slightly to 61.2 percent by 1977.[73] Furthermore, the bulk of such imports was of single origin: as in the late 1970s, more than 75 percent of technological imports came from Japan.[74]

This need not be the last word on the electronics industry. At the root of all the Korean hue and cry of the 1980s—technological "leapfrogging," concentration on computer and semi-conductor industries, increased R&D, and massive training of scientists and technicians—is the determination to get out from under the Japanese technological grip. The relatively quick product cycle in electronics, rendering existing technologies obsolescent overnight (64K RAM chips, etc.), may make the Korean leapfrog possible in this somewhat anomalous industry.

Conclusion

The year 1972 opened on an ominous note. In his New Year's speech, Park Chung Hee complained of a democratic distemper: "while the affairs of state are publicly debated and decided through the ballot box here, the North Koreans are of one mind, obsessed with making guns, mortars, and tanks."[75] Thus, out went the ballot boxes, and South Korea became of one mind, like their Northern brethren, concentrating on building basic industries that were indispensable for defense. Park finally thought that the gap had closed by the end of the decade. In a visit to the Ministry of Defense, he would remark that South Korea "has come a long way, finally at par with North Korea in defense capabilities. The future will see us ahead of them."[76] Korea at the decade's end was capable of manufacturing, notwithstanding American protests, M-16 rifles, M-60 machine guns, M-48 tanks, model 500 helicopters, "fast boats," medium- and long-range land-to-land missiles and fighter aircraft.[77]

The period covered in this chapter is the distance between these two pronouncements. The Korean "industrial deepening" of the 1970s was unthinkable apart from the security threat, real and perceived, from outside. And the timing makes no sense without paying attention to the decline in American prowess that left Korea out in the cold. This was really what set Korea apart from the Latin American version of the "industrial deepening," the latter orchestrated in the absence of a massive security threat. It underlines our judgment that Korea should be classified as a late developer: industrialization amidst intense competition, but also with a perceived security threat.

6

The Political Economy
of Korea, Inc.:
The State, Finance, and
the Chaebôl

*T*HE BIG PUSH was a success. Korea's GNP grew—on average—by
11 percent each year from 1973 to 1978, an outstanding achievement even in the annals of the twentieth century's most prodigious
economic performances. Success, however, never begot popularity.
For many, the Big Push was a big shove by a big government that
bullied workers, coerced entrepreneurs, and distorted the market. If
the achievement looked big in the aggregate, it was thought to have
happened *in spite of*, rather than *because of*, the government's role:
predictably, economists at home and abroad lambasted the 1970s'
program.

The reality was a bit more complicated than that, and went beyond the issue of market intervention by a strong state. The 1970s
gave us a model of the Korean political economy. Through its media-
tion of enormous amounts of finance capital, the state achieved its
autonomy and its capacity to shape the market, firms, and society at

large. Here we describe the mechanism; the industrialization that we described in the previous chapter was the outcome.

The era of financial reform, we recall, came to a grinding halt in 1972. The seven-year experiment—what Ronald McKinnon called "reform without tears"[1]—had fallen short of liberalization, whereby financial prices would be set at equilibrium in a unified market; rather, it had been a catch-as-catch-can compromise, a state attempt at efficient resource allocation by hiking interest rates, thereby mimicking the market price of money. Then came the August 3rd Decree that massively drove down the price of capital, and ended, once and for all, the "reform," which had been a travesty of market liberalization.

From that point on, bank loans became subsidies for the chosen —the entrepreneurs who had already proven their mettle through good export records, the risk-takers who entered into heavy and chemical industries, and the faithful who plunged into the untried sea of international competition with *new products*, relying on the state's good offices to rescue them. It was really these entrepreneurs who made the Big Push possible, the drive for heavy and chemical industrialization and industrial maturation.

To join the hallowed chosen few, enterprises had to be big; but to remain chosen, they had to be gigantic: size was an effective deterrent against default—something that would threaten not only the financial but the economic stability of the country—forcing government into the role of the lender of last resort. The importance of size in this sense cannot be overemphasized, since highly leveraged firms (which characterized virtually all Korean conglomerates) live with a constant specter of default. It was for this reason that the expression "octopus-like spread of the chaebôl" *(chaebôl ûi munôbal-sik hwak-jang)* came into wide circulation in Korea. But the chaebôl tentacles gripped not only the economy but the state as well: big state and big business would have to sink or swim together. A credit-based financial system, mediated by an interventionist authoritarian state, became the basis of Korea Inc.

A chaebôl is a family-owned and managed group of companies that exercises monopolistic or oligopolistic control in product lines and industries. The conventional way to differentiate the chaebôl from its Japanese counterpart, the prewar zaibatsu, is to note the conspicuous absence of a banking institution at the core of the former (although that may very well change with a more complete financial liberalization in the future). Some business historians of Japan argue, however, that it was the general trading companies that formed the core of the prewar zaibatsu.[2] In Korea, general trading companies have also acted as the core of a number of large chaebôl groups, mimicking the structures of, say, prewar Mitsui and Mitsubishi (for reasons that will be explained later.) Even so, Korean general-trading firms had no financial clout apart from the state, and the chaebôl groups possessed no banks that could back up the trading firms.

In lieu of a group-affiliated bank, then, the state mediates the flow of capital (domestic and foreign) to the chaebôl and supervises its operations through a designated bank (the *chukôrae ûnhaeng)*, whose role might be likened to that of German banks prior to World War I.[3] The growth of the chaebôl is predicated on state provision of industrial capital, and furthermore (as we will argue later) on the fungibility of this bank credit. Unlike Japan, the chaebôl do not guarantee employment to workers (through internal shifting from declining to expanding sectors).[4]

In what follows, we will examine the financial policies and political consequence of the Big Push. As in other chapters (save chapter 5), we will look into, first, the way the state mobilized foreign and domestic savings; second, the way it refracted the nation's financial resources to bring about the sort of industrialization discussed in chapter 5; and finally, the way it created and recreated a class of world-size industrial conglomerates.

Sovereign Risk and the Politics of Foreign Debt

By the 1970s, Korea was no longer a global mendicant, having taken off in the 1960s; moreover, the world was floating in petrodollars without political strings attached—just an incessant search for borrowers. The availability of private loans was truly critical and made all the difference for Korea. The money Korea needed for the Big Push was now handed them on a silver platter by the world's eager moneylenders, who delighted in Korea, the developmental wunderkind.[5] With all this, Koreans finally gained greater autonomy in their conduct of domestic affairs.

To anticipate the argument, we may say that Korean debt-politik had three different aims, seemingly disparate, but all invariably aiding in the search for greater security and autonomy. The first was an attempt to increase the American and Japanese *economic* stake in Korea through debt: this was insurance against hard times when Korea might need a quick injection of rescue loans, as it indeed received in the early 1980s. The second was to use economic interdependence as collateral to secure America's *political* commitment in Korea after the war in Vietnam. This was not unlike what Taiwan, in the wake of Nixon's opening to China, sought to do by wooing American direct investment.[6] The third aim does not require an explanation: it was to finance industrialization. In the absence of foreign lending, the annual growth rate for 1962–1982 would perhaps have been 4.9 percent, not the actual 8.2 percent.[7] Heavy concentration of foreign loans in the portfolio of external liabilities provides little countercyclical hedge in times of global recession. But it did accord Koreans greater autonomy in the conduct of the domestic economy—with less kibitzing than with bilateral aid. With this new autonomy, the state now made a move to turn a textile exporting economy into an industrial powerhouse, and the domestic financial system became the transmission belt.

The timing of the Korean entry into the global loan market was fortuitous. Domestic saving, as a proportion of investment, increased sharply in the 1970s, thanks mostly to a high level of government and business savings. But the absolute amount needed to pay for the heavy industrialization push remained mammoth. Investment as a percentage of GNP often hovered over 30 percent in the 1970s, but savings at no point touched the 30 percent barrier (this historic "ceiling on savings" was only broken in 1987): in 1974, when the Big Push was being launched, the level of investment was 31.65 percent of GNP, and savings at 20.65 percent, with fully 11 percent of GNP financed through foreign savings: in 1975, investment was at 30.02 percent of GNP, domestic savings at 20.18 percent, and the gap at 9.84 percent of GNP.

On the supply side of international finance, great changes were also taking place, to satisfy the developing economies' thirst for capital: the explosive growth of Euromarket capital and also sovereign-risk lending by multinational banks, all occurring outside the regulatory framework. Large U.S. banks raked in upwards of half of their earnings from foreign lending. The 1970s also saw (especially after the departures of Nixon and Simon) a resurgence in the IMF's activities—both as the good cop (the lender of last resort) and the bad cop (imposing stabilization) of international finance—that created some stability and order in the global money bazaar.[8] For Korea, this meant that the IMF, and not the State Department, was the new watchdog of Korea's political economy. In this brave new world, the flow of foreign monies followed a simple rule: a low spread and abundant credit if Korean exports soared, a high spread and less plentiful loans if Korea had balance of payments problems.

So Korea plunged into the loan market in a big way around 1973–1974. To outsiders the Korean entry at first looked like an innocuous part of a large picture in which many non–oil-producing developing countries, capitalist and communist, jostled for more money to finance oil imports and other industrial projects. That changed quickly, however, as Korea became, in scarcely half a decade, the world's third largest developing debtor nation. Table 6.1 gives a comparative perspective on the magnitude of Korean debts in Eurocurrency bank credits.

Table 6.2 shows the velocity of debt accumulation by breaking down the total external debt by period, and also by source. It indicates that the total external debt for all LDCs grew approximately 6.89-fold in the eleven years from 1967 to 1978, ninefold for Brazil in the same period, tenfold for Mexico, but fifteenfold for Korea—that is, more than double the average LDC rate. The figure for private, short-term loans is even more revealing: the LDC debt in the international financial market grew 17.05 times in the eleven-year period, 40 times for Brazil, 18 times for Mexico, but the Korean reliance on private money market increase almost 100 times over. By 1984, Brazil topped the list with $92.4 billion, Mexico with $86.2 billion, Korea with $43.5 billion, and Argentina with $40.6 billion. It was only by the late 1980s that Korea, through extraordinary

TABLE 6.1. Eurocurrency Bank Credits to Non-OPEC Countries, January 1976–December 1979

	Amount	*As Percent*
Total	84,114	100.0
Mexico	19,895	23.7
Brazil	17,440	20.7
South Korea	7,312	8.7
Argentina	6,074	7.2
Philippines	5,725	6.8
Chile	2,639	3.1
Morocco	2,543	3.0
Malaysia	2,145	2.6
Taiwan	2,094	2.5
Peru	1,180	1.4
Other	17,066	20.3

SOURCE: Morgan Guaranty Trust Company of New York, *World Financial Market*, December 1979, p. 10.

export growth, was able to lower its outstanding debt to about $37 billion.[9]

This quantum leap in private borrowing—in comparison even with the world's most intrepid borrowers—was critical for the successful completion of the Big Push, a program with few supporters in international development agencies like the World Bank. It was private—not public—loans that financed the industries we spoke of in the previous chapter. By 1981, industries in the manufacturing sector had claimed 60.3 percent of total private loans, in comparison with 37.5 percent for social capital, and 1.6 percent for the primary sector. If one considers social capital—roads, harbor, and transportation—as infrastructure indispensable for manufacturing indus-

TABLE 6.2. External Debt (Including Undisbursed Portion) of Brazil, Mexico, and South Korea

	1967	1971	1973	1975	1978
Brazil					
All lenders	3434.4	6295.4	9176.7	14707.8	31275.7
Official sources	2598.3	3487.7	4545.4	5812.9	9754.4
Suppliers + others	395.7	1587.1	1863.0	1723.3	4246.3
Financial markets	440.4	1220.6	2768.3	7171.6	17730.3
Mexico					
All lenders	2675.5	4206.5	7249.3	13547.7	27021.5
Official sources	1154.8	1702.8	2708.4	3649.8	5345.6
Suppliers + others	370.1	365.0	318.5	499.1	404.5
Financial markets	1150.6	2138.7	4222.2	9398.8	21271.3
South Korea					
All lenders	1199.2	3243.8	4940.0	7173.9	18146.3
Official sources	434.7	1415.7	2730.7	3796.8	8210.9
Suppliers + others	703.3	1327.8	1308.8	1466.2	3921.6
Financial markets	61.3	500.3	900.5	1910.9	6013.8
Total, all LDCs					
All lenders	45069.5	76158.5	109763.0	167446.8	310598.0
Official sources	31890.3	53715.0	73516.1	103884.6	166573.7
Suppliers + others	6492.6	12508.5	13588.0	19146.2	29916.9
Financial markets	6686.6	9874.9	22659.1	44416.0	114017.3

SOURCE: Friedan, "Third World Indebted Industrialization," p. 414.

tries, then 97.8 percent of all private loans were used for manufacturing and related industries. The industries that received the most loans were steel and iron, automobile, machine-building, shipping, petrochemical, nonferrous metal, and nuclear energy.[10]

By contrast, public (long-term) loans mostly financed agriculture and infrastructural facilities, as well as the development of the tertiary sectors, like banking; and the EXIM bank loans financed imports from the United States. Of the total of public loans, only 2.5 percent was spent on manufacturing.

The massive infusion of foreign capital was critical in fulfilling Korea's hefty investment ambition, which ran as much as 33 percent of the GNP by 1979 (25 percent is the historical average for investment.) In the 1977–1979 period, heavy industry absorbed more than 70 percent of the total investment in manufacturing. As table 6.4 shows, targets were often fulfilled earlier than planned in the 1977–1981 period. Investment in machine building, for instance, was greater than the initial projection by 30 percent, and investment in the chemical industry also outpaced the projection. By contrast, the actual investment in light industry was less than half the initial projection.

The global money market was an economically expedient means to industrialization and also politically fortuitous for Koreans. High finance went hand in hand with high politics, and with international security—with the structural interest of the home country looming

TABLE 6.3. Official Loans Received by Use

	Amount	Percentage
Agriculture, fishery, and forestry	2,086	15.0
Mining	44	0.3
Manufacturing	372	2.7
Electricity, gas, and waterworks	3,630	26.1
Construction	2,184	15.7
Transportation	2,066	14.9
Banking, insurance, and real estate	1,992	14.3
Social service	1,510	10.8
Total	13,884	100.0

SOURCE: Ministry of Finance, ROK.

large in bankers' bottom-line calculations.[11] The logic of this political economy is not difficult to plumb: there are some countries whose strategic importance to the United States makes them practically undefaultable (Mexico, Korea, Egypt, the Philippines), and some banks so huge that they can only go belly-up at great risk to the home economy (BankAmerica, Citibank, Chase, etc.). For such borrowers and lenders, America is the lender of last resort, and bankers do well by lending big, and to countries that are American-supported through and through.

This was not the only reason for lending big to countries like Korea. But it adds to the prevailing explanations—all more or less economistic—on the debt crisis: the rational-choice argument that bankers (a priori rational) merely responded to the market disequilibria by lending to major developing countries that promised higher returns; the technological explanation that emphasizes large banks' competitive edge with regards to information and banking techniques; or the business-cycle argument that chastises the economics profession for having miscalculated the usual boom-and-bust recurrence in international banking.[12]

A cursory look at the U.S. multinational banks' loan portfolios supports the haute finance/haute politics argument: e.g., the disproportionate share of U.S. bank loans in Latin America and Asia. Massive loans to Korea and the Philippines perpetuated and reinforced the American commitment in those countries, as did the prompt rescue of Turkey from its impending bankruptcy in 1979 and

---

TABLE 6.4. Investment in Manufacturing for 1977–1981 (in billions of won, 1975 price)

	A Plan	B Achievement	B/A Percentage
Heavy Industry	2,893	2,806	97
Basic metals and			
machinery, etc.	731	951	130
Shipbuilding, etc.	1,145	827	72
Chemicals, etc.	1,017	1,028	102
Light Industry	1,621	746	46
Textiles	900	447	50
Other	721	302	42
Total	4,515	3,555	78

SOURCE: Economic Planning Board, ROK.

Mexico in the early 1980s, to cite only a few. The large "money-centers" might or might not be the "true foreign aid policy makers of the United States," as Representative Jim Leach said, but their portfolio decisions were far from apolitical.[13]

Official lending also had its political favoritism, which may be seen in the U.S. EXIM bank loans: in 1973, for example, seven of the top ten LDCs most favored by the EXIM had been recipients of $1 billion or more in net aid-flow in the past (a figure that, of course, includes Korea), a sign that the global security structure is perpetuated through economic means as well.[14] In IMF borrowings, too, the countries with U.S. backing and/or the NATO connection could easily count on less rigid imposition of economic programs as a condition of drawing over 100 percent of their quotas. For instance, the economic program imposed on Egypt in July 1978 for drawing the Fund facility equivalent to 163 percent to Egypt's quotas had been considerably "watered-down."[15] The lending pattern of the Asian Development Bank (ADB), the most scruplous and conservative of all international development banks, also reflected the political order and interest in the region: throughout the 1970s, as in the preceding decade, Korea remained the top borrower, with the Philippines a distant second.[16]

American private bankers took their cue from their government, and loaned to Korea because "the American government is," as one U.S. banker put it, "the guarantor of the whole South Korean government, lock, stock and barrel."[17] They lent even at a time when Korea was widely considered by international banking circles as the most likely nation to default, and cited as such in the *Wall Street Journal*.[18] The Institute for International Economic Policy devoted the inaugural issue of its journal to the impending debt crisis in Korea, an account based on confidential estimates being circulated at the State and Treasury departments.[19] That was in 1974–1976, Korea's first period of worries about default since 1970. The country had not only acquired a huge external debt in the aftermath of the first oil shock, but its debt-service capacity was in serious doubt: in a rare admission of helplessness, the Bank of Korea had projected growth for 1975–1980 at 4.1 percent to 4.8 percent, well below half the rate achieved for the first half of the decade.[20]

The Morgan Guaranty Bank of New York, it was reported, had "absolutely no confidence in Korea's balance of payment position," but that apparently did not prevent the bank from being the syndicate leader in the world's most closely watched "risk loan of the year."[21] American bank claims on Korea rose by 62 percent to a record $1.7 billion (of which $1.5 billion was short-term) in the first nine months of 1975, in the thick of the default gloom.[22] The U.S. share in foreign loans to Korea came to a remarkable 80 percent of the total outstanding. Table 6.5 breaks down the U.S. share by institutions, as of August 1975. The largest Japanese exposure was $53.7 million by The Bank of Tokyo, making six of the seven largest lenders American. (The Japanese had opted for retrenchment in this period and were not active in the international money market. In the late 1970s, however, Japan came back with vengeance.)

Amid growing concerns over the stability of the First National City and Chase Manhattan banks, the Treasury pondered the possibility of bailing out Korea, which would have required an emergency infusion of quick disbursing concessional commitments on an unprecedented scale.[23] Late 1976 was a nasty time for the American creditors of the Korean debt. Congress had just passed new Human Rights Amendments, and many bankers worried that the American government was reducing its commitment to Korea.[24]

Korea did not default, of course, thus obviating a possibility of placing the U.S. Congress and the administration at loggerheads on rescuing Korea. The country was out of trouble by 1976, having balanced its current account (after inducing a severe recession) several years ahead of the World Bank prediction.[25] In an incredible turnaround that was complete by 1978, Korea even "threatened" to repay (much to the consternation of the bankers worried about loss of income) the outstanding $114 million from the particularly usurious $200 million debt negotiated in 1975.[26] After that, foreign credit became much cheaper and considerably more plentiful: loans

TABLE 6.5. Foreign Banks with Credit Outstanding in Korea, August 1975

	$ million
Chase Manhattan	298.4
First National City New York	272.8
Manhattan Trust	257.4
Bankers Trust	226.6
Chemical Bank	126.0
Fidelity of Philadelphia	61.1
Irving Trust	36.4
Girard Bank of Philadelphia	30.0

SOURCE: *The New York Times*, November 21, 1975.

were provided to state banks without specific government guarantees, spreads on syndicated loans were "relentlessly" narrowing, and money was literally pushed on Korea.[27]

Just as Korea skirted a possible debt crisis, a new headache of an entirely different order was in store for the Ministry of Finance officials: the newly infused credit (post-1978) was not mainly American in origin, but arrived bearing motley national flags. Koreans knew from past experience in raising money abroad (and perhaps from their mercantilist instincts) that international finance and security were usually interlocked, that it was simply not good politics to fritter away "debtor leverage" by borrowing too little from too many countries that do not have significant security interests in Korea. As American bankers played brinkmanship with their home government over international debt, Koreans too had sought to play the debt game against the hegemon. Despite Korean preference for American leaders, the share of Japanese and European banks grew by leaps and bounds in the late 1970s. Given Japan's security stake in Korea, its loans posed no problem, but European money was none too useful politically.

The combined share of Japanese and European banks had been a mere 12 percent in 1976, but grew to 33 percent in 1978, then leaped to 70 percent of total funds provided in 1979. They had entered Korea with ruthless determination, fighting off American competitors through price-cutting and trading profit for a larger market share.[28] Americans sat on the sidelines; if Koreans wanted to reverse the trend, they had better make the sacrifices. So the Korean government chose to bypass the cheaper European credit in favor of the more expensive *but* indelibly American loans. In one well-publicized instance in 1979, Korea turned down a European offer of a straight 0.625 percent over LIBOR for ten years, and instead opted for a syndicate loan with 0.625 percent over LIBOR, (the first five years) and 0.75 percent (the next five years), managed by the Bank of America and Bankers Trust, and with a greater number of American banks participating.[29] By 1981, the share of American banks jumped again, claiming $2.3 billion of the total $3.4 billion in net lending by international banks. Korea's portfolio of external liabilities eventually contained only two loan sources, in effect: American and Japanese. Even bond flotations, which became increasingly important in the early 1980s and accounted for about 24 percent of gross external financing in 1984, were mostly absorbed by American and Japanese banks.[30]

Koreans thus wooed American multinational banks as the interconnecting putty between nations and their financial systems, so that they may rise and fall, sink and swim together. Through the politics of foreign debt, Koreans sought to wrest autonomy through interdependence, to cleave into the international system so as to be freed from abject dependence.

The Politics of Financial Allocation

The main goal of Korea's finance was to hemorrhage as much capital as possible into the heavy industrialization program. To that end, the financial policy of the *yushin* was this: the government set financial prices at an artificial low to subsidize import-substituting, heavy, chemical, and export industries, which inevitably led to a bifurcation of the financial market: business and government savings remained captives of the banking system to finance (along with foreign loans) major industries, and household savings by and large stayed in the "curb" to finance the rest of the economy (the needs of medium and small enterprises and consumers).

The political economy of this bifurcated financial system was illiberal, undemocratic, and statist. The ubiquitous curb, a vital part of the nation's economic life, was outside the protection, and at the mercy, of the state, which retained for itself the prerogative to shake up, freeze, and destroy the private money market so as to unclog business cash flow in times of recession. The curb rate reflected the high risk of dealing in an unstable market. It was unfair to curb-borrowers and to taxpayers: the state, partly to compensate for tax revenues lost in private money, resorted to a myriad of regressive indirect taxes, as well as direct taxation on wage income.[31]

In an otherwise thriving capitalist nation of scrupulous entrepreneurs, the formal financial sector remained most backward. Every bank in the nation was owned and controled by the state; bankers were bureaucrats and not entreprenuers, they thought in terms of GNP and not profit, and they loaned to those favored by the state. The monetary authority—the Bank of Korea—forfeited what little autonomy it had during the days of reform (1965–1972); in its stead, the Ministry of Finance came to direct monetary policies, the Economic Planning Board to oversee bank budgets, and the Ministry of Commerce to influence the flow of export and other policy loans.

Table 6.6 shows that bank loans were almost always below the GNP deflator. From that, we calculate that the average real cost of bank loan for 1974–1980 came to minus 6.7 percent. On the other hand, the curb rate was always positive, well above inflation: for the same time period, the average cost of borrowing in the curb was about 18.5 percent. The difference in average between the two money markets was, then, a whopping 25.2 percentage points.

Table 6.7 shows that the total domestic savings vacillated between 18.06 percent and 22.59 percent of GNP from 1972 through 1980. Business savings remained remarkably stable at around 10 percent of GNP; government savings steadily rose; but household savings showed sensitivity to the increases in interest rates in the 1977–1979 period (as can be seen in table 6.6), only to plummet again in 1980.

The Korean ratio of government and business savings to the GDP was really not meretricious, and was comparable to rates achieved in Japan and Taiwan. But household savers could not be cajoled into depositing their money in the banking system so long as interest rates remained low. A survey conducted in 1980 indicated that more than 70 percent of household savings may have stayed in the curb.

The ordinary tools of monetary control—the reserve requirement, discount, and open market operation policies—were, mostly, ineffective. The reserve requirement policy changed so frequently that it destabilized the M1, M2 supply multipliers; and despite frequent changes, the ratio always remained too high, cutting into bank profitability and prompting the BOK to extend special loans to cover the banks' reserve deficiencies, in addition to paying interest on reserves. All of these considerations undermined the monetary instrument's raison d'être. Such counterproductive behavior may be explained by the government's wish for tighter control over banks.

TABLE 6.6. Interest Rates on Curb and Bank Loans

Year	Inflation (GNP deflator)	Curb Market Nominal	Curb Market Real	Bank Loan (general) Nominal	Bank Loan (general) Real
1974	29.5	40.6	11.1	15.5	−14.0
1975	25.7	41.3	15.6	15.5	−10.2
1976	20.7	40.5	19.8	18.0	− 2.7
1977	15.7	38.1	22.4	16.0	0.3
1978	21.4	41.2	19.8	19.0	− 2.4
1979	21.2	42.4	21.2	19.0	− 2.2
1980	25.6	44.9	19.3	20.0	− 5.6

SOURCE: The Bank of Korea.

TABLE 6.7. Domestic Savings, 1972–1980, as Percent of GNP

	General Government (1)	Public and Private Corporations (2)	Household and Nonprofit Organizations (3)	Domestic Savings (1) + (2) + (3)
1972	3.64	8.72	5.70	18.06
1973	3.99	11.17	8.98	24.14
1974	2.25	11.36	7.04	20.65
1975	3.76	9.81	6.61	20.18
1976	6.05	10.21	8.81	25.07
1977	5.11	10.68	12.30	28.09
1978	6.17	9.94	13.28	29.40
1979	6.74	9.75	12.29	28.28
1980	5.67	10.29	6.63	22.59

SOURCE: The Bank of Korea.

High required reserve ratio tends to reduce the DMBs'—and increase the BOK's—liabilities. This way, the BOK has a larger role in credit allocation than would otherwise be the case. Open market operations, moreover, were all but moribund;[32] finally, the impact of BOK discount policy on money supply was nil. With bank interest at negative real rates, the demand for loans was never satiated, and variations in discount rates (i.e., supplying credit to the banking system through rediscounting commercial bills) made little difference: the DMBs always clamored to borrow more from the central bank.

How, then, was money-creation regulated? The state simply invoked its fiat to settle the matter by nonprice mechanisms. The extraordinary demand on BOK resources was curtailed through a

TABLE 6.8. Urban Household Saving Deposit Pattern in 1980

Organized Financial Market	29.8%
Banks	(22.3%)
Nonbank financial institutions	(6.4%)
Securities	(1.1%)
Unorganized Financial Market	70.2%
Total	100.0%

SOURCE: Citizens National Bank.

mixture of absolute ceilings and quotas on rediscounts and loans, rejection of applications, and restriction on bills eligible for rediscounting. Every year, the government set ceilings on the BOK rediscount/loan availability, and parceled out resources among DMBs, taking their reserve positions into consideration. There were no ceilings, however, on export and other policy loans, which were sacrosanct and automatically approved.

This last point, the exemption of policy loans from regulatory ceilings, was an albatross that further eroded the effectiveness of monetary policy (such as it was) for macroeconomic adjustment: for instance, if exports expanded, so did the amount of the automatically approved export loans, which in turn increased the money supply and inflationary pressure. So long as the rising industries were financed by BOK currency issuance, the money supply could not become an effective countercyclical tool for economic stabilization. The magnitude of this problem can be gleaned from table 6.9. The automatic rediscount issued by the BOK was 38.6 percent of the total BOK reserve base (high powered money) in 1975, but reached an amazing 70.2 percent by the end of 1981.

What were "policy loans"? In Korea, all bank credits were business subsidies, their allocation scrutinized by the state. In some

TABLE 6.9. Policy Loans Issued by the Bank of Korea
(in 100 million won, percent)

	1975	1978	1980	1981
Export Loan	3,797	7,751	12,915	16,279
Supporting Loan for Energy Conservation	—	—	5	711
Special Support for Export Industries	—	—	—	1,266
Agricultural Loan	260	—	711	611
Fishery Loan	55	284	500	619
Support Loan for Military Industry	—	90	167	119
Others	41	1,140	253	4
Total (A)	4,153	9,265	14,511	19,659
Total BOK loan (B)	7,961	11,785	24,450	33,711
(A)/(B)	52.2%	78.6%	59.3%	58.3%
Reserve Base (C)	10,770	28,020	32,439	28,016
(A)/(C)	38.6%	33.1%	44.7%	70.2%

SOURCE: Kim and Pak, *Hanguk kyôngje wa kûmyung* [Korea's Economy and Finance], p. 359.

sense, therefore, all loans were policy loans. Nonetheless bank credits fell into two categories, policy and general. "Policy loans" carried exceedingly low rates (lower even than the subsidy rates of "general loans") with longer maturity, and were virtually nondefaultable because of state backing. They claimed over 40 percent of total domestic credits, 74 percent of total loan categories, and bolstered industries and projects supervised by eleven different government ministries.[33]

There were essentially three ways of generating policy loans for desirable industries. One was through the banking system: the BOK rediscount shown in table 6.9 claimed the major portion of resources garnered through financial means, but there were others, such as the "specialized banking funds," the "directive" loans (i.e., ad hoc policy loans designated by the government and not covered through BOK rediscount), and "compensation for interest rate differentials." The second source of policy loans was fiscal, taken out of the state budget. The third was the National Investment Fund (NIF). As can be seen in table 6.10, policy loans accounted for 43.5 percent of total domestic credit in 1978, 40.8 percent in 1979, and 42.8 percent in 1980. These funds were distributed to exporters and other preferential borrowers through DMBs.

Table 6.11 shows the rates carried by policy loans; parts of table 6.6 are inserted here to underscore differences from the market (curb)

TABLE 6.10. Policy Loans by Source and as Percent of Total Domestic Credit

	1978	1979	1980	1981
I. Banking System	35.9%	34.2%	36.7%	39.8%
a. BOK rediscount	15.4%	13.3%	13.6%	14.2%
b. compensation for interest rate diff.	6.3%	5.8%	5.6%	6.7%
c. special banking fund	8.2%	9.7%	10.0%	10.8%
d. directive loan	6.0%	5.4%	7.5%	8.1%
II. Government Budget	3.9%	3.2%	3.4%	3.3%
III. NIF	3.7%	3.4%	2.7%	2.6%
IV. Total Policy Loan (I + II + III)	43.5%	40.8%	42.8%	45.7%
V. General Loans	56.5%	59.2%	57.2%	55.3%
VI. Total Domestic Loan	100.0%	100.0%	100.0%	100.0%

SOURCE: Kim and Pak, *Hanguk kyôngje wa kûmyung* [Korea's Economy and Finance], p. 354.

and general bank rates. Export loans were the cheapest by far, at almost a quarter of general bank rates in 1971, stabilizing at about half by the decade's end. Rates on National Investment and Machinery Industry Promotion Funds more closely trailed general rates.

Of all policy loans, export credits and National Investment Fund were the most compelling for the Big Push. Export loans at real interest rate anywhere between minus 19.73 (1975) and minus 10.6 (1980) were not only giveaways, but were the most plentiful and easiest of all loans to get: exporters merely had to produce letters of credit from foreign buyers to turn on the loan spigot. Soon, an institution emerged to absorb a lion's share of these credits: the general trading companies (GTC) *(chonghap sangsa)*, or *sogo shosha*, as these East Asian behemoths came to be known. These were really mercantilist instruments par excellence. The Japanese *sogo shosha* originated in the late nineteenth century to strike at western traders who often abused Japan's infant industries. The Korean GTCs did the same to the Japanese: the establishment of GTCs in 1975 was decreed when the Japanese *sogo shosha*, in the thick of growing U.S. protectionism, avoided handling Korean exports.[34] It proved a terribly expensive retaliation: the financial system hemorrhaged limitless credit into GTCs, which often exported at a loss but survived on credit-subsidy. And the Korean chaebôl, forbidden to own banks (unlike their Japanese counterparts), in turn relied on GTC export

TABLE 6.11. Interest Rates on Various Loans

Year	Curb Loans	Corporate Bond	Bank Loans General	Bank Loans Export	Bank Loans MIPF[a]	NIF	GNP Deflator
1971	46.41	—	22.0	6.0	—	—	13.92
1972	38.97	—	19.0	6.0	—	—	16.11
1973	33.30	—	15.5	7.0	10.0	—	13.40
1974	40.56	—	15.5	9.0	12.0	12.0	29.54
1975	41.31	20.1	15.5	9.0	12.0	12.0	25.73
1976	40.47	20.4	17.0	8.0	13.0	14.0	20.73
1977	38.07	20.1	15.0	8.0	13.0	14.0	15.67
1978	41.22	21.1	18.5	9.0	15.0	16.0	21.39
1979	42.39	26.7	18.5	9.0	15.0	16.0	21.20
1980	44.94	30.1	24.5	15.0	20.0	22.0	25.60
1981	35.25	24.4	17.5	15.0	11.0	16.5	15.90

SOURCE: The Bank of Korea.
[a] MIPF: Machinery Industry Promotion Fund.

credits to finance their sprawling industrial empires. In that sense, the Korean chaebôl looks like a concentric circle emanating from a GTC at its core, with the energy coming from the state's extraordinary policy loans.

In 1975, five GTCs were licensed; in 1976, nine; in 1977, eleven; in 1978, thirteen; and in 1979, twelve. By 1979, half of the nation's total exports were handled by the GTCs. GTCs have spearheaded diversification of exports, and are credited for having promoted heavy industrial product sales such as industrial plant machinery. The proportion of heavy and chemical goods exports accomplished by GTCs rose to 68.4 percent in 1984, up from 22.6 percent in 1976.[35]

The state was munificent, but also a harsh disciplinarian. It supplied the cold bath that the market could not. Export credits were wonderful gifts to the chaebôl, but to get it, one had to be deserving: otherwise, licenses were immediately revoked. Every year, the state slapped stringent performance criteria on the GTCs with respect to capital, total export volume, and the minimum number of export items, destinations, and overseas branches required. GTCs meeting these requirements were allowed the dollar amount of the L/C at favorable exchange and interest rates. (In 1976, for instance, the GTCs might be allowed 420 won to a dollar instead of the official rate at 480 won, and at 8 percent interest rate instead of the 17 percent for general bank loans.) Some GTCs with exceptional export records were even exempted from showing L/C to receive credit, and could borrow up to 1.5 month's worth of their past export records.[36]

The National Investment Fund, established in 1973 with the express purpose of financing heavy and chemical industries, was neither as plentiful nor as cheap as export credit. But it was extensive enough to maneuver the financially leveraged chaebôl into new heavy sectors of shipbuilding, automobiles, machinebuilding, chemicals, and electronics. The size of the fund was 4.4 percent of total domestic credit in 1979 and the rate of interest subsidy ranged between minus 17.54 percent in real interest in 1974 to minus 3.60 percent in 1980.

NIF bonds were mostly absorbed by banking institutions, which provided about half of total NIF resources: the rest were split between insurance companies and government agencies.[37] Table 6.12 breaks down NIF use by industry and shows that heavy, chemical, and power industries combined, claimed anywhere between 78.8 percent (1976) and 86.9 percent (1978) of the total. (The *Saemaul* on the fourth line is a program for rural industrialization.)

Thus our evidence shows that the state, through massive and

liberal use of policy loans, fostered the growth of export and heavy/ chemical industries. A bird's-eye view of the overall lending pattern reinforces the same conclusion. Table 6.13 reveals that the average cost of all loans—bank, foreign, nonbank financial intermediaries, bond, etc.—for export industries was almost always cheaper than that for industries producing for domestic consumption, and loans to heavy industries were always significantly lower than that to light industries. What is further remarkable is the concurrence of the same phenomenon when borrowing firms are divided by size: large manufacturers had greater access to cheaper loans than did small manufacturers.

The magnitude of the bias and subsidy is clear when we look at not only the cost but the size of the total bank and foreign loans received, as shown in table 6.14. Export and heavy industrial sectors again fared well in their access to borrowing, computed here as the ratio of total loans over total assets. Large firms, likewise, did well at the expense of small firms.

The Korean bias toward export industries was by no means unique to Korea: Taiwan, another super-exporter in East Asia, also had an effective system of export credit subsidy. But, Korean favoritism toward heavy industries and large firms was really sui generis. This eventuated by necessity: the economies of scale demanded by heavy industry could be met only by the large—the chaebôl—firms, ergo policy loans to big business. At times, the chaebôl might buy influ-

TABLE 6.12. Uses of National Investment Fund, Selected Years

Uses	1974	1976	1978	1980
Heavy & chemical industries	44,120 (58.5)	100,677 (56.4)	239,447 (62.7)	266,704 (60.8)
Power industries	17,000 (22.5)	40,000 (22.4)	92,000 (24.2)	120,000 (27.4)
Agricultural industries	10,547 (14.0)	19,415 (10.9)	14,946 (13.9)	21,711 (5.0)
Saemaul factories	3,740 (5.0)	8,450 (4.7)	4,222 (1.5)	—
Export on deferred payment	—	10,000 (5.6)	29,684 (6.2)	30,000 (6.8)
Total	75,407	178,542	380,229	438,415

SOURCE: The World Bank, *Korea: Managing the Industrial Transition*, 2:111.

TABLE 6.13. Average Cost of Borrowing by Each Sector

	1974	1975	1976	1977	1978	1980
Export industry (1)	9.82	9.82	11.34	12.87	12.68	16.01
Domestic industry (2)	10.88	12.60	12.25	13.24	12.25	21.03
(2)–(1)	1.06	2.78	0.91	0.37	−0.43	5.02
Heavy industry (1)	10.38	10.24	10.14	11.50	10.09	17.58
Light industry (2)	10.59	12.16	13.70	14.29	15.85	20.05
(2)–(1)	0.21	1.92	3.56	2.79	5.76	2.47
Large firms (1)	10.49	11.19	11.80	11.91	11.91	18.42
Small firms (2)	11.41	13.92	14.39	13.80	15.55	20.74
(2)–(1)	0.92	2.73	2.59	1.89	3.64	2.32

SOURCE: Bank of Korea, *Financial Statement Analysis,* various issues.

ence through political contributions or promises of what is known as the *amakudari* in the literature on Japan.[38] Table 6.15 shows how the chaebôl expanded by partaking in the Big Push. With very few exceptions that are marked with asterisks, all acquisitions are post-1973. It was not uncommon for the chaebôl to triple their affiliates in the years 1974 to 1978, with new acquisitions often in the heavy and chemical sectors.

Bankers' bottom-line considerations also made the bias toward bigness prevail in the disposition of funds under their allocationary discretion (about 60 percent of total domestic loans). When loans rates are kept artificially low under a ceiling, as was the case in

TABLE 6.14. Access to Borrowing by Each Sector

	1974	1975	1976	1977	1978	1980
Export industry (1)	49.28	45.07	43.11	44.06	42.85	48.57
Domestic industry (2)	42.93	36.62	39.91	39.83	37.54	31.66
(1)–(2)	6.85	8.45	3.20	4.23	5.31	16.90
Heavy industry (1)	41.25	38.52	41.59	42.53	41.60	39.67
Light industry (2)	49.05	41.96	40.32	40.04	35.94	37.11
(1)–(2)	−7.79	−3.44	1.27	2.48	5.66	2.56
Large firms (1)	45.65	40.93	41.36	41.38	39.69	39.25
Small firms (2)	25.44	27.38	34.98	40.79	37.02	33.79
(1)–(2)	21.10	13.56	6.38	0.59	2.67	5.46

SOURCE: Bank of Korea, *Financial Statement Analysis,* various issues.

Korea, bankers have no compelling incentive to seek out truly enter-prising borrowers: the maximum return on loans, no matter how well and enterprisingly spent by borrowers, is always limited. Thus, bankers become cautious, not venturesome: they seek to protect their moderate profit by avoiding bad loans and reducing default-risk; and with what economists call "imperfect information," bank-ers usually end up loaning to known entities. In the Korean context, that meant loans to the chaebôl, who also enjoyed state support.[39]

The combination of state industrial policy and bankers' bureau-

TABLE 6.15. Chaebôl Participation in Heavy and Chemical Industries

Chaebôl	Number of Affiliates		Acquisitions in HC Industries
	1974	*1978*	
Hyundai	9	31	automobile*, machinery*, iron & steel, shipbuilding, aluminum, oil refining, heavy electrical, heavy machinery
Samsung	24	33	shipbuilding, general machinery, electric switching system, petrochemicals
Daewoo	10	35	machinery, automobile, shipbuilding
Lucky	17	43	petrochemicals*, oil refining*, electronics*
Hyosông	8	24	heavy electrical, machinery, auto parts, petrochemicals
Kukje	7	22	iron & steel, machinery
Sunkyung	8	23	chemical, machinery
Samhwa	10	30	electrical, machinery
Ssangyong	17	20	cement*, heavy machinery, shipbuilding, heavy electrical
Kûmho	15	22	iron & steel, petrochemicals
Kolon	6	22	heavy electrical, petrochemicals

SOURCE: Kim, "From Dominance to Symbiosis."

cratic inertia conspired to reward the sectors that were often less productive. Table 6.16 shows that the average rates of return on investment for the credit-gobbling trio were always lower than those of their counterparts. This meant that firms exported even though it was far more profitable to sell at home, and the chaebôl moved into heavy industries even though returns on their investments were slow in coming. The gap between these and opportunity cost was presumably paid with credit subsidies.

Now it was possible for the state to argue the case for subsidizing exports (after all, exports paid for imports and serviced gigantic debts, and even dumping had the virtue of expanding the market share abroad), and for heavy industries (which provided backward-linkage and were also important for national security). But having well-fattened chaebôl on welfare was something else: as the chaebôl grew big—even gargantuan—so did handouts. And so did criticism. Detractors framed the issue as a noisome, cynical alliance of big business and corrupt officials.[40]

The truth was graver and deeper than that, however, and the solution to the problem more intractable: the chaebôl in Korea, for all practical purposes, was a private agency of public purpose. Park Chung Hee had eradicated the distinction between public and private when he pumped the chaebôl, back in 1973, as the muscle of the Big Push. By the end of the decade the chickens were coming home to roost.

TABLE 6.16. Average Rate of Return on Investment by Each Sector

	1974	1975	1976	1977	1978	1980
Export industry (1)	8.21	7.75	9.10	8.75	8.53	9.22
Domestic industry (2)	12.25	10.82	11.08	11.12	12.33	9.08
(2)–(1)	4.04	3.07	1.98	2.37	3.80	−0.14
Heavy industry (1)	12.45	9.34	9.41	8.96	9.69	7.36
Light industry (2)	9.45	9.65	11.50	11.57	13.80	11.40
(2)–(1)	−3.0	0.31	2.09	2.61	4.11	4.04
Large firms (1)	10.86	9.43	10.37	10.06	10.82	8.84
Small firms (2)	12.81	10.87	11.22	12.25	12.23	11.10
(2)–(1)	1.95	1.44	0.85	2.19	1.41	2.26

SOURCE: Bank of Korea, *Financial Statement Analysis,* various issues.

Socializing Risk: The Economic Basis of Korea, Inc.

The extraordinary concentration of domestic credit *in* the chaebôl might be gleaned from the following: 400 large firms belonging to 137 different chaebôl claimed (in 1983) 69.6 percent of total bank and 47.6 percent of total financial institution loans outstanding. (In Taiwan, by comparison, the share of the top 100 firms was 11.6 percent, and the top 333, 18 percent of the total domestic credit.)[41] The share of the 50 largest chaebôl in total domestic credit came to 26.5 percent, and the combined share of the three largest (Hyundai, Daewoo, and Samsung) was over 10 percent of the total.[42] The ratio of debt to equity in the 50 largest chaebôl was conservatively estimated at 524 percent in 1980, and 454.8 percent in 1985.[43] Seven of the top 50 have staggering debt ratios of over 1,000 percent: of them, some were over 10,000 percent, and one stood at 47,699 percent.[44]

Such credit concentration and corporate debt-leverage is extremely destabilizing for the economy in times of global recession and slacking exports; even in good times, huge nonperforming loans, accumulated through the years, cast a thick pall over the health of the banking system. In 1983, the sum of nonperforming loans[45] in the banking sector came to 13.7 percent of total domestic credit, and in 1985, to 17 percent: in the latter year, the portion of bad loans held by each city bank was anywhere between to two to five times its paid-up capital.[46]

Since banks are understandably reticent in divulging information on their clients' credit standing, we cannot know what percentage of nonperforming loans is attributable to the chaebôl. But a number of facts make the case for overwhelming chaebôl share in the bad debts outstanding in the Korean financial system. First, banks mostly loan to large enterprises, which almost always belong to the chaebôl; second, the chaebôl are more leveraged than other firms; third, the chaebôl's profitability, say, in manufacturing, is much lower—by more than a third—than for others;[47] four, "financially unsound" industries in the late 1970s were heavy industries and automobiles, and in the 1980s, construction, shipping, and General Trading (GTCs), which are all chaebôl oligopolies.[48] Finally, only the chaebôl were allowed collateral that fell short of the loan amount, and this type of loan is often labeled as bad or nonperforming loans.[49]

The chaebôl, however, rarely go belly-up, save when the state lets one or two die at a great interval in a case of exemplary justice. (The selection of sacrificial lambs was often political, as when Yulsan, an intrepid corporation that ballooned on export credits, supported an opposition politician.) The chaebôl leverage against bankruptcy is, very simply, its size and its impact on employment. Table 6.17 is an illustration of that point. The sales of the top 10 chaebôl (which were among the 28 developing country firms listed in the Fortune-500 list of largest non-U.S. industrial companies) were 30.2 percent of the total manufacturing, and the top 30 absorbed about one-fifth of the total workforce in manufacturing.

This is a Korean version of what Theodore Lowi called "permanent receivership," whereby institutions large enough to be a significant factor in the community get their stability underwritten.[50] The financing of this permanent receivership is public in three ways. The most obvious is taxation, but it is also the most problematic (even in an authoritarian state): by the end of 1980, the amount and variety of direct, regressive taxes reached intolerable limits, and a higher tax on corporations, already groaning with huge financial expense, was considered infeasible.

But a second one was routinely used: taxation through inflation.[51] From 1972 to 1982, the central bank issued 130 billion won in rescue loans to DMBs at a 5 percent nominal interest rate, which were used by the latter to write off and to reschedule bad loans: as of 1985, about half of the rescue loans were returned to the banking system. But that was a drop in the bucket, since nonperforming loans were estimated at 4 trillion won as of 1985. Hence, the Bank of Korea was forced to expand, in 1985, the category of rescue loan eligibility and to drive down the rate to 3 percent. The DMBs would then reschedule loans at nominal 11.5 percent, and use the 8.5 percent margin to make up for the loss. As of April, 1985, the total BOK credit to the DMBs was equal at 42 percent of the total DMB loans outstanding.[52]

Finally, as a third measure, the state can grab the bull by the horns, and forcibly "reorganize" the troubled industry: the number

TABLE 6.17. The Chaebôl Share in Manufacturing (Percent)

	Sales			Employment		
	1978	*1980*	*1981*	*1978*	*1980*	*1981*
Top 5 chaebôl	15.7	16.9	22.6	9.5	9.1	8.4
Top 10	21.1	23.8	30.2	13.9	12.8	12.2
Top 20	29.3	31.4	36.6	18.2	17.9	16.0
Top 30	34.1	36.0	40.7	22.2	22.4	18.6

SOURCE: Lee, "Conglomerates and Business Concentration."

of chaebôl participants can be winnowed down to a few profitable
ones, through a state fiat ordering mergers. Yet since the state cra-
dles the enterprises from birth to grave, the chosen few receive
newly-infused support loans and the losers are compensated with,
say, monopoly concessions (and more credit) in other industries. Or
the state can mix financial and fiscal palliatives to get their houses
in order: tax exemptions and BOK rescue funds for the chaebôl willing to improve their financial structure by shifting resources away
from areas that are not profitable, outside of their main concentration, or real estate. In either case—whether reorganization is at the
enterprise or industry level—the public ends up bearing the cost.

How did the chaebôl grow so big, so destabilizing to the economy,
and so burdensome to the state? The greater part of the story is
already told: it occurred through state manipulation of the financial
system to herd business—no matter how inevitably inexperienced
and inept in a developing country—into selective industries, and
also because economies of scale were deemed critical to survive fires
of international competition. But once set in motion, the process
could be neither stopped nor reversed.

Whenever credit allocation shows a bias for size, it sets in motion
a powerful tendency toward market concentration: chaebôl firms
can use their easy accessibility to bank loans to either keep small
firms from entering the market (by making the cost of entry prohib-
itively high), or to squeeze out competitors through predatory pric-
ing. Table 6.18 shows that the market share of industries characterized as uncompetitive (monopolies, duopolies, and oligopolies)
increased, both in terms of number of commodities and sales value,
between 1970–1982. The shares of monopolies and duopolies rose in
1970–1977 (years of the Big Push); they dropped in 1977–1982, but
the drop, we see, is not translated into an increase in the share of
competitive firms but of oligopolistic firms. This sharp rise in shares
of oligopolies points to the chaebôl tendency to create beachheads in
a variety of industries: hence chaebôl-level concentration is probably
much higher than is reflected here.

Discriminatory financial cost and accessibility, by firm size, also
intensify the aggregate economic concentration by the chaebôl. Taking advantage of their credit accessibility, large firms can perform
leveraged buy-outs, and small competitors often go along, because a
merger of this kind (i.e., becoming chaebôl affiliates) has the virtue
of bringing in much-needed capital. According to the White Paper
on Fair Trading, one half of all mergers occurring in the 32-months
period between April 1981 and December 1983 involved the nation's

thirty largest chaebôl. A breakdown in the direction of such mergers shows that horizontal mergers (i.e., with firms making same type of products) accounted for 13.5 percent, and vertical mergers (i.e., with firms producing for use by the next) claimed 24.7 percent, but the mergers with firms entirely unrelated both in market and production process came to a whopping 61.8 percent of the total. The directional rates for other mergers (unrelated to the thirty *chaebôl*) were 29.8 percent, 25.5 percent, and 44.7 percent, respectively.[53]

In addition to market monopoly and merger, the chaebôl found other and (really much more nefarious) ways of using the banks' fungible credit to serve the ends of expansion: investment in the curb market and speculation in real estate. The arbitrage between the two money markets promised, of course, a windfall. (We know from table 6.6 that the average real interest rate on the curb was 18.5 percent for 1974–1980, and that the same on bank loans was −6.5 percent.) The extent of such practices is, however, impossible to investigate: an estimate of the money market arbitrage by the chaebôl is, to the best of my knowledge, unavailable.[54] Chaebôl speculation in real estate, on the other hand, became the eye of a political

TABLE 6.18. Market Structure of Korean Manufacturing (Percent)

	1970	1974	1977	1982
Monopoly[a]				
Commodities	29.6	30.8	31.6	23.6
Sales	8.7	12.7	16.3	11.4
Duopoly[b]				
Commodities	18.7	17.9	20.1	11.1
Sales	16.3	12.6	11.0	6.6
Oligopoly[c]				
Commodities	33.2	34.2	32.0	47.6
Sales	35.1	38.6	33.9	50.6
Noncompetitive				
Commodities	81.5	82.8	83.7	82.1
Sales	61.1	63.9	61.2	68.6
Competitive				
Commodities	18.5	17.2	16.3	17.9
Sales	39.9	36.1	38.8	31.4

Source: World Bank, *Korea: Managing the Industrial Transition*, 2:30.

[a] A firm concentration exceeding 80 percent.

[b] A two-firm concentration over 80 percent.

[c] Top three produce more than 60 percent.

storm, as the price of real estate skyrocketed in the inflationary spiral of the late 1970s, caused by the monetization of foreign borrowing and vast liquidity flows from the Middle East.

In an analysis of corporate financial structure, the Bank of Korea revealed that chaebôl investment in fixed assets was dangerously high as ratios both of net worth, and of long term capital, and that a substantial portion of the chaebôl's fixed assets was in holdings of real estate unrelated to business operation.[55] This tendency to invest in fixed assets (over and beyond the available long-term capital) was much more pronounced in export industries than in industries producing for domestic consumption, which strongly implied that the short-term export policy loans found their way into the purchase of real estate. Heavy industries also had higher ratios of fixed assets to long-term capital, meaning that both long-term loans through NIF and additional short-term DMB might have gone into real estate.

Real estate speculation by the chaebôl had egregious influence on the economy in more ways that one: it not only made the cost of home ownership prohibitive for ordinary citizens, but further destabilized the financial system. This was because the chaebôl, their cash flow in trouble yet unwilling (and sometimes unable) to liquidate landholdings, often turned to the central bank for rescue loans. The BOK threatened retaliation by making corporate landowners ineligible for rescue loans[56], but the threat only turned tragedy into farce, a catch-22: to get the BOK rescue loans, the chaebôl had to liquidate their landholdings, but without land, there was insufficient collateral for the DMB loans.[57] Thus, the state warning remained just that, a warning: the barking dog could not bite.

Now, all of this is not to say that the state was feckless, ineffectual, or passive. In fact, the state enacted numerous draconian decrees all through the 1970s and into the 1980s, designed to curtail the worst abuse by the chaebôl. The most notable was the attempt to reduce chaebôl reliance on bank credits by forcing the chaebôl to go public.

In 1972, after the August 3rd Decree, almost as a quid-pro-quo for having rescued the chaebôl from collective bankruptcy, the state selected what it considered "blue chip" firms (based on profitability, equity, and asset position) and forced them to go public. This was done by threats of slapping the recalcitrants with a whopping 40 percent corporate tax (versus the 27 percent usual) and to deny itemized reductions. Overnight, new public stock offerings valued at $48 million innundated the Seoul Stock Exchange and the number of companies listed jumped 50 percent.[58] The stock market received a further boost in 1974, when a special presidential decree tightened the audit and supervision of bank credit for all nonlisted (but listable, according to the government) firms.[59] Many more measures like these followed throughout the remainder of the 1970s.

The government sought to control the securities market by setting low prices on new issues and determining dividends and corporate reinvestment decisions. The chaebôl found themselves, then, between a rock and a hard place: between the state's punitive measures and the costs of going public, which meant the lack of autonomy in business decision making, bypassing cheap bank credits, high cost of raising undervalued equity capital, and government intervention in corporate management. Some firms decided that it was better to resist the government order, pay the tax, and bypass the palliatives that the government offered to listed firms. Others obeyed the government, but without truly complying: the owners themselves absorbed much of the newly issued stocks.

Conclusion

Given the state's inefficacy in correcting the abuses of the chaebôl, it is tempting to conclude here that what we have in Korea is a case of private power circumventing the public purpose. That conclusion is ipso facto logical, but it flows from a false distinction between public and private. Social scientists are wont to see the government (or state) and social groups (or class) as "actors" in the political "arena," vying for "power," sometimes in "antagonistic", sometimes in "cooperative" (or corporative) ways.

We beg to differ: we posit that the private and the public in Korea is rolled into one, into what one might term "Korea Inc." As we have explained in this chapter, the mercantilist state raised industrial capital abroad and at home, and refracted it in ways commensurate with its purpose, in the process rewarding the chaebôl, which it deemed the most fit agent to carry out the state's purpose. But then the state was forced to socialize the risk created by the chaebôl's destabilizing presence in the financial system. The problem of the chaebôl is a political one, too, a question of equity, as critics have pointed out. But in the overall scheme of things, the state saw the problems raised by the chaebôl as a nefarious part of the beneficial whole in the long march toward industrial transformation. As the chaebôl groups—the very spearhead of exports—soared, so did the state, and so did the economy. Such, for good or ill, is the makeup of Korea Inc.

7

Slouching Toward the Market: Financial Liberalization in the 1980s

A DIACHRONIC approach to political economy denies, a fortiori, the possibility of a miracle; and so does this study, which has shown that the stunning economic success of Korea must be traced to the first few decades of the Japanese imperium. That was when Korea entered the world system first as Japan's semiperiphery, its security buffer, its industrial addendum, and then its clone. Liberated, Korean leaders parodied the alchemy of the prewar Japanese economic success, from political exclusion of the masses to the financial legerdemain that turned the young and restless into the *shinko zaibatsu*, or in the Korean instance, the *chaebôl*, the private agencies of public purpose. Now, the story beginning some three quarters of a century back may be winding to an end as authoritarianism gives way—however fitfully—to electoral politics, financial control to liberalization, and abroad, cold war to glasnost, hinting at the possibility of Nordpolitik at home. Thus, the mosaic of strong state, global security, financial control, and the ascendence of the chaebôl that had formed the gestalt of Korean late development may be coming unstuck, with recidivism always a possibility byt not an impending one.

This chapter is concerned with changes in Korean politics and economy, especially finance, in recent years. The method of inquiry we use here is the same as in other chapters: it is diachronic, and not synchronic, and it sees the 1980s not as a departure but as a long and complex codicil, in which the historic tasks set by the first generation of postwar Korean economic architects came to completion, but not without unraveling some contradictions in Korean political economy as discussed in this book. We will first examine some of the economic problems surfacing at the end of the 1970s that set the stage for economic restructuring. After that, we will traverse, as we have done chapter after chapter, the realm of international relations, to understand the paradox of hegemonic influence: the eddies of pressure for market opening combining, clashing, whirling with the traditional support for dictatorship. In the end, it was global capitalism that won over national capitalism, and economics that took command over politics, so that by 1990, Korea found itself not only with a more liberal and open market but its political counterpart, a state that is less interventionist, and often halted by the growing power of the monied class. The final portion of the chapter focuses on the domestic origins of the change toward the market, on the *Rashomon*-like understanding of the state, the chaebôl, and (less importantly) the popular opposition regarding the political impact of economic liberalization, the most significant of which has taken place in the financial realm.

Time of Troubles: Recession, Insurrection, and Reaction

The era of the Big Push ended with a bang in 1979. Park Chung Hee was assassinated by his henchman, inflation was at the decade's highest, the current account deficit tripled, and the GNP growth rate slowed down to 6.5 percent in 1979—from over 10 percent—and then nosedived, to hit a dismal minus 5.2 percent in the year after, a cataclysmic figure in the Korean context. Riots had spread like wild fire in the summer of 1979, touched off by outraged female workers in, significantly, the textile sector, which was still the largest earner of foreign currency but crippled by the appreciating exchange rate,[1] eclipsed by heavy industries in the view of policy makers, and rapidly losing what export competitiveness it had.[2]

Liberal economists at home pinned the blame for this performance on the Big Push, as did foreign observers and officials at international development agencies, clucking their tongues at the Korean tendency to do too much, too quickly, too injudiciously;[3] and they swore to reform the economy by undoing the regulatory maze of the Big Push and liberalizing the market, which was also in conformity to the latest (Reaganite) global creed. So began the stabilization-cum-liberalization program, extending five years beyond 1980, its tab picked up through three IMF standbys and two structural adjustment loans from the World Bank.[4]

This program, hailed as the triumph of "orthodox stabilization policies"[5] was really neither very orthodox nor consistent, and was more an imbrication of three tendencies. The first tendency, from 1980 to 1982, was idiosyncratic to the Korean way of dealing with crisis: incurring more debt to absorb exogenous shock, more stimulative financial policy, more devaluation, and more export. The second tendency, commenced in 1983, was a vintage IMF prescription and sought to bolster creditor confidence by eliminating inflation, reducing the rate of growth of external debt, and improving maturity structure. It entailed, among other things, a sharp reduction in public sector deficit and credit expansion as well as a real depreciation of currency. This, then, led the way to the third tendency, to the Valhalla of a liberalized market, which would be the ultimate guerdon for the five years of painful and costly structural adjustment. When the stabilization component of the program was over in 1985, inflation was squeezed out, the current account began showing sizable surplus, and the country was on a growth spurt that saw GNP leaping by 12 percent each year through 1988, to become the envy of nations even in East Asia. Such, briefly, is the chronicle of the last ten years.

It would be profoundly wrong, however, to interpret the 1980s as the triumph of the IMF's will and technique—what Hirschman calls money doctoring;[6] nor is it correct to see the decade as the overcoming, the correcting, of the 1970s. If anything, the adjustments were revelatory of the *tenacity* of the Korean economy, the first glint that Korea could stay on the beam even when faced with the sort of global recession that distributed wreckage in other semiperipheral nations. The adjustments proved, in other words, the essential correctness and prescience of the Big Push, with its goals of basic industries, a greater measure of economic self-sufficiency, and habits of thinking in long and strategic terms. But to evaluate the merits of the stabilization cum liberalization, we have to reexamine the nature of the crisis and the actual process of crisis management in the 1980s.

The crisis in 1979–1980, termed "the sternest test since the end of the Korean War" by *The Wall Street Journal*,[7] was really a conflation of three phenomena. The first was that some of the heavy industries built in the 1970s, just coming on stream, were severely hit in the global recession of 1979–1980, creating huge excess capacity in machine building, construction, and most damagingly, in shipbuilding. In hard times, this looked like stupid waste, another example of Korean recklessness. But the truth was that it also held a promise of great recovery with an upturn in the global economy— fruits of the forced march in the 1970s would be reaped not in 1980, but a few years later. In this, the Korean situation was not unlike that in Brazil in the first half of the 1980s: a recovery that is less a result of routine market reaction to maxi-devaluation but to the maturing of the ultimate stage of import-substituting industrialization.[8]

Thus, Koreans did what was rational under the circumstance: they girded their loins, bided their time, and sought to bolster the competitiveness of those heavy industries. And they did this with the Korean style *pan y palo,* called "industrial reorganization," which meant resuscitation through monetary infusion of those heavy industrial firms likely to be competitive in the world market and forced mergers for the less likely: the weeding worked because the state controlled credit. Hyundai, Daewoo, and Samsung were ordered to give up the production of power generating and heavy construction equipment and merge into Korea Heavy Industries and Construction (KHIC); Saehan Motors was ordered merged with Hyundai in 1980 so that there would be only two makers of passenger cars for the international market, Daewoo and Hyundai; Kia and Tong-a were merged into a monopoly on trucks and buses; production of marine diesel engines over 6,000 horsepower became the exclusive right of Hyundai and KHIC, those below 6,000 horsepower went to Ssangyong, which had taken over a subsidiary of Daewoo; the heavy electric subsidiaries of Ssangyong and Kolon were merged with Hyosông; production of electronic switching system became a duopoly of Samsung and Lucky-Goldstar; copper refining became a monopoly of Korea Mining and Refining Company, and so on.[9]

The second problem fueling the 1979–1980 debacle was inflation. The source of this inflation was massive infusion of foreign capital into heavy industries, strong exports, a huge liquidity flow from the Middle East construction boom (and related to it, wage increases at home). The last point merits some explanation. In the early 1970s, the Korean government began a major push for construction contracts in the Middle East, forming an overseas construction corporation with equity ownership by twenty-five construction firms and subsidizing it with export (concessional) loans and a 50 percent corporate tax reduction.[10] Thus, Koreans earned not a penny from Middle East construction in 1973, but, by 1978, they were receiving $15 billion in contracts. Such massive export of labor fueled inflation in two ways. First, the influx of money sent home by the overseas workers helped push up prices, much as Spanish gold helped produce European inflation in the sixteenth century;[11] on top of the already high domestic liquidity, the broadly defined money supply jumped by 40 percent without a corresponding increase in domestic production.[12] Second, the exodus of skilled labor put pressure on wages, such that raiding and competitive outbidding became a common labor practice.[13] In fact, a perusal of macroeconomic indicators for the two decades prior to 1984 reveals that the real wage was running ahead of the increase in productivity during the 1977–1979 period, something that had never happened before. Labor's share of income (as measured by compensation of employees/value added) also recorded stunning increases, reaching a peak of 51.2 percent in 1978, which is remarkable given the absence in Korea of the practice of productivity bargain (gain-sharing.)[14]

The bout with inflation became the opening salvo of import liberalization that moved with breathless speed all throughout the 1980s. The last years of the 1970s saw attempts to liberalize imports of consumer goods and semiprocessed goods to soak up the increase in spending power, estimated to be growing, even after inflation, at 15 percent annually.[15] Another response to inflation was the stabilization program, which brought down domestic credit expansion from 41 percent in 1980 to 30 percent in 1982, but most spectacularly, to 16 percent in 1983 and 13 percent in 1984.[16] But, if one of the sources of inflation at the end of the Big Push could be pinned on the cost-push from wage increases, the authoritarian government knew exactly what it had to do: it cracked down on labor.[17]

In 1981, real wages actually *fell* by 1 percent, while labor productivity leaped by 18 percent. The annual increase in labor productivity for 1980–1984 averaged 12.1 percent while the average increase in real wages straggled at only 3.1 percent: a precipitous drop indeed, from 15.8 percent in 1977–1979.[18] The productivity increase might have been obtained through utilization of excess capacity in the early 1980s, but wage restraints were an artifact of sheer political terror that, by contrast, made even the Yushin years appear like halcyon days. The number of labor disputes recorded by the Ministry of Labor plummeted from 407 incidents in the particularly cantankerous year of 1980 to 186 in 1981, then only 88 in 1982.[19] Workers were also massively laid off (as can be seen in table 7.1), more so in large enterprises than in small ones, thus giving the lie to the claim of paternalism in chaebôl companies. Repression during the Chun Doo Hwan regime (1980–1988), greater even than that during the Park Chung Hee years (1961–1979), was such as to give credence to the argument–essentially of Latin American origin–that extreme levels of coercion have more to do with stabilization policies than with any particular regime form.[20]

The crisis of 1979–1980 was due to global economic malaise that slowed down demands and pushed up interest rates and oil prices, and in that sense Koreans shared their woe with other non–oil-producing developing countries. The price of oil leaped from $13 per barrel in 1978 to $36 in 1981, which meant that Koreans, who had been paying $2.2 billion for oil in 1978, now found themselves footing the bill for $6.5 billion in 1981. The burden of interest payment on external debt leaped from a LIBOR at 8.8 percent in 1978 to 16.8 percent in 1981, which, in the Korean context, translated into a payment of $3.5 billion, compared to $900 million in 1978; this was a fourfold jump.[21]

Koreans responded to this external shock exactly the same way they did during the first round of the oil crisis: they absorbed it through devaluation, more export, and more borrowing. As a result, Korean external debt, which stood at $20.3 billion in 1979, snowballed to $40 billion in 1983, and $46.7 billion in 1985.[22] At the end of 1980, Korea was the developing world's second largest borrower after Brazil, and Asia's biggest.[23] It was also one of the riskiest: *Euromoney*'s country risk, for instance, ranked Korea only 35th out of 67, trailing far behind Taiwan (19th), Mexico (21st), Brazil (23rd), and the Philippines (24th).[24] This bad report card, however, was no

TABLE 7.1. Employment Adjustment by Firm Size (in percentage)

Number of employees	5–99	100–299	300 or more	Total
1980	4.9	−5.9	−9.1	−3.8
1981	0.1	−1.9	−5.5	−2.5

SOURCE: You, "Is Fordism Coming to Korea?" p. 28.

deterrent to international bankers who clamored to lend to Korea, at attractive terms,[25] so that Korea had no difficulty raising more than $6 billion, more than half of that in long-term loans—and in the midst of a crisis.[26] Part of the reason for this was the backing that the United States and Japan extended to Korea in the pivotal year 1980, as will appear in the next section.

An economic crisis like the 1979–1980 one, caused by the confluence of factors we have just mentioned—excess industrial capacity during global economic recession, inflation through transfer of income from abroad, and external shocks—might be considered a *conjunctural* crisis. There was, of course, a deep structural flaw in the Korean economy—financial stability—that was built into Korea's capital-poor, credit-based system. That is one of the main arguments in this book. But what happened in 1979–1980 could easily be, and was, corrected with the tools and habits of this same flawed economy: industrial reoganization by fiat, labor repression, foreign loans to ride out bad times—and then simply a wait for the end of global recession, when the factories would run at full capacity. Why, then, was there such eagerness to unlearn the past, to do away with the Big Push, to "liberalize" the economy, to "structurally" adjust it? Why were policy makers, who so long resisted the sagacious advice of international agencies and domestic economists, suddenly all ears? The reasons for this turnaround were deeply political, but also ideological and economic.

Antinomies of Hegemonic Influence

The Big Push was over because it was a success and not because it was a failure. It was dismantled because its mission was largely completed, so its raison d'être was no more—and not because the economic "reformers" willed it.[27] The Big Push, which had its origin with the Nixon Doctrine and its apotheosis during Carter's human rights crusade, had been a nationalist response to the vicissitudes in "big power politics," as Park was wont to say. So its demise should not be surprising, given the volte-face in Carter's policy toward East Asia and Korea, made increasingly clear from the beginning of 1978, and then crystal clear by 1979, as Carter reneged on his pledge to pull all U.S. troops and nuclear weapons out of Korea.

This new policy toward East Asia, inaugurated during the Carter administration and consolidated in the Reagan era, sought to counter the Soviets in the Far East through tight U.S. economic *and* security ties with Japan, Korea, and the People's Republic of China and—

what is much more problematic—among these nations themselves. The logic of this sort of regional consolidation led to, as we shall discuss in some detail below, a swift U.S. embrace and support of the new dictatorship in Korea. Japan was no less forthcoming, infusing, at U.S. prodding, billions of dollars in financial aid to the new regime.

This happy ménage à trois ultimately came to an unhappy end, however. The cause for that, to anticipate our argument, rested with the antinomy of politics and economics in Reagan's foreign policy, the ultimate incommensurability between its intense patronage of Chun's strong state—more so than any other American administration toward Korea—and its economic ideology intent on denying and eradicting economic functions of that same state. In a way, this was an old conundrum in American foreign policy, and it was usually resolved with politics taking command—at least in the heyday of Pax Americana. But the 1980s version was different. This time, the American economic agenda arrived with big fangs: first, structural monetarism, pullulating out of Stanford and applied earlier in the Southern Cone of Latin America[28], and second, ceaseless pressure to pry open Korea's market to American imports and service industries. This commingling of right-wing political orthodoxy and militant monetarism begat a result that had been unforeseen and unintended—at least, from the Korean perspective: the "structural" adjustment and liberalization program resulted in chipping away at the state's many prerogatives, to create ultimately what Alfred Stepan calls—in the Chilean instance—a "small state, strong state."[29] This really set the stage for the political regime change toward the end of the 1980s, and explains why the United States and the Korean haute bourgeoisie sat on the sidelines and watched the military regime collapse. But to understand how things got to be like that requires going back more than a decade.

Nixon pulled a division out of Korea in 1971 because the American troop commitment—a trip wire in the event of war—stood in the way of his "grand design," a more flexible competition with the Soviets, which included an offshore naval nuclear strategy that avoided American involvement in risky regional conflicts.[30] Carter sought to complete Nixon's Korea agenda, but for different reasons: he wanted to slap wrists because of human rights abuses, and his trilateralist view stressed economic interdependence, diplomacy, and arms control instead of containment.

A recent dissertation based on interviews with officials in the Carter administration found, however, that Carter's Korea policy was fiercely resisted and eventually subverted through the concerted effort of, predictably, the U.S. Army, and less predictably, officials in the State Department. Richard Holbrooke, Assistant Secretary of State for East Asian and Pacific Affairs, along with Leslie Gelb from the State Department and Morton Abramowitz and Michael Armacost from the Pentagon, successfully persuaded Senators Sam Nunn, John Glenn, and Gary Hart, who in turn brought over powerful Democratic party military reformers to oppose Carter's policy.[31] The U.S. Defense Intelligence Agency's 1976 reassessment—and its confirmation by the CIA in 1977—that dramatically increased the number of North Korean military personnel became grist for the mill reversing Carter's Korea agenda. By 1978, the House Armed Services Committee issued a comprehensive attack on the withdrawal policy, and by January of 1979, the whole Senate was overwhelmingly in favor of totally dropping the withdrawals.[32] The Carter agenda was, for all practical purpose, dead.

Thus, by early 1979, if not earlier, Park Chung Hee was a dictator who came in from the cold. And the year after that, the United States was extending hospitality to another general, releasing (at his request) troops from the combined United States-South Korea Command for use in the Kwangju massacre,[33] and soon afterwards, the head of the combined forces was publicly endorsing the coup d'état.[34] At a senior staff meeting at the State Department, Richard Holbrooke reportedly urged upon Edmund Muskie, who had just become Secretary of State, a prudent silence on Korea, since there was "so much attention to Kwangjoo [sic]" at the cost of "broader questions."[35]

What, then, were these broader questions, the woods in which Kwangju was merely a tree, and an inconvenient one at that? The most important of these questions must have involved the reconfiguration of regional security, which now tightly drew into its orbit the People's Republic of China, with which the United States finally normalized relationships in 1978.

This new security map showed a triangulation of the area into two zones, which both required and reinforced the stability and security of South Korea. One such triangular zone was composed of United States-China and United States-Japan security relations, and completed with Sino-Japanese economic relations with minimal security cooperation (no more than exchange of views and information) thrown in. A foreign policy cause célèbre in the Carter administration, this was in place by 1978 and requires little elaboration.[36] But the second zone was less well known: a triangle of United

States-South Korea and the United State-Japan security relationships, *tied into South Korean–Japanese security cooperation* mediated by the United States. These two triangles touched base, literally speaking, on United States-Japan security relations, thus linking Japanese and Chinese security dependence on the United States to the fate of its ally, South Korea.[37]

The idea of security cooperation between Japan and South Korea was really traced to the Nixon-Sato Communiqué of 1969 when Sato publicly acknowledged, as a first step in the Nixonian "burden sharing," that the security of Korea was Japan's concern. But this idea, when it resurfaced at the end of the 1970s, was devoid of the tortuous diplomatic subtlety and ellipses of the past, and brazenly argued that Korea was really armed to the teeth for Japan's benefit, and that the least Japan could do was to pay for its hired gun. This notion of Korea as Japan's fortress had been adumbrated in the American stationing of the nuclear forces in Korea as a way of circumventing the Japanese nuclear "allergy," a perfect conjoining of the State Department's interest in Japan with the Army's in Korea. As Richard "Dixie" Walker, who would later become Reagan's ambassador to Korea, wrote in 1975:

> The presence of American conventional and even tactical nuclear forces in Korea helps to confirm strategic guarantees for Tokyo and to discourage any Japanese thoughts about a French solution: a force de frappe of their own. This is a fact well understood by leaders of many political persuasions in Tokyo and also appreciated in Peking.[38]

Because Washington, too, understood this well, in 1980, Secretary of Defense Harold Brown would ask three directors of Japan's Self-Defense Agency for a loan for Korea's military modernization efforts.[39] But it really took Reagan, with his global strategy that emphasized confrontation with the Soviets and greater defense burdens for allies, to designate Korea's DMZ as the Asian equivalent of the European central front, and thus explicitly couple the security of Korea with that of Japan.

As soon as Reagan entered office, he chose Chun Doo Hwan as the first foreign head of state to visit Washington, sold him 36 F-16 jetfighters and related equipment for $900 million, and had his Secretary of Defense Weinberger resume United States-South Korea security meetings and promise sophisticated weapons and economic concessions. Simultaneously, Weinberger was calling on Japan to do its part in the "common defense," in the "rational division of burdens," which was said to be a part and parcel of the new "global" (i.e., not Eurocentric) strategy.[40]

This meant, among other things, that the Japanese should patrol the seas and the skies west of Guam and north of the Philippines to keep open the sea lanes through which ships carrying most of Japan's oil and other vital supplies pass; build ships, aircraft, and mines able to close off the straits leading from the Sea of Japan to the Pacific Ocean, thus bottling up the Soviet submarines and surface fleet based at Vlasdivostok; and stockpile ammunition, supplies, and other logistical support for the ships, planes, and other weapons currently in their armed forces.[41] Zenko Suzuki, Japan's Prime Minister, agreed to provide "naval protection" for a perimeter of several hundred miles around Japan and in commercial lanes extending 1,000 nautical miles from Japan.[42]

The Reagan and Suzuki agreement—publicly released in the form of a communiqué—really affirmed the existence of the dual security triangle in East Asia, gridlocked by the United States-Japan security treaty. So, Japan agreed to a continuing expansion in cooperative relations with the PRC (the first security triangle), and to "promote the maintenance of peace on the Korean peninsula as important for peace and security in East Asia, including Japan" (the second triangle),[43] and to do all that not bilaterally, but from the perspective of anti-Soviet strategy.[44] As a way of cementing the second triangle, Japan promised the United State to pay—in effect—for Korea's security.

All of this could not have been more opportune and fortuitous for a Korean regime grappling with economic crisis, massive popular disaffection, and—just to top it off—a disastrous harvest. Thus the Korean government, encouraged and emboldened by the United States, presented Japan with a bill: $10 billion in aid and loans from Japan over a five-year period starting in 1982. This was a twentyfold increase in Japanese aid to Korea, which had been running at $80.2 million a year.[45] Eventually, Koreans cut the bill down to $6 billion, which was still a fourteenfold increase in aid.

If the first Korean solicitation of Japanese money in 1965 had the trappings of a tragedy—Koreans had stormed the street in anguish, caught between need and pride, the wish to forget and to remember —the second solicitation had all the trappings of a brazen farce. So, the Chun Doo Hwan regime, buoyed by Reagan, fancying itself "pro-American" and "anti-Japanese," demanded the $6 billion not only for defending Japan but as a payola for sealed lips on the past *yu-*

chaku.[46] The outraged Japanese foreign minister called it extortion, lectured the Koreans on their economic failure, and threatened to break off the aid talks if they did not shut up about doing Japan's defense.[47] All of this was against the backdrop of Japanese big business cheering the Koreans on and pressuring their own government to increase Korean aid.[48]

When it was over, Korea was to receive from Japan $4 billion, consisting of $1.85 billion in governmental loans and $2.15 billion in loans from Japan's EXIM Bank, most of that in supplier's credit, to be paid over seven years from 1983.[49] It was nearly 13 percent of Korea's net external debt, more than 5 percent of the GNP, and almost a fifth of total investment in 1983.

This Japanese aid, a particularly dramatic example of the linkage between security and development finance, was by no means an isolated incident in the early 1980s. The helping hands of Korea's hegemons had been there already and working busily. The chairman of the U.S. EXIM bank traveled to Korea in the thick of the economic crisis, sending signals to American and western European banks that EXIM's largest market, at $3.1 billion in loans outstanding, was a sound enough investment for more loans.[50] Japanese bankers, while not eager to increase their exposure in Korea, were also busy making loans, as one banker put it, for reasons of politics.[51] These loans were followed by highly visible visits from Nobusuke Kishi, David Rockefeller, and William Spenser, and it was not long before foreign banks were competing to make loans to Korea, at the best available terms.[52]

Thus Korea's foreign guarantors helped the Chun Doo Hwan regime weather the economic storm that had threatened to undo the coup, and imparted the man on horseback with a new claim to legitimacy: to wit, he saw eye to eye with Reagan, Suzuki, and later, Nakasone. But that was only half the story in Korea's critical foreign relations; the other half was, for the Korean President, a much less amusing affair. America took with one hand what it gave with the other, as it pummeled Koreans to open the market to American goods.

Trade liberalization was really an agenda without a noticeable domestic constituency, and deeply resented even by Korean consumers, the would-be beneficiaries of free trade. It might have been because Koreans had a mindset that found greater virtue in self-reliance than in mere thrift, in nationalism than in individualism, or in the argot of political science, in moral economy than in rational choice. Be that as it may, Americans were unrelenting in their resolve, turning the threat of protectionism as the means toward the ends of laissez faire and, with the Bentsen-Rostenkowski bill and the Gephardt Amendment, to bully those with a big trade surplus.

Protectionist retaliation was not a threat that a trading nation like Korea could take lightly. Korea's exports subject to import restrictions in industrialized countries had already increased from 32.3 percent in 1981 to 42.9 percent of the total in 1982, and the number of Korean cases brought under antidumping and countervailing charges jumped from thirteen in 1981 to twenty-three in 1983, and then to thirty in 1984. The volume of Korean exports subject to antidumping measures—which is, really, protectionism against the poorer nations—rose from 8.2 percent of Korea's total exports to 12.4 percent in 1983, to reach 17.9 percent in 1984.[53]

The new regime in Korea moved swiftly to accommodate the American wish, which meant dismantling the Big Push. By 1978, this push had caused the estimated effective rate of protection for all industries to leap threefold over that in 1968.[54] But now import restriction for products in steel, machinery, petrochemicals, and shipbuilding had to be scrapped rapidly, and the sector that had received most protection in the 1970s, agriculture, was now pried open to receive American rice, wheat, grains, pulses, and tobacco.[55] Pressure was also applied across the board on consumer goods.

The Korean government began shifting large number of items from its import restriction list to the "automatic approval list," so that the latter, which had included 68.6 percent of imported goods categories in 1980, covered 74.5 percent in 1981, 87.7 percent in 1985, and by the end of the decade, was projected to include nearly 100 percent of the total imported goods category. The tariff structure, while less important as a protection device than quantitative restrictions, also saw an overhaul that included phased general reductions in tariff levels and changes aimed at producing greater uniformity of tariff levels. Thus, in terms of tariff reduction, the simple arithmetic average of tariff rates, which had been at 31.7 percent in 1982, came down to 23.7 percent in 1983, and then to 21.9 percent in 1984 and 18 percent in 1988. Tariffs above 50 percent, which had been slapped on 15.5 percent of total imports in 1983, were imposed on only 5.5 percent in the year after, and even tariffs over 30 percent became a rarity by 1988.[56] The change was so swift that by the summer of 1989, the average tariff in Korea was among the lowest for the non-OECD countries, enabling it to dodge the new crowbar of Super 301.[57]

No other *economic* issue fueled such intense resentment and anti-Americanism in Korea as trade liberalization. For some, like farmers, it was simply a matter of livelihood. In protest they herded cows to downtown Seoul, not unlike the Americans who smashed Japanese cars in public. But for others, like students, the trade issue was just another humiliating symbol of Korean lackeyism, of a state so ruthless at home but so feckless abroad. This bitterness, combined with the suspicion that the United States really stood in the way of Korean unification (and judging from the Kwangju massacre, Korean democratization as well) propelled students into a replay of the sort of anti-Americanism that might have been found in Latin America more than two decades ago.

Even so, the concessions on import liberalization were not so problematic as those on finance, nor did they have as profound an impact on the state, economy, and social classes; as Rudiger Dornbusch put it, importing alfalfa was far less costly and far more salubrious than giving in on the issue of financial reform.[58] What, then, was this financial liberalization, so alarming that even alfalfa ought to be palatable to Koreans in power?

The idea of financial liberalization was, we recall, nothing new to Korea: practically everyone who had been opposed to the regime had advocated it, one way or another. In the 1950s, Americans like Arthur Bloomfield advocated independence of the state's financial apparatus to curtail the inflation issuing from government deficit spending, and Kim Dae Jung—Korea's most prominent oppositionist —made passionate pleas for it in the 1960s as a way of severing the Gordian knot between the state and the chaebôl. In the late 1960s, there was a change in interest rate structure, which was a lackadaisical attempt at financial reform, and even *that* was dropped with the *Yushin*.

In the 1980s, however, financial liberalization came as part and parcel of the long stablilization mentioned earlier, and this time, there was nothing lackadaisical about it. This was true of Korea as it was of the Latin American Southern Cone, as both began to experiment with what came to be known as "structural monetarism." This new creed insisted, in a curious parallel to the Keynesian way of thinking, that fundamental economic changes were required to cope with ills—or symptoms—such as inflation. In this way, it distinguished itself from the monetarism of the 1950s and 1960s, which had been a sort of a quick fix for the economy, using instruments such as control of money supply, reduction of the government deficit, exchange rate devaluation, freeing of prices, and eliminating subsidies. But it was also a radical repudiation of Keynesianism in that it sought economic redemption through "modernization," i.e., development of a domestic capital market, and articulating with the world economy by deepening ties with international financial institutions—an idea that received a sympathetic hearing from a former stockbroker now ensconced as chief of staff at the White House. It was also inexorably free market, probusiness, and anti-big state.[59]

This new evangelism hit Latin America before Korea, and the result there had been disastrous, a fulfillment of the worst possible fears about financial liberalization. In Chile and Argentina, high interest rates (high cost of capital is a sine qua non in the structural monetarist—or debt-intermediation—view, for scaring up savings and ensuring allocation efficiency) choked business, which, combined with an already large proportion of bad loans in the banking sector, precipitated a collapse of the financial sector; internationalization of finance led not to efficient allocation of resources but to conglomerate *(grupo)* control of banks, the resources of which were used in turn to buy firms that were being privatized. In the end, both Chile and Argentina had to bail out banks and to reimpose control over the financial sector.[60]

The lessons of Latin America were not lost on Korea, but they worked in the direction of firing up rather than dampening the enthusiasm for financial liberalization. Having blamed the failure in Latin America on inadequate *preparation* for financial liberalization, some money doctors were now scalpel-happy to find a country ready for it, a country without the Latin American-caliber inflation, without a serious fiscal deficit, and with an external sector that was relatively open.[61] The fact that Korea had already begun to liberalize imports, both to soak up inflation and to placate America, also obviated the handwringing about correct sequencing of liberalization (that is, whether liberalization should be simultaneous in both capital and commodity markets or not, and if not, which market to liberalize first, which was more responsive to a new set of relative price information and signals emanating from liberalization in the other market.[62])

The quest to liberalize Korean finance was carried out by transnational elites now ensconced as economic technocrats, men such as Kim Chae-ik, a freshly minted Stanford Ph.D. who, after brief duty at the Economic Planning Board, became Chun Doo Hwan's economic Svengali; also Shin Pyông-hyôn, Kim Man-je, Sakong Il, Kim Ki-hwan, and Pak Yông-chôl, all experts on finance, all with

American Ph.D.s, and all professing allegiance to the goal of liberalization, as well as the entire panoply of thirty-five men at the Korea Development Institute, every last one of them a Ph.D. from American universities.[63] Ideological osmosis could not have been more complete.

This was a major contrast from the past, when economic architects meant men who had been educated under the Japanese, who cut their financial teeth in Japanese banks in colonial Korea, and who were wont to look to Japan for guidance.[64] Another difference was that Korea's new presidents in the 1980s were, by their admission, tabulae rasae in economics, and as a result, exoticized that discipline and gave *tecnicos* a greater margin of policy maneuver. This was so unlike what happened under Park Chung Hee, a homespun economist with a fierce contempt for transnational eremites in ivory towers. So, Chun Doo Hwan, echoing his American-educated ventriloquists, pledged in his 1980 inaugural that economic liberalization was henceforth the aim of the new republic; and Roh Tae Woo would supinely impart the wisdom that while the supreme leader could "never be too knowledgeable" in political affairs, in affairs of economics, it was "better to know less."[65] The affairs of politics and economics, however, were not so readily separable.

Economics Takes Command

Repression of finance is, as argued in this book, what imparted strength to the state in Korea. Throughout its history, the state has insulated its small financial market from the world, negotiated and brokered the flow of foreign capital, kept Gorgon's eyes on capital flight, and in so doing avoided some of the worst tribulations of dependency. Inside the prophylactic domain thus obtained, the state owned banking institutions and set financial prices, usually so low that money was really transfered from savers to investors—mostly the chaebôl—and savers would be rewarded, eventually, as wage-earners and not as savers. This sort of arrangement was irrational from the perspective of allocative efficiency, as it prompted investors to produce at a loss what pleased the government simply to receive financing, but efficiency by and in itself was never a virtue or goal in Korea. Koreans wanted industrialization, and they got that by giving cheap money to the chaebôl, forcing them to build industries and to export more, and threatening to withdraw the honey pot if they failed. This is how the state in Korea got to be so Brumairean or how it got to be called Korea Inc., which are really two different sides of the same coin.

Financial liberalization meant the end of all that. It meant that Korea's financial market would be *internationalized,* and not protected: foreigners would enter banking, insurance, and capital markets to compete with domestic institutions, granted as a quid pro quo for Korea's entry into foreign financial markets. To compete at the world level, Korean financial firms had to behave like capitalists and not bureaucrats, think profit and not control. That meant *privatization* of banks in Korea. But as banks cannot thrive in situations of financial repression (which does not reward financial intermediaries well,) finance would have to be deregulated, ceilings on interest rates lifted, the practice of policy loans abandoned, and return on financial assets made positive so that saving and financial intermediating could become profitable. The high cost of capital thus issued would finally lead the chaebôl to find other sources of financing, which, combined with the growing surplus since 1985 in current accounts, would result in the blossoming of capital market. In this way, internationalization, privatization, financial deregulation, and development of capital market formed inseparable aspects of financial liberalization. For the state, the implication of these changes was colossal.

The reasons why the state, despite its many political drawbacks, was moved to liberalize finance were legion, but the most important one was already given in the last chapter: the desire to reduce the burden of socializing risk—the problem of default—in a system where the state was creditor. This desire turned into an imperative as the amount of nonperforming loans skyrocketed in the 1980s, making extremely credible the threat of massive financial collapse. Financial scandals at the time—a large scale fraud by a woman peddling political connections, for example—also fueled the old passion against the curb and a new determination to unify the nation's financial market. Finally, there was the pressure of the Open Door, which was the straw that broke the camel's back.

Giving up economic control—and political rents that used to accrue from it—has not been easy for the state. Financial liberalization in Korea has been a protracted process, crawling at a snail's pace, and a decade after the salvo of economic liberalization and many pledges to carry it out, it still remains incomplete. It is a struggle that has locked foreigners in with the state and chaebôl in Korea, all pushing and elbowing others to get the best of liberalization, even if it took partial readings and deliberate misreadings of the letter of financial liberalization.

For foreigners—mostly Americans—financial liberalization has meant internationalization, especially since the U.S. banks in Seoul were making money hand over fist: in 1980 the Bank of America, Citibank, Chase Manhattan, and Manufacturers Hanover recorded returns on capital that were as high as 359 percent.[66] And profits kept going up. In 1984, foreign banks saw a 26.6 percent increase in net profit from the year before, with the size of that net profit now almost equal that of Korean banks which were groaning with bad loans and policy loans.[67] Table 7.2 illustrates the varying fortunes of domestic and foreign banks in Korea.

For foreign banks, operations in Korea were all gravy, for they were virtually risk-free: in addition to the guarantee on a given margin, exchange risk was eliminated by the swap facility, default risk was reduced by the payment guarantee either by the domestic bank or the principal firm of the chaebôl group, and through the freedom, denied to domestic banks, to lend to credit-worthy firms only. As a result, more American and European banks clamored to get into the Korean market, and the existing ones demanded freedom to expand their operation. The Reagan administration tightened the screws on Korean government on behalf of these banks.

Senator E. J. Garn, one of the authors of the proposed Senate bill linking permission for foreign bank operation in the United States with that country's treatment of American banks, visited Korea in the fall of 1983, demanding the easing of restrictions for American banks operating in Seoul. Donald Regan was reported to have demanded "equal treatment" for American financial institutions doing domestic business in Korea.[68] The Reagan administration's insistence on the financial Open Door grew even stronger as years went by.

Americans, of course, did not really want *equal* treatment with

TABLE 7.2. Rate of Return to Total Assets

	1978	1979	1980	1981	1982	1983	1984	1985
Foreign banks	1.4	1.6	1.6	1.7	1.4	1.3	1.4	1.6
Domestic banks	0.7	0.6	0.7	0.5	0.2	0.2	n/a	n/a

SOURCE: Young K. Lee, "Internationalization of Major Financial Sector in Korea," quoted in Cho, "Liberalization of Korea's Financial Market in the 1980s," p. 24.

Korean banks, not so long as Koreans were saddled with policy loans and other allocation orders from the higher-ups. What the Open Door meant, instead, was an equal chance to benefit from munificent banking policies, like receiving the Bank of Korea rediscount on export loans, and the freedom to avoid making politically imperative but economically unlucrative loans. By 1985, Americans got more or less what they demanded: permission to expand their working capital, to venture into trust banking, to join the National Banks Association and the Clearing House, and most importantly, to receive the BOK rediscount on export loans. (In 1985, commercial banks charged 10 percent interest on export financing, 70 percent of which was rediscounted at the BOK at 5 percent interest rate; this 5 percent margin makes export financing extremely lucrative.)[69]

Insurance was another market pried open through U.S. pressure. Life insurance, which in Korea works like a time deposit (only 10 percent of premiums are paid directly for insurance), was enormously lucrative and strictly off-limits for foreign firms.[70] The situation came under investigation for possible violation of Section 301 of the U.S. Trade Act, so that Koreans had to open up life insurance to American participation, lest America retaliate by restricting Korean commodity exports.[71]

Koreans have been extremely wary, however, of opening up the stock market, which has been undergoing explosive growth since 1985. Part of the reason for this reluctance was short-term, and had to do with concern that the low price of Korean stocks would result in the shift of substantial rent to foreigners, and that there would be a massive inflow of short-term foreign capital atop a large current account surplus. But the fundamental question here was one of foreign control of Korean industries—no idle worry in an era when big New York financial firms made extraordinary profit by orchestrating hostile takeovers. Thus, foreigners have been allowed only indirect investment through mutual funds,[72] with direct investment postponed to 1987, then to 1989, and now to 1992. But it seems only a matter of time before Korea's stock market will be weaned from the state, especially if Japan is the mirror for Korea's future.

The loss of a tight grip on money supply, either through foreign capital inflow as described above or Korean capital outflow (increasingly encouraged to soak up the trade surplus since 1985,) can be traumatic for any interventionist state, be it Japan, France, or—in the most extreme instance—Korea. But as the French experience with financial liberalization in the 1980s reveals, the world market does, in the end, place effective limits on the power of the state.[73] In

our unprecedented bourgeois era at the end of this century, economics, to reverse Mao, has taken command.

The global financial market, knocking at Korea's door, created
another agenda for the state: privatization. In theory, nothing really
doomed state-owned banking enterprises to mediocrity, unable to
compete at the world level; but neither were there compelling reasons to keep banks nationalized if they had to be transformed from
conveyers of industrial policy to lucrative capitalist outfits. This,
the chaebôl's favorite interpretation of financial liberalization, deeply
troubled the state.

The fear was not unwarranted: privatization in the Latin American Southern Cone had its conglomerates running amok, buying up
banks to buy up other enterprises, stacking up loan portfolios with
loans made out to affiliated firms, and skyrocketing interest rates
with "false demands" caused by rolling over debts of related firms.
Pell-mell deregulation thus led to Chilean and Argentine *grupos*
profiting like bandits, and contributing to the collapse of financial
sectors in these countries.[74] It was entirely possible that Korea's
chaebôl, with their egregious financial structure and bottomless appetite for expansion, might be tempted to use newly acquired banks
to finance their expansion and to deny credit to competitors. Public
opinion, to the extent that it mattered, was also against the chaebôl
acquisition of nation's city banks, with all three parliamentary opposition parties denouncing the favoritism shown the chaebôl, and
calling for an end to chaebôl domination of the economy.[75]

The move toward privatization was therefore extremely cautious.
Before the state proceeded with selling its bank shares, it tried to
tackle the problem of nonperforming loans, and so called upon the
chaebôl to put their financial houses in order by selling off all non–
business-related land and affiliate enterprises defined as "nonmain-
stream," i.e., enterprises in which the group has no competitive
edge.[76] Paralleling this financial surveillance, the Economic Planning Board launched a campaign—the Fair Trade Act—to check
market monopoly by the chaebôl. All of these probably created more
sound and fury than anything else, but they did signal to the chaebôl
that acquisition of finance capital was not going to be smooth
sailing.

Divesture from city banks of government-owned stocks began in
1981 (one city bank had already been privatized in 1978,) and by
1983, all of Korea's five banks plus two new additions were privatized. This privatization was, however, in name only, with catch-as-
catch-can restrictions inserted to prevent chaebôl control of these

banks. Ceilings were imposed on the percentage of shares a single shareholder might hold (less than 10 percent), as well as on the percentage of loans and loan guarantees extended to the chaebôl. The chaebôl have tried to beat the system by purchasing stocks in more than one bank. That does add up to a hefty amount, but it is still a far cry (as of 1989), from the structure of the Japanese zaibatsu that emanates from a bank at the group's core. Management of banks also continued to be the state's prerogative, which frequently made the rapidly rotating offices of bank presidency into political sinecures.[77] Most importantly, the state still retained the right to set financial prices, decided policy loans, and kibbitzed on who should receive credit allocation. Thus, Korea's city banks became privatized, only to be restrained from doing anything of their free will.

But if the state retained the right to set financial prices, in what sense was finance liberalized in Korea? As of the end of the 1980s, it really was not. But the state manipulated the financial market to make it *look* as if it were, by squeezing out inflation and setting high real deposit rates that more closely approximated the market price, in what some scholars have called "de facto financial liberalization."[78] As can be seen from table 7.3, the real bank deposit rates have steadily increased, especially in contrast to the 1970s, although not quite as high as the curb rates that incorporate high risk premiums.

Loan rates, which had been negative in real terms throughout the 1970s, also became positive starting in 1981. Table 7.4 shows that, by 1982, inflation was controlled at the 7.6 percent level, leading to real interest rates of 2.4 percent for general bank loans, thence leaping to 7 percent as inflation dropped further to the 3 percent level. Also noteworthy is that, by 1982, the Korean government did away with special rates for major policy loans, such as export loans, MIPF, and NIF. From then on, the rates on *all* bank loans became uniform at around 10 percent.

Nonbank financial intermediaries (NBFI) were another route to de facto liberalization, the most important of which are investment and finance companies for dealing in short term commercial papers, and life insurance companies and investment trust companies, both of which attract longer term funds for investment in corporate bonds or direct loans to business. The NBFIs had been established in the wake of the August 3 Decree, with the permission to pay higher interest rate on deposit in order to soak up funds from the curb. With financial liberalization, the state accelerated deregulation of the NBFIs, allowing them private ownerships, and greater flexibility in interest rates and management; lifting ceilings on commercial papers and unsecured corporate bonds that the NBFIs deal in; removing the burden of making policy loans; relaxing entry barriers; and permitting a wide variety of financial services. So, the business of NBFIs soared in the 1980s, with the number of investment and finance companies jumping from 20 in 1980 to 32 in 1987, and mutual savings and finance companies from 191 in 1980 to 239 in 1984.[79] The share of NBFI deposit as the percentage of the total had been less than 20 percent in 1975, but it was 30.1 percent in 1980, 45.5 percent in 1984, and by 1987, it was 51.3 percent—now, more deposits headed to the NBFIs than to the banks.[80]

From a statist perspective the relaxation of control over the NBFIs was really very ingenious, for it eased the pressure on the financial jugular of the country without relinquishing state surveillance of the financial system: the money fed into the NBFI probably flowed out from the curb, anyway. In other words the uncontrolled, unofficial financial market was being supplanted by a more deregulated, but official, financial market. The state killed two birds with one stone.

This sort of liberalization was riddled with problems for the chaebôl. The chaebôl got their first taste of owning finance capital through acquisition of the NBFIs and a limited portion of bank shares, but

TABLE 7.3. Bank Deposit and Curb Market Rates

Year	Inflation (GNP Deflator)	Bank Deposit		Curb Market	
		Nominal	Real	Nominal	Real
1972	16.2	15.0	−1.0	39.0	19.7
1973	13.4	12.0	−1.2	33.3	17.5
1974	29.5	14.8	−11.4	40.6	8.5
1975	25.7	15.0	−8.5	41.3	12.4
1976	20.7	15.5	−4.3	40.5	16.4
1977	15.7	15.8	0.1	38.1	19.4
1978	21.9	16.7	−4.3	41.2	15.8
1979	21.3	18.6	−2.2	42.4	17.4
1980	25.6	22.9	−2.2	45.0	15.4
1981	15.9	19.3	2.9	35.3	16.7
1982	7.1	11.0	3.6	30.6	22.8
1983	2.9	8.0	5.0	25.8	22.3
1984	3.9	9.0	4.9	24.7	20.0
1985	3.8	10.0	6.0	24.0	19.5
1986	2.7	10.0	7.1	23.1	22.0

SOURCE: Bank of Korea.

such rewards paled in the face of meeting the cost of capital, which got heftier with the rising bank interest rate. This rate was, to be sure, still lower than the would-be domestic market rate, but any crawl upward immediately translated into a major burden, since in Korean firms, financial cost was more than a quarter of the cost of manufacturing.[81] The Federation of Korean Industrialists, representing more than 300 big enterprises, lobbied hard to keep the lid on interest rates, but the salad days of the chaebôl—when loans were like Christmas presents—were rapidly coming to a close.

However, the chaebôl did not wish to go on record as having stood in the way of laissez faire finance, if that were the wave of future; as Marx once said, the bourgeoisie may not be heroic but it has a need for heroism. Thus, the Federation of Korean Industrialists touted and defended liberalization—but it should happen (to borrow a vexing and useful phrase from America's desegregation ruling), with all deliberate speed. The chaebôl endorsement was not just tongue-in-cheek, however; Korea's haute bourgeoisie had reasons for wanting to get the state out of its hair.

TABLE 7.4. Interest Rates on Various Loans

			Bank Loans				
	Curb	*Corporate*	*General*	*Selected Policy Loans*			*GNP*
Year	*Market*	*Bond*		*Export*	*MIPF*[a]	*NIF*[b]	*Deflator*
1973	33.3	—	15.5	7.0	10.0	—	13.40
1974	40.56	—	15.1	9.0	12.0	12.0	29.54
1975	41.31	20.1	15.5	9.0	12.0	12.0	25.73
1976	40.47	20.4	17.0	8.0	13.0	14.0	20.73
1977	38.07	20.1	15.0	8.0	13.0	14.0	15.67
1978	41.22	21.1	18.5	9.0	15.0	16.0	21.39
1979	42.39	26.7	18.5	9.0	15.0	16.0	21.20
1980	44.94	30.1	24.5	15.0	20.0	22.0	25.6
1981	35.25	24.2	17.5	15.0	11.0	16.5	15.9
1982	33.12	17.3	10.0	10.0	10.0	10.0	7.6
1983	25.77	14.2	10.0	10.0	10.0	10.0	3.0
1984	24.84	14.1	10–11.5	10.0	10–11.5	10–11.5	3.9
1985	24.0	14.2	10–11.5	10.0	10–11.5	10–11.5	3.8
1986	23.1	12.8	10–11.5	10.0	10–11.5	10–11.5	2.2

SOURCE: Bank of Korea.

[a] Machinery Industry Promotion Fund.

[b] National Investment Fund.

One reason was that the cost of currying favor with the authoritarian state to obtain financing was simply getting out of hand. A convenient measure, if incomplete, of propitiary offerings made to the state was entered in corporate ledgers under "secondary tax (chunjose)." This included various fees and dues paid out by corporations (konggwase), corporate social expeditures (sahoejôk ômmu kwangge piyông), and most illustrative, "contributions (kibukûm.)"[82] The last category is widely understood as a financial forced draft to stay on the good side of the state, and constituted in 1983 some 0.85 percent of the corporate value added, which was 2.4 times higher than that in Japan at 0.35 percent—and it has increased by 45.3 percent each year since 1976. The total secondary tax in 1983 was 7.79 percent of the corporate value added, which topped the corporate tax payment at 5.21 percent of the value added. In terms of total sales volume, secondary taxation was equivalent of 1.37 percent of total sales, as versus 1.03 percent for tax payment.[83] The "contributions" made by firms listed in Seoul Stock Exchange were equivalent to 22 percent of their net profit in 1985, with some firms reportedly making the "contributions" as they verged on bankruptcy.[84]

These expenditures were by no means as corrupt, extortive, or voluminous as "political contributions." The full extent of political contributions might never be known, but a glimpse of the greasing of Korea Inc. occurred on the extraordinary occasion of the investigation into financial misconduct during the Chun regime. At the hearing in the democratically-elected parliament, the founder of the Hyundai group admitted to donating close to $2.5 million to the "Ilhae Foundation," Chun's retirement home-cum-think tank (because it was "more convenient that way"); he also made donations to the political party coffer "always in the amount asked."[85] Groups like Daelim, Shindonga, P'ungsan, and Koryô likewise made hefty donations to Ilhae, for which they were alleged to have received not only bank financing but lucrative concessions.[86] Those who did not make satisfactory donations ended up staring into the corporate abyss of credit severance: Yang Chông-mo, the founder of the Kukje group (Korea's seventh largest conglomerate that capsized a few years earlier) bitterly complained that Kukje's destruction was owing to his indolent compliance with government requests for donations.[87]

These examples were but the tip of the iceberg; but they are revelatory of the operational method of the patronage network in Korea Inc., far more arbitrary and jagged than that in Japan Inc.: in the Korean instance, a racketeering state became the flip side of the benign developmentalist state.

Another reason for the growing state-chaebôl discord, probably vastly more important than the resentment over state racketeering, had to do with the regulations and restrictions that the state imposed on them. Thus, in the 1980s, the bigwigs of the Federation of Korean Industrialists bewailed the state's microeconomic interventions, which were of course made possible by dangling the carrot of bank credit. In one revelatory meeting with the nation's top economic technocrats, Korea's richest industrialists blew their collective top, accusing the government of a multitude of sins: not providing sufficient business financing while frequently ordering corporate restructuring; causing industrial downturns through mismanagement of finance; placing an albatross around the nation's industrial neck through maintaining a mediocre financial system; creating instability and corporate default through arbitrary standards and whimsical decrees; and refusing to privatize banks, in the true sense of the word.[88] Other drumbeats of rebuke in the 1980s included resentment over quantitative ceilings imposed on loans to the chaebôl and the adoption of an arbitrarily defined "healthy" debt-equity ratio before firms could be determined eligible for bank loans.[89] To cap it all, Chông Chu-yông, the patriarch of Hyundai and Korea's most influential industrialist, made a public plea for ending state interventionism, eliminating secondary taxations, and eventually granting full autonomy to the financial sector.[90]

Such confidence and independence as the chaebôl came to express in the late 1980s would not have been possible had it not been for this: the securities and stock markets had blasted off in the 1980s to become important sources of financing for the chaebôl. As can be gleaned from table 7.5, the number of companies listed in the Seoul stock exchange increased from 352 firms at the beginning of the decade to 523 as of May of 1989; listed capital shot up from 2.4 trillion won in 1980 to 13.7 trillion won in May of 1989, which is more than a fivefold increase; total market value increased twenty-eight times in the same time period; and the composite price index, at 100 in January 1980, was 932.76 by May of 1989. The greatest spurt occurred in the three years from the end of 1985 to 1988, which saw the total market value multiply almost ten times, and the composite price index, by almost six. The size of this bustling stock market may be brought home better if we consider the total market value as a ratio of GNP, which was only 9 percent at the end of 1985, but (56.6 percent) three years later. In terms of market capitalization, the Korean stock market was now the ninth largest in the world in 1990, and according to some estimates, could easily grow into the fourth largest in ten years.[91]

Growing corporate reliance on the equity market—and nonbank intermediaries—really overdetermined the political disposition of the chaebôl. They no longer had much need for the state to run interference on their behalf. Additionally, there was always the danger that the state could just as easily use its muscle to shield someone else, such as, for example, the long neglected medium-sized industries—thus bump off the chaebôl as socially undesirable. Chông Chu-yông wondered if the state might not be tempted now to confiscate the chaebôl property outright[92]—a worry that was neither idle nor fantastic since each military regime used the chaebôl to discredit its predecessor. In an age of "deepening" finance and maturing capitalism, then, the chaebôl eschewed a capricious political order that so casually mixed benevolence with terror; instead, it came to desire greater stability and the rule of law, even if that meant liberal democracy (*especially* if that meant "liberal democracy" along Japanese lines.) Thus, Ku Cha-kyông, the head of the Federation for Korean Industrialists, pledged an end to the chaebôl contribution to political parties or "nonparliamentary forces" that did not respect principles of the free market or the rules of liberal democracy.[93]

TABLE 7.5. Stock Market Indicators—End of Year, Except 1989 (in 100 million wons)

	1980	1985	1986	1987	1988	1989 May
Listed companies	352	342	355	389	502	523
Listed stocks	437	414	485	603	970	689
Listed capital	24,214	46,654	56,497	75,949	125,604	137,079
Total market value	25,266	65,704	119,942	261,722	645,437	703,115
(Percent of GNP)	6.9%	9.0%	14.3%	26.8%	56.6%	—
Composite price index	106.87	163.37	272.61	525.11	907.20	932.76

SOURCE: Korea Stock Exchange.

Conclusion

When asked what he thought about the French Revolution, Mao Ze-dong is said to have replied that it was too early to tell. Judged by that standard, a study of Korean industrialization in the century past, let alone the past ten years that occupied this chapter, would appear an exercise in jejune judgment. But the recent past is important, not because it happened (and thus was there to be discussed), but because—if the argument in this book is correct—the 1980s were really the slow beginning of the end of the Korean variant of late industrialization. The dissipating alchemy of Korea Inc.—which we have defined as the political and economic uses of finance for industrialization and the promotion of a huge entreprenuerial constellation—brings an effective close to this book: our story has a beginning, a middle, and an end.

My argument addresses (and redresses) the Kantian bias in 1980s punditry that finds in the present an incontrovertible and ineluctible process, so that economic liberalization becomes a correction of the "mistakes" of the Big Push, electoral politics an entry (after so many decades of riding on the shoulder) onto the correct lane of political development, and the 1988 Seoul Olympics a gala to celebrate all this "progress"—the symbol that Korea indeed has come a long way to join the comity of the richer nations: Korea in the 1980s, embodiment of a perpetual improvement.

The telos of the Korean political economy, however, was usually painted in broad strokes in either New York or Washington, in the epicenters of world capitalism and politics. Korea was allowed the luxury of deviation, a state-led and late development, as long as it remained in the interstices of global capitalism and on the forefront of the cold war. The story of the 1980s, then, is not the story of Korea "reforming," rehabilitating from the bad habits of the past, but adjusting to the new reality in Washington and plunging into the whirlwind of world capitalism with an eye to becoming, say, a proper member of the OECD.

That, however, required a reshaping of Korea's political economy, for the truth was that America's brave "laissez faire" world often meant protectionism at home and free trade abroad for the United States, but in such a world, a strong and interventionist state like Korea's, even if an ally, could not be sustained. The best known instance of American pressure and American success has been in the sphere of trade, in the issue of import liberalization. But finance, as argued in this book, is the stuff power is made of, and the attempt to liberalize finance in Korea—ten years in the making and still not complete—has precipitated a silent revolution, surreptitiously altering the relationship between state and society.

The path of financial liberalization, to be sure, has been tentative and halting, with two steps forward and one step back: but when all is said and done, financial liberalization marks the coming of age for Korea's entrepreneurs and the close of the era when the state nursed big business from the cradle to the grave. It heralds the end of the willful confusion between a state that purports to supplement but actually supplants the market. It is the beginning of the end of the Leviathan state.

Notes

1. Theoretical Considerations

1. Friedman, *A Program for Monetary Stability*, p. 8.
2. Fitzgerald, "The State and the Management of the Accumulation in the Periphery."
3. Huntington, *Political Order in Changing Societies*; Skocpol, *States and Social Revolutions*; Krasner, *Defending the National Interest*; Stepan, *The State and Society* and *Rethinking Military Politics*.
4. Hintze, *The Historical Essays of Otto Hintze*; Weber, *Economy and Society*.
5. Poulantzas, *Political Power and Social Classes*; Miliband, "The Capitalist State: Reply to Nicos Poulantas," and "Poulanzas and the Capitalist State"; Offe in various issues of *Kapitalistate*; Therborn, *What Does the Ruling Class Do When It Rules?*
6. Offe, "The Capitalist State and the Problem of Policy Formation," and "Advanced Capitalism and the Welfare State"; O'Connor, *The Fiscal Crisis of the State*; Wolfe, *America's Impasse*.

7. Exceptions include Joachim Hirsch who places the development of state in the need to develop counter tendencies against the falling rate of profit, and thus pays attention to monetary policies as countercyclical tools. Also, see Epstein, "Domestic Stagflation and Monetary Policy," and Greider, *Secrets of the Temple*.

8. For representative writings of "organizational approach," see Katzenstein, *Small States in World Markets*; Hall, *Governing the Market*; Loriaux, *Reforming the Overdraft Economy*; and Zysman, *Governments, Markets, and Growth*.

9. A representative writing of ECLA structuralism is Furtado, *Economic Development of Latin America*. For the problem of unequal exchange, see Emmanuel, *Unequal Exchange*. The process of the development of underdevelopment is discussed in Frank, *Capitalism and Underdevelopment in Latin America*, and Amin, *Accumulation on a World Scale*. For the perspective on dependent development, see Cardoso and Falleto, *Dependency and Development in Latin America*, and Evans, *Dependent Development*. For an argument that uses imperialism as the critical variable in economic backwardness, see Baran, *The Political Economy of Growth*. Recently, Becker used the idea of "post-imperialism" and denationalized bourgeoisie to discuss the spread of capitalism in Latin America. See his *The New Bourgeoisie and the Limits of Dependency*.

10. Kaufman, "Democratic and Authoritarian Response to the Debt Issue"; Frenkel and O'Donell, "The 'Stabilization Programs' of the International Monetary Fund and Their International Impacts"; Whitehead, "Debt, Diversification, and Dependency"; and Stallings, *Banker to the Third World*, and "Peru and the U.S. Banks."

11. Calder and Hofheinz, *The Eastasia Edge*; Pye, *Asian Power and Politics*; and Morishima, *Why Has Japan Succeeded?*

12. Norman, *The Establishment of a Modern State in Japan*; Lockwood, *The Economic Development of Japan*; Johnson, *MITI and the Japanese Miracle*; Samuels, *The Business of Japanese State*. The "seamless web" problem is quoted from Lockwood, and is cited by Samuels, p. 288.

13. For the "patterned pluralism" problem, see Krauss and Muramatsu, "Japanese Political Economy Today." Okimoto argues the case of the "societal state" in "Japan the Societal State." Pempel argues that Japan is a "state-led capitalism" in his *Policy and Politics in Japan*. The notion of "adaptive communitarianism" appears in Vogel, "Japan: Adaptive Communitarianism."

14. See, for instance, the studies on the economic and social modernization of Korea undertaken jointly by the Harvard Institute of International Development and the Korea Development Institute (KDI): Kim and Roemer, *Growth and Structural Transformation*; Krueger, *The Developmental Role of the Foreign Sector and Aid*; Jones and Sakong, *Government, Business, and Entrepreneurship in Economic Develop-*

ment; and Mason et al., *The Economic and Social Modernization of the Republic of Korea*.

15. Amsden, *Asia's Next Giant*; Deyo, ed., *The Political Economy of the New Asian Industrialism*; Gold, *State and Society in the Taiwan Miracle*; Luedde-Neurath, *Import Controls and Export Oriented Development*; Wade, *Governing the Market*; Winkler and Greenhalgh, eds., *Contending Approaches to the Political Economy of Taiwan*.

16. Stepan, *The State and Society* and *Rethinking Military Politics*, p. 4.

17. Krasner, *Defending the National Interest*, p. 57. In fact, Krasner has called the Korean state "a strong state that could resist domestic pressures" in his *Structural Conflict*, p. 49.

18. Gerschenkron, *Economic Backwardness in Historical Perspective*; Hirschman, "The Political Economy of Import Substitution Industrialization in Latin America."

19. Keohane, "The Big Influence of Small States."

20. *Maeil Kyôngje Shinmun*, March 12, 1985.

21. Korea's open trade regime is discussed in Frank, Kim, and Westphal, *Foreign Trade Regimes and Economic Development*; Hasan, *Korea: Problems and Issues in a Rapidly Growing Economy*; Hong and Krueger, eds., *Trade and Development in Korea*; and Krueger, *Foreign Trade Regimes and Economic Development*.

22. Strange, "Protectionism and World Politics."

23. Zysman, *Governments, Markets, and Growth*.

24. Pempel, "Japanese Foreign Economic Policy," p. 152.

25. Wade, "The Role of Government in Overcoming Market Failure."

26. Kim Byông-ju and Pak Yông-chôl, *Hanguk kyôngje wa kûmyung*. p. 352.

27. Lowi, *The End of Liberalism*, and "Toward a Politics of Economics." He argues that the federal government of the United States increasingly and inexorably underwrites risk for established and well-organized interests.

28. Mason et al., *The Economic and Social Modernization of the Republic of Korea*.

29. Moore, *Social Origins of Dictatorship and Democracy*. The suppression of peasants in the 1945–1947 period is documented in Cumings, *The Origins of the Korean War*: Liberation.

30. See McKinnon, *Money and Capital in Economic Development*, and Cole and Park, *Financial Development in Korea*. For the discussion on financial liberalization, see chapter 7 of this book.

2. *Soldiers, Bankers, and the Zaibatsu in Colonial Korea*

1. One exception is Bruce Cumings, who argues that industrialization in Korea and Taiwan had complex colonial origins. Cumings, "The Origins and Development of the Northeast Asian Political Economy,"

and *The Origins of the Korean War: Liberation*, ch. 1–2. Other studies have also argued the case for the colonial origins of Korean capitalism, but in terms of continuity in entrepreneurial or bank personnel. See Eckert, "The Origins of Korean Capitalism"; McNamara, *Colonial Origins of Korean Enterprise*; and Moskowitz, "Current Assets." An excellent work that examines the formation of colonial labor force is Park, "The Emergence of Factory Labor Force in Colonial Korea."

2. Most Korean language literature on the colonial period do this. See, for example, Kim, *Ilbon chekukjuûi ûi t'ongch'i* [The Reign of Japanese Imperialism], and Kang, *Hankguk hyôndaesa* [The Contemporary History of Korea]. In English, see Suh, *Growth and Structural Changes in the Korean Economy*. A recent work of Korean "late industrialization" finds Korea's colonial experience under the Japanese, the world's most celebrated late-industrializer, of no developmental consequence. See Amsden, *Asia's Next Giant*, pp. 31–35.

3. For instance, see Jones and Sakong, *Government, Business, and Entrepreneurship in Economic Development*, pp. 30–37; Mason et al., *The Economic and Social Modernization of the Republic of Korea*; and Fei, Ohkawa, and Ranis, "Economic Development in Historical Perspective."

4. The role of Korea's industrial infrastructure in political mobilization is discussed in detail in Cumings, *The Origins of the Korean War: Liberation*, especially p. 12; on the importance of railroad networks, see Granjdanzev, *Modern Korea*, p. 185.

5. This argument on product cycle is advanced in Cumings, "The Origins and Development of the Northeast Asian Political Economy"; on Korean inheritance of Japan's obsolete industries and new regional division of labor, see Granjdanzev, "Korea Under Changing Orders," p. 295. For an excellent study of the product cycle in textiles, as production shifted from Japan to Korea and then to Manchuria, see Eckert, "The Origins of Korean Capitalism."

6. Jensen, "Modernization and Foreign Policy in Meiji Japan," p. 182.

7. Peattie, "Introduction," in Peattie and Myers, *The Japanese Colonial Empire, 1895–1945*, p. 5.

8. Hirschman, *National Power and the Structure of Foreign Trade.*

9. I do not use this term in its historical sense of the sixteenth to eighteenth-century economic practices in Europe. Rather, I mean by this an emphasis toward balancing trade, state management, state building, and autarky. See an excellent discussion on mercantilism in Schumpeter, *History of Economic Analysis*, pp. 335–378.

10. Peattie, "Introduction," p. 11.

11. Anderson, *The Lineages of the Absolutist States.*

12. Cumings, *The Origins of the Korean War: Liberation*, ch. 1–2.

13. For further discussion of the cadastral survey, see Kang Man-gil, *Hanguk hyôndaesa* [The Contemporary History of Korea], pp. 90–93.

14. Park, "The Emergence of Factory Labor Force in Colonial Korea," pp. 16–17.

15. Kang, *Hanguk hyôndaesa* p. 118; Park, "The Emergence of Factory Labor Force, p. 17.

16. Junosuke Inoue, Governor of the Bank of Japan (1918–1923), quoted in Nakamura, *Economic Growth in Prewar Japan*, p. 152.

17. Yasuda, "Politics of Industrial Financing Policy," p. 381.

18. Nakamura, *Economic Growth*, p. 152; Yasuda, "Politics of Industrial Financing Policy," p. 415.

19. Park, "The Emergence of Factory Labor Force," p. 39.

20. Chosôn Ch'ongdokbu, *Chosôn kyôngje yônbo* [The Economic Yearbook of Chosun].

21. Kang, *Hanguk hyôndaesa*, p. 121.

22. The argument is advanced in Suh Sang Chul *Growth and Structural Changes in the Korean Economy, 1910–1942.*

23. The Japanese emigration into colonies is discussed in Gold, "Entrepreurs, State, and Multinationals in Taiwan." The influx of Japanese labor was so massive that colonial Taiwan never formed native proletariats.

24. Mitsubishi Economic Research Bureau, *Japanese Trade and Industry, Present and Future*, p. 424.

25. Yasuda, "Politics of Industrial Financing Policy," p. 347.

26. Kobayashi, *War and Armament Loans of Japan*, p. 95.

27. Moskowitz, "Current Assets," p. 26.

28. Duus, "Economic Dimensions of Meiji Imperialism," pp. 154–155.

29. Kang Man-gil, *Hanguk kûndaesa* [The Modern History of Korea], p. 269.

30. Ibid., p. 268.

31. *Hwangsông shinmun*, quoted in Kang, *Hanguk kûndaeasa*, p. 272.

32. Patrick, "Financial Development and Economic Growth in Underdeveloped Countries," p. 175. Also see, Patrick, "Japan 1868–1914."

33. Bix, "Japanese Imperialism and the Manchurian Economy," pp. 439–440; Young, *Japan's Special Position in Manchuria*, pp. 242–243.

34. Grajdanzev, *Modern Korea*, p. 204.

35. Lockwood, *The Economic Development of Japan*, pp. 516–517. Doubts about the raison d'être of the Bank of Chosen as the central bank of Korea were often raised by banking circles in Japan, not just because of the bank's prolific foreign activities but also because of the worsening balance of payment situation in Korea. The annual import excess of Korea vis-à-vis Japan made it extremely difficult for the central bank to maintain its gold species at the required ration. In fact, the idea of merging the Bank of Chosen with the Bank of Japan surfaced many

times in the early period of colonial rule. Bank of Chosen, *Economic History of Manchuria*.

36. Chang, "Japanese Corporations and the Political Economy of South Korean-Japanese Relations, 1965–1979," p. 33.

37. Cohen, *Japan's Economy in War and Reconstruction*, p. 34.

38. Cheil ûnhaeng, *History of the First City Bank of Korea*, p. 28.

39. Moskowitz, "Current Assets," pp. 356, 372.

40. "Kûmyunggye rûl chibae han inmaek p'ando" [Lineages of Men Who Dominated Banking], *ûnhaengga*, March 1971, pp. 32–37.

41. Eckert, "The Origins of Korean Capitalism", McNamara, *Colonial Origins of Korean Enterprise*, ch. 3.

42. Nakamura, *Economic Growth in Prewar Japan*, p. 142; Ho, "Colonialism and Development," p. 364.

43. Nakamura, *Economic Growth*, pp. 232–238.

44. Grajdanzev, "Korea Under Changing Order," p. 292.

45. Park, "The Emergence of Factory Labor Force," p. 48.

46. Ho, "Colonialism and Development," pp. 365–366.

47. Jerome Cohen, *Japan's Economy*, p. 37.

48. Duus, "Economic Dimensions of Meiji Imperialism," p. 155.

49. Wales, "Rebel Korea," p. 29.

50. Park, "The Emergence of Factory Labor," p. 50.

51. McNamara, "Colonial Origins of Korean Enterprise," ch. 3.

52. Mizoguchi and Yamamoto, "Capital Formation in Taiwan and Korea," p. 411.

53. Nakamura, *Economic Growth in Prewar Japan*, pp. 239–262.

54. Nakamura, *Economic Growth*, pp. 299–300.

55. Jerome Cohen, *Japan's Economy in War and Reconstruction*, p. 18.

56. Cohen, *Japanese Economy*, p. 21.

57. Kant, "The Perpetual Peace," p. 88.

58. Nakamura, *Economic Growth*, p. 288.

59. Norman, *The Establishment of a Modern State in Japan*, pp. 218–221.

60. McNamara, *Colonial Origins of Korean Enterprise*, ch. 4.

61. Eckert, "The Origins of Korean Capitalism".

62. McNamara, *Colonial Origins*, ch. 4.

63. Park, "The Emergence of Factory Labor Force," p. 39.

64. E. B. Schumpeter, *The Industrialization of Japan and Manchuria*, p. 374.

65. Park, "The Emergence of Factory Labor Force," p. 52.

66. Kang, Man-gil, *Hanguk hyôndaesa*, pp. 121–122; McNamara, *Colonial Origins*, ch. 4; Jerome Cohen, *Japan's Economy in War and Reconstruction*, p. 36.

67. Grajdanzev, *Modern Korea*, ch. 3.

68. Park, "The Emergence of Factory Labor Force," p. 53.

69. Grajdanzev, *Modern Korea*, p. 154.

70. Lockwood, *The Economic Development of Japan*, p. 533.

71. Jerome Cohen, *Japan's Economy in War and Reconstruction*, p. 114.

72. Cohen, *Japan's Economy*, p. 138.

73. Japan's bomb project was moved to the area around Hŭngnam, and there, the Japanese processed more than 90% of the monazite mined in Korea in 1944, seeking to recover sufficient amounts of thorium for a bomb. Wilcox, *Japan's Secret War*, pp. 25, 35–38, 151–152, 166.

74. Peattie, "Introduction," p. 27.

75. For a distinction between state and societal corporatism, see Schmitter, "Still the Century of Corporatism?"

76. Cumings, *The Origins of the Korean War: Liberation*, pp. 27–28; for details of mobilization in the last decade of the colonial rule, see Kim Un-tae, *Ilbon chequkjujŭi ŭi hanguk t'ongchi*, pp. 415–488.

77. Park, *Korea Reborn*, p. 132.

78. Jerome Cohen, *Japan's Economy in War and Reconstruction*, p. 36. Other data show an even worse concentration of Japanese ownership in all these industries.; See, for example, Kang, *Hangk, Hyŏnsdaesa*, p. 123.

79. Park, "The Emergence of Factory Labor Force," p. 54.

3. A Method to His Madness

1. The most succinct exposition of the flaws of import-substitution industrialization is found by Krueger, "Export-led Industrial Growth Reconsidered." Elaborations on the egregious political outcome of the ISI, the "rent-seeking society," are in Buchanan et al., *Toward a Theory of the Rent-Seeking Society*. In particular, see Krueger, "The Political Economy of the Rent-Seeking Society"; Buchanan, "Rent-Seeking and Profit Seeking"; Tullock, "Rent-Seeking as a Negative-Sum Game," and "The Welfare Costs of Tariffs, Monopolies, and Theft."

2. The term is from Huntington, *Political Order in Changing Societies*. This type of assessment is so prevalent that it is impossible to cite the sources. For representative writings on the 1950s, see Chin et al., *1950 nyŏndae ŭi inshik* [Understanding the 1950s]; in English, see Hahn-been Lee, *Korea: Time, Change, and Administration*.

3. For instance, Cole and Lyman, *Korean Development*; Kim and Roemer, *Growth and Structural Transformation*; Krueger, *The Developmental Role of the Foreign Sector and Aid*; Jones and Sakong, *Government, Business, and Entrepreneurship*; and Mason et al., *The Economic and Social Modernization of the Republic of Korea*.

4. John Foster Dulles, NSC Meeting, August 8, 1957, NSC Series, Box 9, AW File, Eisenhower Liberary (henceforth DDE Library).

5. D. Eisenhower, NSC Meeting, January 31, 1957, NSC Series, Box 8, AW File, DDE Library.

6. Gourevitch, "The Second Image Reversed."

7. Frank, "The Unequal and Uneven Historical Development in the World Economy," p. 92.

8. Evans, *Dependent Development*.

9. Mason et al., *The Economic and Social Modernization*, p. 165.

10. Cumings, "The Origins and Development of the Northeast Asian Political Economy," p. 67.

11. "Briefings by the Joint Chief of Staff," January 15, 1959, Dodge Papers, Box 2, CFEP File, DDE Library.

12. "Conference with Members of ICA on Korea," October 15, 1956, Randall Series, Trips Sub-series, Box 2, CFEP File, DDE Library. The figure of $1 billion a year to support Korea also appears in the record of NSC Meeting, October 6, 1955, NSC Series, Box 7, DDE Library.

13. "State Department Briefing to Dodge," January 16, 1959, Dodge Papers, Box 2, CFEP File, DDE Library.

14. There is an econometric calculation, conducted by David Cole, of per capita GNP growth rates in the absence of aid under varying assumptions about substitution of aid for domestic savings. According to that computation, Korea would have seen GNP per capita growth of −1.5 in the period between 1953–1962 in total absence of aid, and 0 if only one half of aid had come through. Cole et al., *The Korean Economy*, p. 16. While this sort of computation is interesting, the behavioralist assumption of *ceteris paribus* ultimately obfuscates the matter, making it impossible to gauge the impact of foreign resource transfer on the national economy.

15. This is an expression used by C. D. Jackson in a letter to Henry Luce. See Rostow, *Eisenhower, Kennedy, and Foreign Aid*, p. 122.

16. Letter from W. L. Clayton to Joseph Dodge, December 30, 1954, Dodge Series, Correspondence Sub-series, Box 1, CFEP File, DDE Library.

17. Morley, *Japan and Korea*, p.52.

18. Eisenhower argued that "to retreat from Korea now [despite a billion-a-year hemorrhage that Humphrey complained about] would now cost the United States its entire position in the Far East," and was seconded by Dulles and Radford. NSC Meeting, October 6, 1956, NSC Series, Box 7, AW File, DDE Library. Elsewhere he said that "while Korea is of no military importance to us in a general war, it is psychologically and politically of such importance that to lose it would run the risk of the loss of our entire position in the Far East. Accordingly, we have got to carry on in South Korea." NSC Meeting, August 8, 1957, NSC Series, Box 9, AW File, DDE Library.

19. For discussions on development policies in the 1950s and arguments of P. T. Bauer, see Rostow, *Eisenhower, Kennedy, and Foreign Aid*, pp. 38–54; for ICA policy on Korea which emphasizes the role of small industries, see "Conference with Members of ICA on Korea," October 15, 1956, Randall Series, Trip Sub-series, Box 2, CFEP File, DDE Library.

20. Maxfield and Nolt argue that ISI was not merely a Frankenstein

of Third World nationalists. Contrary to the received wisdom that ISI was anathema to Americans, they show that independent U.S. initiatives to promote ISI came from those most associated with liberal trade policy: the executive branch of government, and international business. Maxfield and Nolt, "Protectionism and the Internationalization of Capital."

21. The meetings where concerns over the possibility and bluff of Rhee's march northward were raised are too numerous to list here, but records of these meetings can be found in NSC Series, Boxes 7, 8, and 9, AW File, in DDE Library.

22. Cumings, *Origins of the Korean War*, vol 1.

23. Packenham, *Liberal America and Foreign Aid*, p. 35.

24. Gardner, "Commentary," p. 61.

25. Keohane, "The Big Influence of Small Allies."

26. Wedemeyer, *Report to the President*, pp. 21, 17.

27. Acheson to the Embassy in Korea (Top Secret), U.S. Department of State, *Foreign Relations of the United States, 1949*, 7:975.

28. Ellis Briggs, U.S. Ambassador to Korea 1952–1955, Oral History, AW File, DDE Library.

29. Paul Hoffman testified in the Senate: "[Korea] will be the bastion of democracy in Asia, and it will be a very bright and shining light in the midst of the great darkness on that continent." U.S. Senate, *Economic Assistance to China and Korea*, p. 129.

30. U.S. Department of State, *Foreign Relations of the United States*, 1950, 7:30.

31. Bloomfield and Jenkins, *Banking Reform in South Korea*, p. 59.

32. Ibid., p. 60.

33. U.S. Department of State, *Foreign Relations of the United States*, 1949, vol. 7, passim. In February 1954, Rhee renewed his offer to send an expedition to Laos—one division of Korean troops, this time. While some in the U.S. government thought it would dramatize Asian capability and accelerate the formation of an anticommunist regional security pact, the consensus at the NSC was that it merely widened hostilities in the region. Thus, the offer was declined. "Memorandum for the National Security Council," Top Secret, March 2, 1954, NSC Series, Policy Papers Sub-series, Box 10, WHO File, DDE Library.

34. This is Richard Barrett's arguement. See Barret, "Autonomy and Diversity in the American State on Taiwan," pp. 121–137.

35. Ranis, "Challenge and Opportunities Posed by Asia's Superexporters."

36. Krueger, *The Developmental Role of the Foreign Sector and Aid*, ch. 2.

37. Maxfield and Nolt, "Protectionism and the Internationalization of Capital."

38. Macy, "Report on Korea," October 25, 1956, Randall Series, Trip Sub-series, Box 2, CFEP File, DDE Library.

39. Hirschman, "The Political Economy of Import-Substituting Industrialization in Latin America."

40. Cumings, *The Origins of the Korean War: Liberation,* and *The Origins of the Korean War: The Roaring.*

41. George Kennan to the Secretary of State, August 21, 1950, U.S. Department of State, *Foreign Relations of the United States, 1950,* 7:623–628.

42. See Schaller, *The American Occupation of Japan;* and Borden, *The Pacific Alliance.*

43. Quoted in Cumings, *The Origins of the Korean War: The Roaring,* ch. 15.

44. Ibid.

45. I am referring to the second volume of Bruce Cumings' *The Origins of the Korea War.* See chs. 2, 5, and 15.

46. Dower, *Empire and Aftermath,* p. 316.

47. Dulles, NSC Meeting, March 31, 1953, NSC Series, Box 4, AW File, DDE Library.

48. Eisenhower and Dulles, NSC Meeting, April 8, 1953, NSC Series, Box 4, AW File, DDE Library.

49. "Foreign Minister Shigemitsu Visit: Policy Toward Red China Including China Trade," Secret, August 23, 1955, Dodge Series, Subject Sub-series, Box 3, CFEP File DDE Library; W. L. Clayton to Dodge, December 30, 1954, Dodge Series, Correspondence Sub-series, Box 1, CFEP File, DDE Library.

50. Trade with China without recognition was discussed in NSC Meeting, March 4, 1954, NSC Series, Box 5, AW File, DDE Library; December 9, 1954, NSC Series, Box 6, AW File, DDE Library.

51. These are from Dulles' discussion of his trip to the Far East. NSC Meeting, September 12, 1954, NSC Series, Box 9, AW File, DDE Library.

52. NSC 5506, "Future United States Economic Assistance for Asia," Secret, January 21, 1955, NSC Series, Policy Papers Sub-series, Box 14, WHO File, DDE Library.

53. NSC 5514, "U.S. Policy Toward Japan," Top Secret, March 29, 1955, NSC Series, Policy Papers Sub-series, Box 15, WHO File, DDE Library.

54. "Foreign Minister Shigemitsu Visit: Policy toward Red China Including China Trade," Secret, August 23, 1955, Dodge Series, Subject Sub-series, Box 3, CFEP File, DDE Library.

55. Kenneth Langdon of the Operations Coordinating Board thought that the CFEP project on Asian economic development and its idea of economic regionalism was really prompted by the desire to delay Japan, as long as possible, from reestablishing ties with mainland China. Memo from Kenneth Langdon of OCB to F. Dearborn, October 3, 1957, OCB Series, Subject Sub-series, Box 1, WHO File, DDE Library.

56. Memo from Herbert Hoover Jr. to Joseph Dodge, July 19, 1955, Dodge Series, Subject Sub-series, Box 4, CFEP File, DDE Library.

57. "FM Shegemitsu Visit: Japan-ROK Relations," Secret, August 22, 1955, Dodge Series, Subject Sub-series, Box 3, CFEP File.

58. Rhee to Eisenhower, December 29, 1954, U.S. Department of State, *Foreign Relations of the United States, 1952–1954*, 15:1937.

59. Eisenhower, NSC Meeting, July 23, 1953, NSC Series, Box 4, AW File, DDE Library.

60. Japanese complaints to Americans regarding Rhee's intransigence and supplication to force open Korean market were numerous. See, for instance, Koichi Yoshino (chairman of the Kansai Special Procurement Coordination Service, Osaka Industrial Association) to Joseph Dodge, December 14, 1954, Dodge Series, Correspondence Sub-series, Box 3, CFEP File, DDE Library. General Hall also reported to Eisenhower of Yoshida's dissatisfaction on the Korea trade issue. Record of Conversation between Eisenhower and General Hall, July 22, 1954, AW Diary Series, Box 2, AW File, DDE Library. The complaints of the American Embassy in Tokyo regarding Korea are in Dispatch, Embassy to State, Secret, September 21, 1956, Randall Series, Trips Sub-series, Box 2, CFEP File, DDE Library.

61. Record of Conversation between DDE and van Fleet, July 24, 1954, AW Diary Series, Box 2, AW File, DDE Library.

62. Ibid., p. 115.

63. Ibid., p. 1237.

64. Humphrey, NSC Meeting, March 22, 1956, NSC Series, Box 7, AW File, DDE Library.

65. Krueger, *The Developmental Role of the Foreign Sector and Aid*, pp. 61–62.

66. Import substitution industrialization is intended to *accelerate* the pace of industrialization in late developers. But the Latin American experience shows that various phases of ISI were protracted, stretching through many decades. For periodization of ISI phases in Latin America, see Gustav Ranis, "Challenges and Opportunities Posed by Asia's Super-exporters."

67. McKinnon, *Money and Capital in Economic Development*.

68. Robert R. Nathan Associates, *An Economic Programme for Korean Reconstruction*, p. 158.

69. Hanguk kûmyûng yônkuwon, *Hanguk kûmyung yônggam* [Korean Financial Yearbook], p. 77.

70. Ibid., ch. 11.

71. Robert R. Nathan Associates, *An Economic Programme for Korean Reconstruction*, p. 159.

72. Syngman Rhee often made these arguments in responding to his parliamentary critics. His arguments are so entirely plausible that one wonders why Rhee is deemed a *tabula rasa* in economics.

73. *Tonga-ilbo*, April 12, 1957; March 20, 1957.

74. For misguided Keynsianism as the basis of financial repression, see Shaw, *Financial Deepening in Economic Development*, ch. 2.

75. Cumings, *The Origins of the Korean War*, vol. 1.

76. Jones and Sakong, *Government, Business, and Entrepreneurship in Economic Development*, p. 272.

77. Tonga ilbo pyônjippu, *Haebang 30 nyôn* [Thirty Years Since Liberation], 6:97.

78. Ibid., p. 103.

79. Samyangsa is the oldest Korean chaebôl, its textile capital accumulated in the early period of the colonial rule; the founder of the Tusan Group owned a textile store; Yi Byông-ch'ôl of Samsung possessed a small rice mill, some real estate and a trading concern before the Liberation; Ku In-hoe of Lucky-Goldstar was a textile merchant. See Hanguk ilbo Kyôngjebu, *Hanguk ûi 50 tae chaebôl* [Korea's 50 Largest Chaebôl].

80. Seokki Kim, "Business Concentration and Government Policy," p. 53.

81. Kim Sông-du "Hanguk ûi tokjôm kiôp" [Monopoly Enterprises in Korea].

82. Jones and Sakong, *Government, Business, and Entrepreneurship in Economic Development*, p. 271.

83. Kim Sông-du, "Hanguk ûi tokjôm kiôp" [Monopoly Enterprises in Korea].

84. Hanguk ilbo kyôngjebu, *Hanguk ûi 50 tae chaebôl* [Korea's 50 Largest Chaebôl], pp. 82–85.

85. Krueger, "The Political Economy of the Rent-Seeking Society"; also see Colander, ed., *Neoclassical Political Economy*.

86. There are remarkable similarities in the way that the U.S. counterpart fund was used to create artificial middle classes and to conduct patronage politics in South Vietnam and Korea. For Vietnam, see an excellent discussion by George McT. Kahin, *Intervention*.

87. C. D. Jackson reported to Luce the proceedings of his presentation of the World Economic Plan (W. W. Rostow's brainchild), where he had argued for "giving up the Korean-type aid and the brush fire emergencies in order to concentrate on underdeveloped countries." At one point, Humphrey, the Secretary of Treasury, wailed that America was in a jam, that "our major allies are bust . . . we are pouring money into the pockets of cheap politicians who are taking their countries further . . . from the American way of doing things." Rostow, *Eisenhower, Kennedy, and Foreign Aid*, pp. 122–124.

88. Walt Rostow, Max Millikan, P. N. Rosenstein-Rodan, Everett Hagen, Benjamin Higgins, and Wilfred Malendaum Rostow were some of the people at the Center for International Studies who put economic development in the context of modernization. Rostow, *Eisenhower, Kennedy, and Foreign Aid*, p. 54.

89. For records of communication among W. W. Rostow, C. D. Jackson, and Nelson Rockefeller to draw Eisenhower's attention to Rostow's ideas, see Nelson Rockefeller to Eisenhower, June 17, 1955, Administrative Series, Box 30, AW File, DDE Library; C. D. Jackson wished Nelson

Rockefeller luck in getting Rostow's ideas into the official "think-stream" of the administration in a letter dated November 10, 1955, Administrative Series, Box 30, AW File, DDE Library; Nelson Rockefeller to Eisenhower, August 27, 1955, and December 2, 1955, both in Administrative Series, Box 30, AW File, DDE Library; Letters from C. D. Jackson to Eisenhower, March 6, 1958, and May 6, 1960, both in Administrative Series, Box 22, AW File, DDE Library.

90. "W. W. Rostow's ideas on Cold War," first sent by Rostow to Nelson Rockefeller, then sent by Rockefeller to Eisenhower, June 17, 1955, Administrative Series, Box 30, AW File, DDE Library.

91. Rostow, *Eisenhower, Kennedy, and Foreign Aid*, p. 133.

92. Ibid., p. 141.

93. "On the Fairless Committee," CFEP Papers Series, Box 1, CFEP File, DDE Library.

94. "Report on Johnston Recommendation," March 21, 1957, Administrative Series, Box 30, AW File, DDE Library.

95. "ICA Comments on the Johnston Report," March 18, 1957, Administrative Series, Box 30, AW File, DDE Library.

96. NSC 5702/2: U.S. Policy toward Korea, Top Secret, August 9, 1957, NSC Series, Policy Papers Sub-series, Box 19, WHO File, DDE Library.

97. For a discussion on the Klein-Saks mission, see Hirschman, *Journeys Toward Progress*, pp. 199–217.

4. In the East Asian Cauldron

1. See, for example, Frank, Kim, and Westphal, *South Korea*; Krueger, *The Developmental Role of the Foreign Sector and Aid*; Mason et al., *The Economic and Social Modernization of the Republic of Korea*; Cole and Lyman, *Korean Development*; Cole, Lim, and Kuznets, *The Korean Economy*, etc.

2. After teaching at Columbia, Oxford, and MIT, Rostow was, by 1961, the deputy special assistant to the President, for National Security Affairs; the councilor, and then chairman, of the Policy Planning Council at the State Department from 1961 to 1966; special assistant to the president, 1966–1969 and U.S. representative for the Alliance for Progress, 1964–1966.

3. Keynes, *The General Theory of Employment, Interest, and Money*, pp. 483–484.

4. One Korean pundit characterized phases of U.S. aid as follows: "handing out chocolates" in the immediate post-Liberation years, reconstruction aid in the immediate post-Korean War period, the highly troublesome factory and plant aid in the 1950s, agricultural-surplus-dumping in the early 1960s, and in the mid-1960s, aid-on-the-cheap, packed with advice. *Tonga ilbo*, January 22, 1964.

5. Kojima, *Japan and a New World Economic Order*. pp. 150–151.

6. Jerome Cohen, "Arms Sales and Human Rights: The Case of Korea," p. 258.

7. Memorandum from James Grant to Rostow, "On the ICA Far East Mission Directors' Conference," March 16, 1961, NSF, Box 215, JFK Library.

8. *Far Eastern Economic Review*, April 1, 1965.

9. "NSC 6018: U.S. Policy toward Korea," Top Secret, November 28, 1960, NSC Series, Policy Papers Subseries, Box 29, WHO File, DDE Library.

10. Robert Komer to Rostow, March 9, 1961, NSF, Box 127, JFK Library.

11. Robert Komer to Rostow, June 12, 1961, NSF, Box 127, JFK Library.

12. Hugh D. Farley to Rostow, "Report on Korea," sent by W. W. Rostow to Robert Komer, March 15, 1961, NSF, Box 127, JFK Library.

13. "Presidential Task Force on Korea: Report to the National Security Council," NSF, Box 127, JFK Library.

14. Robert Komer to Rostow, March 15, 1961, NSF, Box 127, JFK Library.

15. Robert Johnson to Rostow, May 23, 1961, NSF, Box 127, JFK Library; "Presidential Task Force on Korea: Report to the National Security Council," NSF, Box 127, JFK Library; Robert Johnson's remark on the Presidential Task Force on Korea, June 9, 1961, NSF, Box 127, JFK Library.

16. Rostow, *The Stages of Economic Growth*. For discussion of the "takeoff," see pp. 36–59.

17. Cable from the U.S. Embassy in Seoul to the Secretary of State, April 11, 1961, NSF, Box 128.

18. U.S. House of Representatives, *Investigation of Korean-American Relations*, p. 166.

19. Hugh Farley, "Report on Korea," March 15, 1961, NSF, Box 127, JFK Library.

20. U.S. Embassy in Seoul to the Secretary of State, March 11, 1961, NSF, Box 127; McConaughy to Dean Rusk, April 11, NSF, Box 128, JFK Library.

21. The term "junta" describes the political arrangement in 1961–1963.

22. Roger Hilsman thought that the military seizure of power in May was "the cleverest communist coup ever pulled off." Memorandum on the Korea Task Force meeting, June 28, 1961, NSF, Box 127; the CIA special report called Park's behavior "partially-veiled anti-Americanism." CIA Special Report, October 11, 1963, NSF, Box 127.

23. Berger to the Secretary of State, August 12, 1961, NSF Box 128, JFK Library.

24. McGeorge Bundy to the President, May 31, 1963, NSF, Box 127, JFK Library.

25. Berger to the Secretary of State, October 28, 1961, NSF, Box 128, JFK Library.

26. Green to the Secretary of State, November 11, 1961, NSF, Box 128.

27. "ICA outline of 10-Year Development Goals," March 9, 1961, NSF, Box 215, JFK Library.

28. Berger to the Secretary of State, November 17, 1961, NSF, Box 128, JFK Library.

29. Ralph Duncan to the President, May 8, 1964, Executive File, Box 22, WHCF, LBJ Library.

30. Joseph A. Schumpeter, *History of Economic Analysis*, pp. 343–344.

31. Rusk to the U.S. Embassy in Seoul, June 29, 1962, NSF Box 128, JFK Library.

32. M. V. Forrestal to MacGeorge Bundy, "U.S. Relations with the Korean Military Junta," March 28, 1963, NSF Box 127, JFK Library.

33. Barnet, *The Alliance*, p. 41.

34. Rusk to the U.S. Ambassador in Seoul, June 29, 1962, NSF Box 128, JFK Library.

35. Kim Sông-du "Hanguk ûi tokjôm kiôp" [Monopoly Enterprises in Korea].

36. Stepan, *The State and Society*.

37. Bundy, untitled and unpublished, ch. 16, The Papers of William Bundy, Box 1, LBJ Library. He also wrote to Bill Moyers about trumpeting the ROK's success as a "direct example for what postwar South Vietnam would look like." William Bundy to Bill Moyers, October 6, 1966, NSC History, Box 45, NSF, LBJ Library.

38. Sustained analysis on the Japan and Vietnam factors in Korean development is, to the best of my knowledge, unavailable. As a matter of fact, the authors of the 7-vol. studies on the Korean economy, published by Harvard University and funded by the USAID and the K.D.I. (Korean Development Institute), admit to having omitted the politically sensitive issues of Japan and Vietnam. See, United States Department of State, "Korean Development," p. 4.

39. Memo of Conversation between Dean Rusk and Prime Minister Hayato Ikeda, November 26, 1963, Country File, Box 250, NSF, LBJ Library.

40. *Far Eastern Economic Review*, April 23, 1964.

41. Politicians in the governing party were involved in myriad scams including stockmarket rigging, importation at windfall of Japanese taxis, and the sale of a large textile company to Japanese interests. Japanese business also made substantial inroads in Korea. Cable to the Secretary of the State, November 19, 1963, NSF, Box 127, JFK Library.

42. CIA, "Special Report: The Future of Korean-Japanese Relations," Secret, March 19, 1966, Country File, Box 251, NSF, LBJ Library.

43. Memo of Conversation between Dean Rusk and Prime Minister Hayato Ikeda, November 26, 1963, Country File, Box 250, NSF, LBJ Library.

44. Memo from R. W. Komer to McGeorge Bundy, Secret, August 12, 1964, Country File, Box 250, NSF, LBJ Library. The letter from Bundy to Reischauer said: "we asked Win Brown to tell you of the President's own interest in bringing about at long last a ROK-Japanese settlement and normalization of relations. This note is simply to follow up and make sure you were told that it's 'top priority,' to use the President's words." MacGeorge Bundy to Edwin Reischauer, August 3, 1964, Country File, Box 250, NSF, LBJ Library.

45. Cable, Embassy to State, Secret, November 17, 1964, Country File, Box 250, NSF, LBJ Library.

46. R. W. Komer to MacGeorge Bundy, April 7, 1964, Country File, Box 237, NSF, LBJ Library.

47. *Far Eastern Economic Review*, May 14, 1964. For the role of individual zaibatsu in the Normalization process and in subsequent political economy of Korea, see Chang, "Japanese Corporations and the Political Economy of South Korean-Japanese Relations, 1965–1979."

48. Hosup Kim, "Policy Making of Japanese Official Development Assistance," pp. 81–85.

49. CIA, "The Future of Korean-Japanese Relations," Secret, March 18, 1966, Country File, Box 251, NSF, LBJ Library.

50. For the argument on the German pattern of trade, see Hirschman, *National Power and the Structure of Foreign Trade.*

51. OCB report on NSC 5516/1: U.S. Policy toward Japan, April 9, 1955, NSC Series, Policy Papers Subseries, Box 15, WHOF, DDE Library.

52. Cable, Embassy in Tokyo to the Secretary of State, on Rostow's visit, May 3, 1965, Country File, Box 250, NSF, LBJ Library.

53. Ozawa, *Multinationalism Japanese Style,* pp. 15, 24.

54. Kawata, "The Asian Situation and Japan's Economic Relations with the Developing Asian Countries."

55. Krasner, "Power Structures and Regional Development Banks."

56. The U.S. tried to downplay its role in creating the ADB, and the link between the latter and the Vietnam War. In a memo to Jack Valenti, Frances Bator praised the President in avoiding direct mention of Vietnam at the signing of the ADB Act. Memo from Frances Bator to Jack Valenti, March 11, 1966, Executive File, Box 18, WHCF, LBJ Library; Valenti also wrote that "the Asian Development Bank is a source of pride to the Asians because we played our role in a very discreet and skillful fashion." Memo from Jack Valenti to the President, February 25, 1966, Executive File, Box 49, WHCF, LBJ Library.

57. Memo from Kenneth Langdon (OCB) to F. Dearborn (NSC), "Comments on the CFEP Paper on Asian Economic Development," October 3, 1957, OCB Series, Subject Sub-series, Box 1, WHO File, DDE Library.

58. Rostow was experienced in matters of regional integration since his days of working on German-Austrian economic problems and then in Geneva in 1947–1949 as a member of the secretariat for ECE. Rostow, *The United States and the Regional Organization of Asia and the Pacific*, p. 34.

59. Rostow, *The United States and the Regional Organization of Asia and the Pacific*, pp. 203–216.

60. Yasutomo, *Japan and the Asian Development Bank.*

61. Maekawa, the Deputy Governor of the Bank of Japan, told Burr that the Japanese had expended too little effort in their own backyard, and that he was now much more sympathetic with the problems that the United States faced with Latin America. Memo from Burr to the Secretary of Treasury, December 6, 1965, Executive File, Box 18, WHCF, LBJ Library.

62. U.S. House of Representatives, *The United States and Multilateral Banks*, pp. 26–27, 71–75, 103.

63. Kershmer, *Japanese Foreign Trade*, p. 149, quoted in Choi, "Asian Development Bank," p. 8.

64. "Manila Conference," October 11, 1966, NSC History, Box 45, NSC File, LBJ Library.

65. Jack Valenti to the President, February 25, 1966, Executive File, Box 49, WHCF, LBJ Library.

66. Prior to 1960, the Korean government used MAP (Military Assistance Program) dollars to purchase "O & M" items rather than investing in up-to-date equipment. From 1960 on, the United States tried to force Koreans to use MAP dollars to purchase equipment to modernize their forces and to spend more of their own funds for O & M purchase. The means used for this was the MAP transfer program, i.e., transferring certain expenditures from MAP to the Korean defense budget. Koreans resisted this. Under the Brown Memorandum, the United States ended up suspending MAP transfer during 1966–1970 period, providing savings to the Korean government of about $93 million. See, U.S. House of Representatives, *Investigation of Korean-American Relations*, p. 175.

67. This text of the Brown Memorandum appears in Baldwin, "America's Rented Troops."

68. Ibid., pp. 37–38. Figures vary depending on sources. According to Senator Symington's Subcommittee on the U.S. Security Agreements and Commitments Abroad, the total U.S. payment to Korea in 1965–1970 came to $927 million. According to USAID computation, the sum total during the same period was $925 million. For a breakdown of U.S. payments to Korea, see U.S. House of Representatives, *Investigation of Korean-American Relations*, p. 175.

69. Naya, "The Vietnam War and Some Aspects of Its Economic Impact on Asian Countries."

70. Jones and Sakong, *Government, Business, and Entreprenuership in Economic Development*, pp. 356, 360.

71. Cole and Nam, "The Pattern and Significance of Economic Planning in Korea," p. 22.

72. All throughout the 1970s, annual reports on Korea prepared by the World Bank expressed serious concern over the Korean ability to finance investment and advised scaling down of investment.

73. Memorandum of William Brubeck to McGeorge Bundy, June 19, 1962, NSF Box 127, JFK Library.

74. Joel Bernstein to Walt Rostow, November 8, 1966, Country File, Box 10, WHCF, LBJ Library.

75. Ibid.

76. Walt Rostow to Chang Ki-yông, November 18, 1966, Country File, Box 10, WHCF, LBJ Library.

77. Frieden, "Third World Indebted Industrialization."

78. For discussions of Japanese foreign investment, see Ozawa, Multinationalism Japanese Style.

79. Chang, "Japanese Corporations and the Political Economy of South Korean-Japanese Relations, 1965–1979."

80. Business Asia, July 11, 1975.

81. Krueger, The Developmental Role of the Foreign Sector and Aid, p. 82.

82. Cole and Nam, "The Pattern and Significance of Economic Planning in Korea," p. 14.

83. Adelman, ed., Practical Approaches to Development Planning; Cole and Park, Financial Development in Korea; Cole and Lyman, Korean Development; Krueger, The Developmental Role of the Foreign Sector and Aid; Mason et al., The Economic and Social Modernization of the Republic of Korea; United States Department of State [author: David Steinberg], "Korean Development: Aid or Sui Generis"; Frank, Kim, and Westphal, South Korea.

84. Edward Shaw was one of the advisers in Korea. His ideas are summarized in McKinnon, Money and Capital in Economic Development, p. 3. McKinnon defines economic development as "the reduction of the great dispersion in social rates of return to existing and new investments under domestic entrepreneurial control." Ibid., p. 9.

85. For assessments of the 1965 reforms, see Cole and Park, Financial Development in Korea; McKinnon, Money and Capital, p. 2, 110.

86. Cho, Hanguk kyôngje ûi hyônshil kwa chillo [Current Position and Prospects of Korean Economy], p. 194.

87. Se-jin Kim argues that "the rise of the military is a reappearance of the administrative authoritarian system long ingrained in the Korean body politic." Se-jin Kim, The Politics of Military Revolution in Korea, p. 3. For as Linzian anaysis of the breakdown of democratic order in Korea, see Han, The Failure of Democracy in South Korea.

88. Some Korean chaebol, dubbed the "gang of five," got jump starts though the infusion of Japanese capital that was mediated by the government. The five are: Sônkyông Textiles, Shinjin Motors, Yônhap Iron and

Steel, Korea Explosives, and Kûkdong Construction. Chang, "Japanese Corporations and the Political Economy of South Korean-Japanese Relations."

89. For information on the details of the Kim-Ohira concord on reparation, see Joungwon Kim, *Divided Korea*, p. 241.

90. CIA, "Special Report: The Future of Korea-Japanese Relations," Secret, March 18, 1966, Country File, Box 251, NSF, LBJ Library.

91. Kim, *Divided Korea*, p. 243.

92. Kim Chin-bae and Pak Chang-rae, "Chagwan" [Foreign Debt], *Sindonga*, December 1968.

93. Ibid.

94. U.S. House of Representatives, *Investigation of Korean-American Relations*, p. 248.

95. Kim and Pak, "Chagwan" [Foreign Debt], *Sindonga*, December 1968.

96. Sogang University Research Institute, *A Study of Money Market and Industrial Investment Financing in Korea*.

97. The 1969 referendum allowed a constitutional amendment for a three-term presidency. Following that, Park Chung Hee was elected President in 1971. This was to be the last presidential election in Korea until 1988.

98. U.S. House of Representatives, *Hearing Before the Subcommittee on International Organizations of the Committee on International Relations*, pp. 190–191.

99. Im Myo-min, "Chaebôl kwa kwollyôk: chônkyôngryôn ûi kaldûng" [The Chaebôl and Political Power: FKI in Conflict], *Sindonga*, April 1983.

100. Sôgang University Research Institute. *A Study of Money Market and Industrial Investment Financing in Korea*, p. 48.

101. "8.3 choch'i ûi chubyôn" [The Circumstances Surrounding the August 3rd Decree], *Singdonga*, October 1972.

102. Ibid.

103. "8.3 choch'i wa hanguk kyôngje" [The August 3rd Decree and Korean economy], *Sindonga*, October 1972.

104. Poulantzas, *The Crisis of the Dictatorships*.

5. The Search for Autonomy

1. Chung Hee, *Korea Reborn*, p. 132.

2. Polanyi, *The Great Transformation*.

3. Crisp, "Russia, 1860–1914."

4. Economic technocrats in Korea believed that a period of intensely free trade would follow the inauguration of a floating exchange regime, offering Korea excellent export prospects. The excessive level of investment in the early 1970s was based, in part, on such flawed projections. When the hope for freer trade was dashed, Korea moved swiftly to

diversify trading partners and to emphasize value-added industrial goods. ROK Economic Planning Board, "The Korean Economy: Current Reforms and Future Prospects," pp. 1–4.

5. *The New York Times Magazine*, February 18, 1968, p. 30.

6. *The New York Times*, February 4, 1968.

7. *The New York Times*, February 8, 1968.

8. Kissinger, *The White House Years*, 1: 321.

9. Nam, *America's Commitment to South Korea*.

10. This is according to the Library of Congress study on Overseas Private Investment Corporation (OPIC) as released by the House Committee on Foreign Affairs, September 4, 1973. Of the worldwide total of $1,409 million, $328 million was issued for U.S. investors in Korea.

11. *The Wall Street Journal*, August 26, 1970.

12. "The Hollingsworth Line," *The Far Eastern Economic Review*, February 27, 1976.

13. At a Pentagon briefing, Deputy Defense Secretary Clemens told thirty-five top Japanese industrialists that Japan must expand its influence as spelled out in the Nixon Doctrine, and that the Japanese conventional forces could be called, as a part of a "United Nations forces" if needed, to fill the "regional vacuum" in the Far East Asia. *Washington Star News*, June 15, 1973.

14. Chang, "Japanese Corporations and the Political Economy of South Korean-Japanese Relations."

15. "The Four Principles of Chou En-lai" barred China from trading with those Japanese firms that (1) ship arms to be used in the American war of aggression in Southeast Asia; (2) are affiliated with an American company; (3) invest in business in Taiwan and the Philippines; and (4) provide technical aid to Taiwan and South Korea. This trade bar was finally lifted in March 1973.

16. Chang, "Japanese Corporations and the Political Economy of South Korean-Japanese Relations."

17. On the Korean Skepticism of U.S. resolve to curtail Korean textile exports, see Chunghwahak kongôp ch'ujin wiwônhoe kihoekdan, *Hanguk kongôphwa paljôn e kwanhan chosa yônku: chôngchaek kyôljông kwajông ûi imyônsa* [The Study of Industrial Progress in Korea: The Background], 3: 263–269.

18. Ibid.

19. U.S. House of Representatives, *Investigation of Korean-American Relations*, p. 192.

20. Moskowitz, "Introduction."

21. Odell, "Growing Trade and Growing Conflict between the Republic of Korea and the United States."

22. This is also pointed out in Yoffie, "The Newly Industrializing Countries and the Political Economy of Protectionism."

23. *The Korea Week*, November 30, 1973.

24. Hang-sheng Cheng, "Alternative Balance of Payments Adjustment Experiences in Korea and Taiwan."

25. The term *yushin* refers to the bureaucratic authoritarian order in the 1972–1979 period. The term, which is translatable as "restoration," is borrowed from the Meiji Restoration.

26. Originally, this Corps belonged to what was called the Committee for Promoting Heavy and Chemical Industries, led by the Deputy Prime Minister (Minister of Economic Planning Board, ex officio). The Corps was later detached from the parent body to become an independent supervisory organ for the heavy industrialization effort.

27. Chunghwahak kongôp ..., *Hanguk kongôphwa paljôn* ... 3: 421.

28. Hirschman, "The Political Economy of Import-Substituting Industrialization in Latin America."

29. Gerschenkron, *Economic Backwardness in Historical Perspective*, pp. 343–344.

30. The World Bank, *Current Economic Position and Prospects of the Republic of Korea*, Report 768-KO, and Report 1490-KO.

31. The World Bank, *Current Economic Position and Prospects of the Republic of Korea*, Report 332-KO, p. 64.

32. Economic Planning Board, cited by Amsden, "Growth and Stabilization in Korea."

33. Park Young Chul, "Korea's Experience with External Debt Management," p. 300.

34. See chapter 2.

35. Chunghwahak kongôp ch'ujin wiwônhoe kihoekdan, *Hanguk kongôphwa paljôn e kwanhan chosa yônku: chunghwahak kongôp paljônsa* [The Study of Industrial Progress in Korea: The History], 1: 262.

36. A group of Korean business leaders, sent to the United States to solicit loans in 1962, had misled Americans about the existence of the so-called Korean Pittsburgh. When some American businessmen expressed interest, the junta, in record time, bought the farmland and mountains in Ulsan, bulldozed through them, and hung up the sign, "Ulsan Industrial Complex." The Van Fleet mission came to naught. Immediately following the contretemps, the junta tried to solict German capital in vain; it also sought to form an international consortium of eight companies, but the project fell through when France pulled out. Chunghwahak kongôp ... *Hanguk kongôphwa paljôn* ..., 3: 28–33.

37. The argument for offering pecuniary and technical assistance to Korea was made by those who had most to gain from it, such as Mitsubishi Corporation. It seized a lion's share of plant order for P'ohang.

38. *The Far Eastern Economic Review*, February 20, 1976.

39. The cheapness of Korean steel accounts for the initial and remarkable inroad made in the U.S. (and Japanese) market. In 1978, the hourly wage for the Korean steel industry was a mere $0.45 compared to $5.44 in the United States.

40. Park Young Chul, "Korea's Experience with External Debt Management."

41. The iron and steel production may be divided into the following three categories: (1) the iron-making process, whereby pig iron is produced in gaint blast furnaces which liquefy the iron ore and oxidize it with coke; (2) the steel-making process, whereby such intermediate products as steel ingots, billets, slabs, and hot coils are produced in converters, electric furnaces, or open-hearth furnaces, using pig iron or scrap iron as starting materials; and (3) the rolling process, whereby billets, slabs, or hot coils are heated to incandescence and then extended and shaped under pressure by means of rollers to produce various types of steel manufactures.

42. Kurth, "The Political Consequences of the Product Cycle."

43. Chunghwahak kongôp ..., Hanguk kongôphwa paljôn ..., 1: 642.

44. For the measures contained in the Shipbuilding Industry Promotion Act of 1967, see ibid., pp. 647–649.

45. Fifty-eight percent of total shipbuilding enterprises produced wooden vessels exclusively.

46. The Far Eastern Economic Review, September 15, 1976.

47. The Far Eastern Economic Review, May 18, 1979.

48. The policy on coexistence and cooperation between small suppliers and large shipmakers, repeatedly urged by President Park, has not been successful, as the chabôl shipbuilders gradually consolidated their production vertically and squeezed small enterprises out of market.

49. In the early 1980s, shipbuilding emerged as one of the problem industries, with combined debt of 2.5 trillion won for 70 companies. Tonga ilbo, February 27, 1985.

50. The Far Eastern Economic Review, July 19, 1984.

51. For useful data and discussion on chemical and petrochemical industry, see Chunghwahak kongôp ch'ujin wiwônhoe kihoekdan, Hanguk kongôphwa paljôn e kwanhan chosa yônku: chunghwahak kongôp paljônsa [The Study of Industrial Progress in Korea: The History], 1: 719–836. The figures quoted here are on p. 721.

52. Brian Levy, "The Perils of Partnership," p. 61.

53. Ibid., pp. 61–74.

54. Chunghwahak kongôp ..., Hanguk kongôphwa paljôn ..., 1: 719–836.

55. This figure is arrived at by adding the existing 155,000 m/t naphtha-cracking capacity existing as of 1978, and adding on 350,000 m/t and 385 m/t capacity that came on stream in 1979 and 1981. Data provided by Hanguk sôkyu hwahak kongôp hyôphoe (The Association of Korean Petrochemical Industries).

56. Economic Planning Board, "Statistical Report on Mining and Manufacturing Industries," quoted in Chunghwahak kongôp ch'ujin wiwônhoe kihoekdan, Hanguk kongôphwa paljôn e kwanhan chosa yônku:

chunghwahak kongôp paljônsa [The Study of Industrial Progress in Korea: The History], 1: 723.

57. Watanabe, "Heavy and Chemical Industrialization and Economic Development in the Republic of Korea," pp. 396–397.

58. Data obtained from the Economic Planning Board Bureau of Statistics.

59. It is highly ironic that the government was accused of not doing enough for machine industries in the early 1970s, then of helping them too excessively in the mid-1970s. All through the late 1960s and early 1970s, journalistic pundits criticised the deleterious effect of turn-key plant imports on the domestic machine-building industry.

60. Data from the Ministry of Commerce.

61. Chunghwahak kongôp . . . , Hanguk kongôphwa paljôn . . . , 1: 478–479.

62. Kim Chuk Kyo and Lee Chul Hee, "The Growth of the Automotive Industry," p. 280.

63. Ibid., p. 281. Domestic component in Saenara was about 21 percent.

64. Korean experience differs from the one in Latin America, which has had a much longer history of the MNC influence in both production and decisions regarding market. Local subsidiaries of automobile MNCs in Latin America have concentrated on assembling foreign parts, for sale in the domestic market—and if not domestic, then within the broad Latin American market. Bennet and Sharpe, "The World Automobile Industry and Its Implications," pp. 208–210.

65. Prior to 1974, the localization clause postulated 21 percent of nonfunctional items in domestic component, but enforcement was lax, and criticism alleging political ties (between Shinjin Automobiles, Toyota, and the Ruling party) very frequent. Kim and Lee, "The Growth of the Automotive Industry," p. 281.

66. Ibid., p. 277.

67. The three are Kia, Hyundai, and Daewoo. Fifteen percent of the stock of Hyundai Motor Company is owned by Mitsubishi, which supplies technology and engines for those Pony Excels sold abroad. Daewoo's export item is the produce of Daewoo-GM joint-venture.

68. One could also argue the connection with machine building through uses of spinning and weaving machines. The greatest contribution of textiles to industrialization is, however, the indirect one of generating capital to invest in other industries, such as railroads.

69. Chunghwahak kongôp . . . , Hanguk kongôphwa paljôn . . . , 1: 536.

70. Ibid., p. 578.

71. The decrees are the Five-Year Plan for the Promotion of the Electronics Industry (1967–1972), and imbricating it, the Eight-Year Plan for Promotion of the Electronics Industry (1969–1976).

72. The major concern of the Ministry of Commerce (later renamed

as the Ministry of Commerce and Industry) has been export promotion. It received much praise as the spearhead of the export-led growth, and also criticism for organizing the economy along the precept, "export or perish."

73. Watanabe, "An Analysis of Structureal Dependence between Japan and Korea," p. 397.

74. Chunghwahak kongôp . . . , *Hanguk kongôphwa paljôn* . . . , 1: 598.

75. Chunghwahak kongôp . . . , *Hanguk kongôphwa paljôn* . . . , 3: 608.

76. Ibid., p. 611.

77. U.S. House of Representatives, *Investigation of Korean-American Relations*, pp. 76–87.

6. The Political Economy of Korea, Inc.

1. McKinnon, *Money and Capital in Economic Development.*

2. Yamazawa and Hirohisa, "Trading Companies and the Expansion of Foreign Trade," p. 430.

3. Gerschenkron, *Economic Backwardness in Historical Perspective,* and Cameron, ed., *Banking and Economic Development.*

4. The World Bank, *Korea: Managing the Industrial Transition,* 1: 32.

5. For a brief history of postwar international finance and the role played by banks in the explosive growth of Third World debt, see Moffitt, *The World's Money;* and Sampson, *Money Lenders.*

6. For political reasons behind Taiwan's encouragement of foreign investments in the 1970s, see Gold, "Dependent Development in Taiwan."

7. The ROK Economic Planning Board, *Woechae Paeksô* [The White Paper on Foreign Debt].

8. The IMF at its nadir had been stripped of its initiatives by Nixon and his Secretary of the Treasury Bill Simon, who intended to protect U.S. dominance in the international monetary scene. Simon's departure, coupled with a deteriorating international debt outlook, prompted a shift in American policy. Kahler, "Politics of International Debt."

9. The ROK Economic Planning Board, *Woechae Paksô,* pp. 14, 67. In 1987, Korea's external debt was $37.1 billion, a drop from $44.5 in 1986. The Bank of Korea's reserve grew to $9.3 billion. *Korea Herald,* December 15, 1987.

10. *Woechae Paksô,* p. 83.

11. For an argument along such lines, see Benjamin Cohen, "High Finance and High Politics," pp. 107–127.

12. Wellons, "International Debt," pp. 441–447.

13. B. Cohen, "High Finance and High Politics," pp. 108–110.

14. Feinberg, "The Lending Patterns of the EXIM Bank," p. 65.

15. *Euromoney*, October 1978, p. 17.

16. As of 1973, Korea had an outstanding loan to ADB of $246.8 million; in the aftermath of the oil crisis, the amount made a threefold jump. By the end of 1977, Korea, together with the Philippines and Malaysia, had taken out $3 billion of the $4.2 billion in total ADB loans. *Euromoney*, April 1978, p. 127.

17. *The Wall Street Journal*, December 13, 1976.

18. *The Wall Street Journal*, February 14, 1975.

19. The inaugural issue was for December 1975, and the substance of the cover story was reported in an independent English language weekly based in Washington, D.C. *Korea Week*, December 15, 1975.

20. *Korea Week*, December 15, 1975.

21. Korea had asked Morgan Guaranty to pay its balance of payment deficit. Morgan refused at first, but then returned with a syndicate of twenty American and Japanese banks, and made the loan at 2 percent over LIBOR. *The Wall Street Journal*, February 14, 1975.

22. *The Far Eastern Economic Review*, January 23, 1976.

23. *The Wall Street Journal*, December 13, 1976.

24. Ibid.

25. *The Wall Street Journal*, August 30, 1977.

26. *The Wall Street Journal*, April 11, 1978.

27. *Far Eastern Economic Review*, July 20, 1979. Narrowing the spread on syndicated loans was, in a way, a regional (East Asia) phenomenon. Even so, foreign bankers' eagerness to lend cheap to the robustly growing economies of the Far East was most pronounced in Korea. In 1979, when Korea expressed the wish to borrow $300 million, the syndicated participants offered instead $747 million. Korea, tempted by the unprecedented low interest on the money, in the end took $600 million.

28. *Euromoney*, July 1979, p. 90.

29. *Far Eastern Economic Review*, July 20, 1979, p. 59.

30. The World Bank, *Korea: Managing the Industrial Transition*, 1: 19.

31. For information on the Korean curb market, see Campbell and Ahn, "Kyes and Mujins: Financial Intermediation in South Korea"; Cole and Park, *Financial Development in Korea*, ch. 4.

32. In the early 1960s, BOK had authorized the issuance of short-term stabilization bonds, with a 90-day maturity and within 10 percent of money supply at the time. But the rates that the bonds carried were 10 percent or less, too low for savers or banks at the time. So, in the absence of demand, they were forced onto the banks, hardly an "open" market operation. In 1965, at the urging of John Gurley, Hugh Patrick, and Edward Shaw, BOK had established the "stabilization account," which had identical mechanisms as the required reserve system but had the effect of open market operation.

33. Kim Byông-ju and Pak Yông-chôl, *Hanguk kyôngje wa kûmyung*. p. 352.

34. The Federation of Korean Industrialists had pleaded for establishment of GTCs since 1968. Establishment was refused on the ground that GTCs would gobble up export credits, but when Daewoo and Samsung proved that their products had been boycotted by Japanese *sogo shosha* in the early 1970s, Park Chung Hee allowed their establishment. Chunghwahak kongôp . . . , *Hanguk kongôphwa paljôn* . . . , 3: 427.

35. *Business Korea,* December 1985, pp. 63–66.

36. *Far Eastern Economic Review,* November 19, 1976, pp. 41–46.

37. The World Bank, *Korea: Managing the Industrial Transition,* 2: 110.

38. Korean bankers, who are state employees, and Ministry of Finance officials might show favoritism to larger enterprises in anticipation of their "retirement" into business.

39. For a discussion of allocation inefficiency under interest rate ceiling, see Cho, "The Role of Finance in Industrial Performance."

40. Examples of books lambasting the government policy on the chaebôl include Yi, *Chaebôl;* Hanguk ilbosa kyôngjebu, *Hanguk ûi 50 dae chaebôl* [Korea's Big 50 Chaebôl]; and Chu Chong-hwan, *Chaebôl kyôngjeron* [Theories on the Chaebôl Economy].

41. Yoonje Cho, "Financial Repression, Efficiency of Capital Allocation, and Economic Concentration."

42. Yi, *Chaebôl,* pp. 208, 209.

43. The real debt/equity is difficult to compute. The ordinary practice, to avoid credit severence, is to inflate equity by temporarily drawing capital from affiliated firms. Among the top ten firms, this intergroup transaction is said to be anywhere between 30.2 percent and 81.4 percent of the declared equity: the average is 60 percent. *Hanguk ilbo,* February 24, 1985.

44. Hanguk ilbosa kyôngjebu, Hanguk ûi 50 dae chaebôl [Korea's Big 50 Chaebôl], p. 13.

45. Nonperforming loans are understood here as loans the principal that is past maturity and uncollected, rescheduled loans that the banks expect to write off as lost, and loans whose principals are uncollectable due to insufficient collateral.

46. Yi, *Chaebôl,* p. 204; *Mail kyôngje shinmun,* February 25, 1985.

47. The average profit for the sales in manufacturing is 1.7 pecent, whereas it is 1.1 percent for the chaebôl. The average for the non-chaebôl firms would be much higher than 1.7 percent, since the average is computed including the chaebôl. *Hanguk ilbo,* February 24, 1985.

48. *Maeil kyôngje shinmun,* February 25, 1985.

49. For instance, the collateral put up by the top ten chaebôl for their loans came to 80 percent only of the principal. Yi, *Chaebôl,* p. 204.

50. Lowi, *The End of Liberalism,* p. 280.

51. Government was already slapping ad hoc, regressive taxes on sales and salaries in the late 1970s—the most notorious of which was the National Defense Tax.

52. Pak Yông-ho, "Hanûn t'ûkyung" [Special Rescue Loans of the Bank of Korea].

53. ROK Economic Planning Board, *Kongjông kôrae paeksô* [The White Paper on Fair Trading].

54. Cole and Park assert, however, that such practices were pervasive. Cole and Park, *Financial Development in Korea*, p. 186.

55. Cited in Yi, *Chaebôl*, p. 184.

56. Big corporations, to propitiate the BOK and the Ministry of Finance, often sold some of their land holdings, only to buy them back later.

57. The Federation of Korean Industrialists once blasted the Prime Minister and the Minister of the Economic Planning Board for "ordering sales of land without proper provisioning through bank loans." *Tong-a ilbo*, March 9, 1985.

58. *The Wall Street Journal*, December 12, 1973.

59. Chunghwahak kongôp ch'ujin wiwônhoe, 3: 317.

7. *Slouching Toward the Market*

1. The Korean won had been pegged to the U.S. dollar since 1974, and during 1975–1978, the effective exchange rate depreciated by 15 percent in line with the movement of the dollar, but appreciated by 13 percent in real terms, because prices rose faster in Korea than in its partner countries. In 1979, a substantial appreciation of the dollar led to the effective exchange rate further appreciating by 15 percent in Korea.

2. In August 1979, women textile workers who were laid off and chased out of their company dormitories appealed for help at opposition party headquarters. They were subsequently attacked by 1,000 riot police. See *The New York Times*, August 11, 1979 and August 14, 1979.

3. This assessment is ubiquitous in writings on Korean economy, both at home and abroad. For example, Aghevli and Marquez-Ruarte, "A Case of Successful Adjustment," The World Bank, *Korea: Managing the Industrial Transition*, vols. 1 and 2; The World Bank, *Korea: Adjusting to a New World Environment;* and The World Bank, *The World Development Report* (1989). A pithy verdict is delivered in Browning, "East Asia in Search of a Second Economic Miracle," p. 127.

4. The program was supported by two one-year standby arrangements with the IMF and a structural adjustment loan from the World Bank for the period from March 1980–February 1982. These were followed by another IMF standby arrangement at SDR 576 million, and another structural adjustment loan from the World Bank in the amount of $300 million starting from July 1983 and ending in March 1985. See Aghevli and Marquez-Ruarte, "A Case of Successful Adjustment," p. 15.

5. Ibid., p. 1.

6. Hirschman, "Inflation in Chile," in *Journeys Toward Progress*.

7. *The Wall Street Journal,* May 15, 1980.

8. Hirschman, "The Political Economy of Latin American Development."

9. *Chugan maekyông,* March 14, 1985, pp. 21–22.

10. Chunghwahak kongôp c̆hujin wiwônhoi kihoekdan, *Hanguk kongôpwha paljôn e kwanhan chosa yônku: chôngchaek kyôljông kwajông ûi imyônsa* [The Study of Industrial Progress in Korea: The Background], 3: 456.

11. Browning, "East Asia in Search of a Second Miracle," p. 128.

12. *Far Eastern Economic Review,* April 13, 1979, p. 47.

13. Chunghwahak kongôp . . . , *Hanguk kongôphwa paljôn* . . . , 3:276.

14. You, "Is Fordism Coming to Korea?", p. 25.

15. *Far Eastern Economic Review,* April 13, 1979, p. 47.

16. Aghevli and Marquez-Ruarte, "A Case of Successful Adjustment," pp. 11, 16.

17. Business groups also made pleas to the government to restrain wage and contain labor activites. The Korean Traders' Association, for instance, made a special entreaty to stop the cost-push. See *Korea Herald,* September 26, 1980.

18. You, "Is Fordism Coming to Korea?" p. 13.

19. Ibid., p. 32.

20. Such an argument may be found in R. Kaufman, "Industrial Change and Authoritarian Rule," and A. O. Hirschman, "The Turn Toward Authoritarianism in Latin America and the Search for Its Economic Determinants," in Collier, ed., *The New Authoritarianism in Latin America;* Skidmore, "Politics of Economic Stabilization in Postwar Latin America," in Malloy, ed., *Authoritarianism and Corporatism in Latin America;* Stallings, "Peru and the U.S. Banks: Privatization of Financial Relations," and Frenkel and O'Donnell, "The 'Stabilization Programs' of the International Monetary Fund and Their Internal Impact," in Fagen, ed., *Capitalism and the State in the U.S.-Latin American Relations.*

21. Kyôngje kihoekwôn, *Ôichae paeksô,* [White Paper on the ROK Economy], p. 6.

22. Ibid., p. 2.

23. *The New York Times,* December 22, 1980.

24. Euromoney, October 1980. Credit worthiness is calculated by factoring in the country's natural, human, and financial resources base, its policy, and the balance of payment outlook. For an explanation of country risk ranking, see *Euromoney,* April 1979, pp. 135–159.

25. *The Wall Street Journal,* May 2, 1980.

26. *The New York Times,* April 14, 1980.

27. A recent study at Harvard sees the economic liberalization from 1978 to date as the idea and the work solely of Korea's economic technocrats. Choi, "Institutionalizing a Liberal Economic Order in Korea."

28. For works on Latin American experiments with structural mo-

netarism, see Foxley, *Latin American Experiments in Neo-Conservative Economics*; Corbo and de Melo, "Liberalization with Stabilization in the Southern Cone of Latin America: Overview and Summary"; Diaz-Alejandro, "Good-Bye Financial Repression, Hello Financial Crash"; Fitzgerald, "The State and the Management of Accumulation in the Periphery"; Galvez and Tybout, "Microeconomic Adjustment in Child during 1977–1981," etc.

29. Stepan, "State Power and the Strength of Civil Society in the Southern Cone of Latin America," p. 324.

30. For an excellent analysis of Nixon's foreign policy, see Schurman, *The Grand Design*.

31. Morton Abramowitz was then the head of International Security Affairs and Michael Armacost was Deputy Assistant Secretary for East Asia Bureau at the Pentagon. Leslie Gelb was at the Political-Military Office at the State Department. See Hayes, "Pacific Powerkeg," ch. 5.

32. Ibid., ch. 5. Also see House Committee on the Armed Forces, *Impact of Intelligence Reassessment on Withdrawal of U.S. Troops from Korea*; House Committee on the Armed Services, *Review of the Policy Decision to Withdraw United States Ground Forces from Korea*; Senate Committee on Foreign Relations, *The Humphrey-Glenn Report*.

33. The Pentagon disclosed that South Korea requested that some of its ground forces—rear-echelon units—be released from the combined United States-South Korea Command for use in crowd control and security work, which was granted by General John A. Wickam, Jr. See *The New York Times*, May 23, 1980. General Chun Doo Hwan also requisitioned front line forces under General Wickam's control, a hanging offense in any other military command structure. See *The New York Times*, June 13, 1980.

34. In early August 1980, General John Wickam, Jr., stated that "provided that he demonstrates over time a broad base of support from the Korean people and does not jeopardize the security of the situation here, we will support him because that, of course, is what we think the Korean people want." This state came while Ch'oe Kyu-ha was still the Acting President. *The New York Times*, August 3, 1980.

35. At the meeting, Richard Holbrooke cautioned Muskie against condemning the generals, arguing that information on the political thinking of the military leaders in Korea was not as "complete as the State Department would have liked," due to "so much attention to Kwangjoo" at the cost of "broader questions," which are "left unanswered." *The New York Times*, May 29, 1980; Holbrooke soon formed and headed a high level interagency group to study situations in Korea. *The New York Times*, June 1, 1980.

36. For U.S. security relations with China, see Cumings, "Chinatown," pp. 210–213.

37. Hayes, "Pacific Powerkeg," ch. 11.

38. Walker, "The Future of U.S. Trans-Pacific Alliances," p. 917; also

quoted in Hayes, "Pacific Powerkeg: American Nuclear Dilemmas in Korea," ch. 4.

39. Chong-sik Lee, *Japan and Korea*, p. 106.

40. *The New York Times*, February 1, 1981; March 27, 1981; April 30, 1981; May 1, 1981; and April 29, 1981.

41. *The New York Times*, May 5, 1981.

42. *The New York Times*, May 9, 1981.

43. *The New York Times*, May 9, 1981.

44. Lee, *Japan and Korea*, p. 115.

45. *The New York Times*, August 12, 1981.

46. A member of Chun Doo Hwan's brain trust told a Japanese diplomat that the new regime was "pro-American and anti-Japanese," and that the "$6 billion loan request was made in the spirit of conducting the second round of the reparation talks of 1965." In the event that Japan does not comply, he threatened, the regime "will not hesitate to expose details of collusion between the Japanese and Koreans during the Park Chung Hee era." Lee, *Japan and Korea*, p. 116. Also see Hosup Kim, "Policy Making of Japanese Official Development Assistance to the Republic of Korea, 1965–1983," p. 158.

47. Ibid., p. 118.

48. *The New York Times*, September 13, 1981.

49. Details of the aid negotiation, from both Japanese and Korean sides, are contained in Hosup Kim, "Policy Making of Japanese Official Development Assistance to the Republic of Korea, 1965–1983."

50. John Moore, Jr., the chairman of the U.S. EXIM Bank arrived in Korea in June to discuss the Korean request for an additional $630 million in EXIM loans to cover fourteen projects. Richard Holbrook gave a personal clearance for this travel, coming so soon after the Kwangju incident. *The New York Times*, June 3, 1980.

51. *Euromoney*, July 1980, pp. 107–108.

52. For the Kishi visit, see *The Korea Herald*, September 2, 1980; for the Rockefeller and Spenser visit, *The New York Times*, September 22, 1980; for competition among foreign banks for Korean market, see *The Wall Street Journal*, March 20, 1981.

53. Byung-Sun Choi, "Institutionalizing Liberal Economic Order in Korea," p. 327.

54. Westphal and Kim, "Industrial Policy and Development," quoted in The World Bank, *Korea: Managing the Industrial Transition*, p. 58.

55. The proportion of iron and steel products on the restricted list jumped from 28 percent in 1967 to 75 percent in 1978 (on an items basis) and from 35 percent to 91 percent (on a value basis.) Similar patterns were discernible in petrochemicals and machinery, which nearly doubled from 34 percent to 61 percent between 1968 to 1978. Ibid., p. 59.

56. Ibid., pp. 68–77.

57. *Business Korea*, June 1989, p. 14.

58. *Business Korea,* October 1986, p. 25.

59. Foxley, *Latin American Experiments in Neo-Conservative Economics,* ch. 1–2.

60. See Corbo and de Melo, "Liberalization with Stabilization in the Southern Cone of Latin America: Overview and Summary"; Diaz-Alejandro, "Good-Bye Financial Repression and Hello Financial Crash"; Glavez and Tybout, "Microeconomic Adjustment in Chile during 1977–1981."

61. For the cause of the failure of the financial liberalization attempt in Chile and Argentina, see McKinnon, "The Order of Economic Liberalization," p. 159–186; The World Bank, *Korea: Managing the Industrial Transition,* 2: 82–83.

62. Ronald McKinnon, for example, hopothesizes that control over public finances is a necessary condition before trade can be liberalized, and should be followed by liberalization of domestic market, and only then, by removal of exchange controls on the capital account of the balance of payment. McKinnon, "The Order of Economic Liberalization," pp. 159–186. On the other hand, if the lessons of Chile and Argentina were that the government had a "credibility problem," one would argue for a blitzkrieg in liberalization attempts. See Stockman, "Comment," pp. 187–192. Also see McKinnon, "Reply to Stockman," pp. 193–198; Frenkel, "A Comment," pp. 199–202. They all appear in Brunner, ed., *Economic Policy in a World of Change.*

63. This was so as of 1983. For the backgrounds of economic technocrats in the Fifth Republic, see 'Che 5 kongwhakuk ûi p'awô eritûdûl," [Power Elites in the Fifth Republic] *Shindonga,* October 1983 and November 1983; "Sowi sôganghakpa kyôngje kanryo ûi kwao," [Errors of The Sogang School Economic Bureaucrats] *Shindonga,* August 1985; "Hanguk ûi kisulgwallyo," [Korea's Technocrats] *Ikonomistû,* April, 1984.

64. This was particularly true of men like T'ae Wansôn, Kim Yongju, and Chang Ki-yông. See Moskowitz, "Current Assets," pp. 356–372.

65. Chun Doo Hwan, *The 1980s: Meeting a New Challenge, Selected Speeches,* p. 7; *Maeil kyôngje shinmun,* March 25, 1985.

66. *The New York Times,* April 14, 1980.

67. *Maeil kyôngje shinmun,* March 15, 1985.

68. *Business Korea,* June 1984, p. 35.

69. Ibid.

70. For details of American pressure to open the insurance market, see *Busines Korea,* October 1985, pp. 27–33.

71. Cho, "Liberalization of Korea's Financial Market in the 1980s," p. 30. The writing of insurance other than life insurance has been partially open to foreign participation since 1968.

72. The most famous among these funds are the Korea Fund, which issues equity shares to American and other foreign investors to finance

the purchase of Korean stocks and is listed on the New York Stock Exchange, and the Korea-Europe Fund, based in London for European investors.

73. See Loriaux, "States and Markets."

74. Galvez and Tybout, "Microeconomic Adjustment in Chile During 1977–1981.

75. *Maeil kyôngje shinmun*, March 25, 1985.

76. Business groups with loans outstanding over a certain ceiling, encompassing 1,217 firms owned by the thirty to forty largest chaebôl groups, were ordered to sell their nonbusiness-related landholdings to improve their financial structure. The twenty largest chaebôl groups were also required to streamline their business and concentrate on what they do best. *Donga ilbo*, October 25, 1980.

77. *Maeil kyôngje shinmun*, February 12, 1985.

78. Cho and Cole, "The Role of The Financial Sector in Korea's Structural Adjustment."

79. Cho, "Liberalization of Korea's Financial Market in the 1980s," pp. 9–10.

80. The figures are from the Ministry of Finance, *Fiscal and Financial Statistics*, Korea, quoted in Cho, p. 13.

81. *Maeil kyôngje shinmun*, February 21, 1985.

82. Dues and fees include those paid out to various business associations, the Red Cross, and a multitude of state-sponsored efforts to promote exports, job training, road pavement, safe traffic, thrifty habits, etc; various user fees; and medical and fire insurance. Social corporate expenditures do not go for local development, as might be expected from the Japanese practice, but to employee relations. "Contributions" include those for victims of flood and other natural disasters, and to the *saemaûl* (new village) movement, the Red Cross, national defense, the Korean equivalent of the USO, anti-communist leagues, welfare organizations, sports organizations, sports-related funds, education-related funds, subway construction, etc. About forty different activities appear under the category, "contributions." *Donga ilbo*, October 22, 1984.

83. Ibid.

84. *Maeil kyôngje shinmun*, March 11, 1985.

85. *Chosun ilbo*, November 12, 1988.

86. There were allegations that Daelim received financing for taking over five bankrupt firms as a quid-pro-quo for its political contributions and construction of a presidential villa; that the Shindonga group was allowed to take over Chônnam University as a result of contributing to the Ilhae Foundation; Poongsan was said to have been repaid for the same endeavor with the right to issue coins for the Asian Games and the 1988 Olympics, etc. *Chosun ilbo*, November 12, 1988.

87. *Chosun ilbo*, November 10, 1988.

88. *Donga ilbo*, March 9, 1985.

89. *Maeil kyôngje shinmun*, March 1, 1985; March 9, 1985.

90. *Maeil kyôngje shinmun*, April 15, 1985.
91. *The Wall Street Journal*, January 27, 1989; *The New York Times*, April 30, 1990.
92. *Donga ilbo*, April 25, 1985.
93. *Chosun ilbo*, November 2, 1988 and December 19, 1988.

Bibliography

Public Records: Unpublished

Dwight D. Eisenhower Presidential Library, Abilene, Kansas.

 Eisenhower Papers (Ann Whitman File), 1953–1961: (Series) Administrative, Cabinet, Diary, Dulles-Herter Series, International, Name, NSC.

 White House Office Papers, 1948–1961: (Series) NSC, OCB.

 Council on Foreign Economic Policy File: (Series) CFEP Papers, Dodge, Office, OCB, Randall, Special Studies.

 Oral History

Lyndon B. Johnson Presidential Library, Austin, Texas.

 White House Central File: Executive File, Confidential File.

 National Security File: Agency File, McGeorge Bundy Papers, Country File, Administrative Histories, Memos to President, Name File, National Intelligence Estimates, NSC Histories, NSC Meetings, Rostow Papers, Vice President Security File.

 Oral History

John F. Kennedy Presidential Library, Boston, Massachusetts.
White House Central File
National Security File

Public Records: Published

Kyôngje kihoekwôn. *Kyôngje paeksô* [White Paper on the ROK Economy]. Seoul: EPF, 1985.

—— *Woechae paeksô* [White Paper on Foreign Debt]. Seoul: EPB, 1985.

—— *Hanguk ûi sahoe chipyo* [The ROK Social Indicators]. Seoul: EPB, 1987.

—— [ROK Economic Planning Board]. "The Korean Economy: Current Reforms and Future Prospects." Seoul: EPB, 1980.

Namchosôn kwado chôngbu, *Chosôn. chongge nyônggam* [The Political Yearbook of Chosen]; Seoul: Namchosôn kwado chôngbu, 1948.

Pauley, Edwin. *Report to President Truman.* Washington, D.C.: GPO, 1946.

Taehan sanggong hoeûiso. *Kûmyung sijang ûi kukjewha wa hanguk kyôngje* [The Internationalization of the Capital Market and Korean Economy]. Seoul: Taehan sanggong hoeûiso hanguk kyôngje yônggu senta, 1977.

—— *Wôlnam hyujôn kwa hanguk kyôngje* [The Truce in Vietnam and the ROK Economy]. Seoul: Taehan sanggong hoeûiso hanguk kyôngje yônggu senta, 1969.

—— *Iljunggong kyôngje hyôpryôk kwa hanguk kyôngje.* [Sino-Japanese Economic Cooperation and the ROK Economy]. Seoul: Taehan sanggong hoeûiso hanguk kyôngje yônggu senta, 1979.

—— *Suchul chiiwôn kûmyung ûi hyûnwhang mit munjejôm* [Current Situation and Problems in Export Subsidy Policy]. Seoul: Taehan sanggong hoeûiso hanguk kyôngje yônggu senta, 1977.

United States Department of State. *Foreign Relations of the United States: 1949,* vol. 7. Washington, D.C.: GPO.

—— *Foreign Relations of the United States: 1950,* vol. 7. Washington, D.C.: GPO.

—— *Foreign Relations of the United States,* 1952–1954, vol. 15. Washington, D.C.: GPO.

—— [author: David Steinberg] "Korean Development: Aid or *Sui Generis?"* Washington, D.C.: GPO

United States General Accounting Office. *Report to the Congress: US Assistance for the Economic Development of the Republic of Korea.* Washington, D.C.: GPO, 1973.

United States House of Representatives, The Committee on Foreign Affairs. *The United States and Multilateral Development Banks.* 93d Congress, 2d sess. Washington, D.C.: GPO, 1974.

—— The Subcommittee on International Organizations of the Committee on International Relations. *Investigation of Korean-American Relations.* Oct. 31, 1978. Washington, D.C.: GPO, 1978.

——*Hearings before the Subcommittee on International Organizations of the Committee on International Relations.* 95th Congress, part 6. Washington, D.C.: GPO, 1978.

——Subcommittee on Asian and Pacific Affairs of the Committee on Foreign Affairs. *Economic Issues Between the United States, Japan, and South Korea.* Washington, D.C.: GPO. Printing Office.

——The Committee on the Armed Forces. *Impact of Intelligence Reassessment on Withdrawl of US Troops from Korea.* Washington, D.C:: GPO.

——The Committee on the Armed Services. *Review of the Policy Decision to Withdraw United States Ground Forces from Korea.* Washington, D.C.: GPO, 1977.

United States Senate, Committee on Foreign Relations. *US Troop Withdrawal from the Republic of Korea: a Report to the Committee on Foreign Relations by Senators Hubert Humphrey and John Glenn.* Washington, D.C.: GPO, 1978.

——Committee on Foreign Relations (Historical Series). Economic Assistance to China and Korea: 1949–1950. Washington, D.C.: GPO, 1974.

——Committee on Foreign Relations. *First and Second Sessions on S. 1063, S. 2319, S. 2845.* Washington, D.C.: GPO, 1950.

Wedemeyer, A. C. *Report to the President.* Washington, D.C.: GPO, 1951.

The World Bank. *Current Economic Position and Prospects of the Republic of Korea.* (2 vols.) Report no. 332-KO. February 20, 1974. Washington, D.C.: The World Bank, 1974.

——*Current Economic Position and Prospects of the Republic of Korea.* Report no. 768-KO, May 28, 1975. Washington, D.C.: The World Bank, 1975.

——*Current Economic Position and Prospects of the Republic of Korea.* Report no. 1490-KO, Feb 23, 1977. Washington, D.C.: The World Bank, 1977.

——*Growth and Prospects of the Korean Economy.* Report no. 1489-KO, February 23, 1977. Washington, D.C.: The World Bank, 1977.

——*Korea: Adjusting to a New World Environment.* Report no. 3885-KO, June 1, 1982. Washington, D.C.: The World Bank, 1982.

——*Korea: Managing the Industrial Transition.* (2 vols.) Washington, D.C.: The World Bank, 1986.

——*Korea: Rapid Growth and Search for New Perspective.* Report no. 2477-KO. Washington, D.C.: The World Bank, 1979.

——*Korea's Development in a Global Context.* Report no. 5102-KO, June 1984. Washington, D.C.: The World Bank, 1984.

——*World Development Report.* Report no. 7682. Washington, D.C.: The World Bank, 1989.

Books and Articles in English

Adelman, Irma, ed. *Practical Approaches to Development Planning.* Baltimore: Johns Hopkins University Press, 1969.

Aghevli, Bijan and Jorge Marquez-Ruarte. "A Case of Successful Adjustment: Korea, 1980–1984." IMF Occasional Paper, June 1985.

Ahn, Kyung-sihk. "Inflation in Open Economies: A Comparison Study of Korea and Taiwan." Ph.D. diss., University of Oregon, 1982.

Almond, Gabriel. "The Development of Political Power." In S. P. Huntington and Myron Weiner, eds., *Understanding Political Development.* Boston: Little, Brown, 1987.

American Chamber of Commerce in Korea. "A Presentation of National Treatment Issues Affecting American Bank Branches in Korea." December 1, 1983.

Ames, Barry. *Political Survival: Politicians and Public Policy in Latin America.* Berkeley: University of California Press, 1987.

Amsden, Alice. *Asia's Next Giant: South Korea and Late Industrialization.* New York: Cambridge University Press, 1989.

Amsden, Alice. "Growth and Stabilization in Korea, 1962–1984." Paper for the Project on Stabilization and Adjustment, United Nations University, Helsinki, August 19–21, 1986.

Amsden, Alice. "Taiwan's Economic History: A Case of Estatisme and a Challenge to Dependency Theory." *Modern China* (1979), 5(3): 341–379.

Anderson, Perry. *The Lineages of the Absolutist State.* London: New Left Books, 1979.

Araki, Mitsutaro. *Financial System in Japan.* New York: Institute of Pacific Relations, 1933.

Aronson, Jonathan. *Money and Power: Banks and the World Monetary System.* Beverly Hills: Sage, 1977.

Asiatic Research Center and Hudson Institute. *International Conference on Korean Futures.* Seoul: Korea University Press, 1975.

Bae, Kyung-il. "Small Business and Small Business Financing in Korea." Ph.D. diss., Cornell University, 1987.

Balassa, Bela. "Export Incentives and Export Performance in Developing Countries." *Weltwirtschaftliches Archiv* (1978), 114(1): 24–61.

Baldwin, Frank. "America's Rented Troops: South Koreans in Vietnam." *Bulletin of Concerned Asian Scholars* (1975), 7(4): 33–40.

Bank of Chosen. *Economic History of Manchuria.* Seoul: Bank of Chosen, 1920.

Barnet, Richard. *The Alliance.* New York: Simon & Schuster, 1983.

Barrett, Richard E. "Autonomy and Diversity in the American State on Taiwan in the Late 1940s." In E. Winckler and S. Greenhalgh, eds., *Contenting Approaches to the Political Economy of Taiwan.* Armonk, N.Y.: M. E. Sharpe, 1989.

Barrett, Richard E. "State and Economy on Taiwan, 1960–1980." Paper (no date).

Beasley, W. G. *Japanese Imperialism, 1894–1945*. Oxford: Clarendon Press, 1987.

Barrett, Richard E. "Autonomy and Diversity in the American State on Taiwan in the Late 1940s." In E. Winckler and S. Greenhalgh, eds., *Contenting Approaches to the Political Economy of Taiwan*. Armonk, N.Y.: M. E. Sharpe, 1989.

Becker, David. *The New Bourgeoisie and the Limits of Dependency: Mining, Class, and Power in "Revolutionary" Peru*. Princeton: Princeton University Press, 1983.

Becker, David, ed. *Post-imperialism: International Capitalism and Development in the Late 20th Century*. Boulder: L. Rienner, 1987.

Bennett, Douglas C. and Kenneth Sharp. "The World Automobile Industry and Its Implications." In Richard Newfarmer, ed., *Profits, Progress, and Poverty*. Notre Dame, Ind.: University of Notre Dame Press, 1985.

Bargsten, C. Fred. "The Threat from the Third World." *Foreign Policy* (1973), 1973(11): 102–124.

Bix, Herbert. "Japanese Imperialism and the Manchurian Economy, 1900–1931." *China Quarterly* (1972), 51(4): 425–443.

Block, Fred. *The Origins of International Economic Disorder*. Los Angeles: University of California Press, 1977.

Block, Fred and Margaret R. Somers. "Beyond the Economistic Fallacy: the Holistic Social Science of Karl Polanyi." In Theda Skocpol, ed., *Vision and Method in Historical Sociology*. Cambridge: Cambridge University Press, 1986.

Bloomfield, Arthur and John Jensen. *Banking Reform in South Korea*. New York: Federal Reserve Bank of New York, March 1951.

Borden, William. *The Pacific Alliance: the United States Foreign Policy and Japanese Trade Recovery, 1947–1955*. Madison: University of Wisconsin Press, 1984.

Bornschier, Volker. "Dependent Industrialization in the World Economy." *Journal of Conflict Resolution* (1981), 25(3): 371–400.

Bornstein, Stephen et al. *The State in Capitalist Europe: A Casebook*. London: G. Allen and Unwin, 1984.

Browning, E. S. "East Asia in Search of a Second Economic Miracle." *Foreign Affairs* (1981), 60(1): 123–147.

Bruneau, Thomas C. and Phillippe Faucher, eds. *Authoritarian Capitalism: Brazil's Contemporary Economic and Political Development*. Boulder, Colo.: Westview Press, 1981.

Brunner, Karl. *Economic Policy in a World of Change*. Amsterdam: North-Holland, 1982.

Buchanan, James M., Robert D. Tollison, and Gordon Tullock, eds. *Toward a Theory of the Rent-Seeking Society*. College Station: Texas A & M University Press, 1980.

Buchanan, James. "Rent-Seeking and Profit Seeking." In James Buchanan, ed., *Toward a Theory of the Rent Seeking Society.* College Station: Texas A & M Press, 1980.

Calder, Kent E. and Roy Hofheinz Jr. *The Eastasia Edge.* New York: Basic Books, 1982.

Caldwell, J. Alexander, "The Financial System in Taiwan." *Asian Survey,* (1976) 16(8): 729–751.

Calleo, David. *The Imperious Economy.* Cambridge: Harvard University Press, 1982.

Calleo, David, ed. *Money and the Coming World Order.* New York: New York University Press, 1976.

Cameron, Rondo et al. *Banking in the Early Stages of Industrialization.* London: Oxford University Press, 1967.

Cameron, Rondo, ed. *Banking and Economic Development.* London: Oxford University Press, 1972.

Campbell, D. C. and C. S. Ahn. "Kyes and Mujins: Financial Intermediation in South Korea." *Economic Development and Culltural Change* (1962), 11(1): 55–68.

Canak, William L. "The Peripheral State Debate: Bureaucratic Authoritarianism and State Capitalism." *Latin American Resarch Review* (1983), 19(1): 3–36.

Carbo, Vittorio and Sang Woo Nam. "The Recent Macroeconomic Evolution of the Republic of Korea: an Overview." Paper for the World Bank (June 1985).

Cardoso, F. H. "The Consumption of Dependency Theory in the United States." *Latin American Resarch Review* (1977), 12(3): 7–24.

Cardoso, F. H. "Entreprenuers and the Transition Process, the Brazilian Case." In Guilldermo O'Donnell, Philippe C. Schmitter, and Laurence Whitehead, eds., *Transitions from Authoritarian Rule: Comparative Perspectives.* Baltimore: Johns Hopkins University Press, 1986.

Carnoy, Martin. *The State and Political Theory.* Princeton: Princeton University Press, 1984.

Carr, E. H. *Nationalism and After.* London: Macmillan, 1945.

Chandler, Alfred D. "The United States: Seedbed of Managerial Capitalism." In Alfred D. Chandler and Herman Deems, eds., *Managerial Hierarchies: Comparative Perspectives on the Rise of the Modern Industrial Empire.* Cambridge: Harvard University Press, 1980.

Chang Dal-joong. *Economic Control and Political Authoritarianism.* Seoul: Sogang University Press, 1986.

Chang Dal-joong. "Japanese Corporations and the Political Economy of South Korean-Japanese Relations, 1965–1979." Ph.D. diss., University of California at Berkeley, 1982.

Chang, Han-yu and Ramon Myers, "Japanese Colonial Development Policy in Taiwan, 1895–1906: a Case of Bureaucratic Entreprenuership." *Journal of Asian Studies* (August 1963), vol. 22.

Chase-Dunn, Christopher K. "A World System Perspective on Dependency and Development in Latin America," *Latin American Research Review* (1982), 17(1): 166–177.

Cheilŭnhaeng, *History of the First City Bank of Korea*. Seoul: Cheilŭnhaeng, 1964.

Cheng, Hang-sheng, "Alternative Balance of Payments Adjustment Experiences in Korea and Taiwan, 1973–1977." *Economic Review* [The Federal Reserve Board of San Francisco] (Summer 1978).

Cheng, Tu-jen. "Sequencing and Implementing Development Strategies: Korea and Taiwan." Paper presented for a conference on developmental strategies in Lain America and East Asia. Center for United States-Mexican Studies, University of California at San Diego, May 4–6, 1986.

Cheng, Tu-jen and Stephen Haggard. *Newly Industrializing Asia in Transition*. Berkeley: Institute of International Studies, 1987.

Cheng, Tu-jen and Stephan Haggard. "The Politics of Adjustment in the East Asian Newly Industrializing Countries." Paper (no date).

Cho, Yoonje. "Financial Repression, Efficiency of Capital Allocation, and Economic Concentration: the Case of Korea and Taiwan." Paper for the World Bank (June 1985).

Cho, Yoonje."Liberalization of Korea's Financial Market in the 1980s." Paper Presented at the East Rock Institute Conference on Dynamics of United State–Korea Trade Relations, Yale University, November 10–12, 1988.

Cho, Yoonje. "The Role of Finance in Industrial Performance." Paper for the World Bank (January 1986).

Cho, Yoonje and David Cole. "The Role of the Financial Sector in Korea's Structural Adjustment." Paper for the World Bank (no date).

Chohŭng ŭnhaeng. *The History of the Bank*. Seoul: Chohŭng ŭnhaeng, 1965.

Choi, Sung. "Asian Development Bank." Paper (May 1989).

Choi Byung-Sun. "Institutionalizing a Liberal Economic Order in Korea: The Strategic Management of Economic Change." Ph.D. diss., Harvard University, 1987.

Choi, Jangjip. "Interest Conflict and Political Control in South Korea: A Case Study of the Labor Unions in Manufacturing Industries, 1961–1980." Ph.D. diss., University of Chicago, 1983.

Chu, Yun-han. "Authoritarian Regimes Under Stress: the Political Economy of Adjustment in the East Asian Newly Industrialized Countries." Ph.D. diss., University of Minnesota, 1987.

Cohen, Benjamin. "High Finance and High Politics." In R. Feinberg and V. Kallab, eds., *Uncertain Future: Commercial Banks and the Third World*. Washington, D.C.: Overseas Development Council, 1984.

Cohen, Benjamin. *In Whose Interest?: International Banking and American Foreign Policy*. New Haven: Yale University Press, 1986.

Cohen, Jerome. *Japan's Economy in War and Reconstruction*. Minneapolis: University of Minnesota Press, 1949.

Cohen, Jerome. "Arms Sales and Human Rights: The Case of South Korea." In Peter Brown and Douglas MacLean, eds., *Human Rights and US Foreign Policy.* Lexington, Mass.: Lexington Books, 1979.

Colander, David, ed. *Neoclassical Political Economy: The Analysis of Rent-Seeking and DUP activities.* Cambridge, Mass.: Ballinger, 1984.

Cole, David and Young Chul Park. *Financial Development in Korea, 1945–1978.* Cambridge: Harvard University Press, 1979.

Cole, David and Princeton Lyman. *Korean Development: The Interplay of Politics and Economics.* Cambridge: Harvard University Press, 1971.

Cole, David, Youngil Lim, and Paul Kuznets. *The Korean Economy: Issues of Development.* Berkeley: University of California Press, 1980.

Cole, David and Young Woo Nam. "The Pattern and Significance of Economic Planning in Korea." In Irma Adelman, ed., *Practical Approaches to Development Planning.* Balitmore: Johns Hopkins University Press, 1969.

Collier, David, ed. *The New Authoritarianism in Latin America.* Princeton: Princeton University Press, 1979.

Corbo, Vittorio, Anne Krueger, and Fernando Ossa, eds. *Export-Oriented Development Strategies: The Success of Five Newly Industrializing Countries.* Boulder, Col.: Westview, 1985.

Corbo, Vittorio and Jamie de Melo. "Liberalization with Stabilization in the Southern Cone of Latin America: Overview and Summary." *World Development* (1985), (13)8: 863–866.

Crisp, Olga. "Russia, 1860–1914." In Rondo Cameron, ed., *Banking in the Early Stages of Industrialization.* New York: Oxford University Press, 1967.

Cumings, Bruce. "The Abortive Abertura: Korean Democratization in the Light of Latin American Experience." Paper Presented at the Annual Meeting of the Latin American Studies Association, New Orleans, 1988.

Cumings, Bruce, ed. *Child of Conflict: The Korean-American Relationship, 1943–1953.* Seattle: University of Washington Press, 1983.

Cumings, Bruce. "Chinatown: Foreign Policy and Elite Realignment." In Thomas Ferguson and Joel Rogers, eds., *The Hidden Election: The Politics and Economics in the 1980 Presidential Campaign.* New York: Pantheon, 1981.

Cumings, Bruce. "Ending the Cold War in Korea." *World Policy Journal* (Summer 1984), 1(4): 1–45.

Cumings, Bruce. "The Origins and Development of the Northeast Asian Political Economy: Industrial Sectors, Product Cycles and Political Consequences." *International Organization* (Winter 1984), 38(1): 1–40.

Cumings, Bruce. *The Origins of the Korean War: Liberation and the Emergence of Separate Regimes, 1945–1947.* Princeton: Princeton University Press, 1979.

Cumings, Bruce. *The Origins of the Korean War: The Roaring of the Cataract.* Princeton: Princeton University Press, 1990.

Curtis, Gerald. *The Japanese Way of Politics.* New York: Columbia University Press, 1988.

Curtis, Gerald. "Big Business and Political Influence." In Ezra Vogel, ed., *Modern Japanese Organization and Decision-Making.* Berkeley: University of California Press, 1975.

Davis, Winston. "Religion and Development: Weber and the East Asian Experience." In Myron Weiner and Samuel Huntington, eds., *Understanding Political Development.* Boston: Little, Brown, 1984.

Dearlove, John. "Economists on the State." *IDS Bulletin* (1987), 18(13): 5–11.

de Castro Andrade, Regis, "The Economics of Underdevelopment, the State and Politics in ECLA's Doctrine, 1949–1964." Occasional Paper no. 29, Institute of Latin American Studies, University of Glasgow, 1979.

Deyo, Fred., ed. *The Political Economy of the New Asian Industrialism.* Ithaca: Cornell University Press, 1987.

Diaz-Alejandro, Carlos. "Good-bye Financial Repression, Hello Financial Crash." *Journal of Development Economics* (1985), 19(1–2): 1–24.

Diaz-Alejandro, Carlos. "Southern Cone Stabilization Plans." In William Cline and S. Weintraub, eds., *Economic Stabilization in Developing Countries.* Washington, D.C.: Brookings 1981.

Diaz-Alejandro, Carlos. "Open Economy, Closed Polity?" In Diana Tussie, ed., *Latin America in the World Economy: New Perspective.* London: Gower, 1983.

Dore, Ronald. *Taking Japan Seriously: A Confucian Perspective on Leading Economic Issues.* Stanford: Stanford University Press, 1987.

Dower, John. *Empire and Aftermath: Yoshida Shigeru and the Japanese Experience, 1878–1954.* Cambridge: Harvard University Press, 1979.

Duus, Peter. "Economic Dimensions of Meiji Imperialism: the Case of Korea, 1895–1910." In R. Meyers and M. Peattie, eds., *The Japanese Colonial Empire, 1895–1945.* Princeton: Princeton University Press, 1984.

Duvall, Raymond and John R. Freeman. "The Techno-Bureaucratic Elite and the Entrepreneurial State in Dependent Industrialization." *American Political Science Review* (1983), 77(3): 569–587.

Eckert, Carter. "The Origins of Korean Capitalism: the Koch'ang Kims and the Kyongsong Spinning and Weaving Company, 1876–1945." Ph.D. diss., University of Washington, 1986.

Enos, John. "Government Intervention in the Transfer of Technology: the Case of South Korea." *IDS Bulletin* (1984), 15(2): 26–31.

Epstein, Gerald. "Domestic Stagflation and Monetary Policy: The Federal Reserve and the Hidden Election." In Tom Ferguson, ed., *The Hidden Election*. New York: Pantheon Books, 1981.

Evans, Peter. *Dependent Development: The Alliance of Multinational, State, and Local Capital in Brazil*. Princeton: Princeton University Press, 1979.

Evans, Peter. "Reinventing the Bourgeoisie: State Entrepreneurship and Class Formation in Dependent Capitalist Development." *American Journal of Sociology* (1982), 88 (supplement): 210–247.

Evans, Peter. "State, Capital, and the Transformation of Dependence: The Brazilian Computer Case." *World Development* (1986), 14(7): 791–808.

Evans, Peter, Theda Skocpol, and Dietrich Rueschemeyer, eds. *Bringing the State Back In*. London: Cambridge University Press, 1985.

Fagen, Richard, ed. *Capitalism and the State in the United States-Latin American Relations*. Stanford: Stanford University Press, 1979.

Fei, John C. H., Kazushi Ohkawa, and Gustav Ranis. "Economic Development in Historical Perspective: Japan, Korea, and Taiwan." In Ohkawa Kazushi, Gustav Ranis, and Larry Meissner, eds., *Japan and the Developing Countries*. New York: Basil Blackwell, 1985.

Feinberg, Richard and V. Kallab, eds. *Uncertain Future: Commercial Banks and the Third World*. Washington, D.C.: Overseas Development Council, 1986.

Felix, David. "Alternative Outcomes of the Latin American Debt Crisis: Lessons from the Past." *Latin American Research Review* (1987), 22(2): 3–46.

Ferguson, Thomas and Joel Rogers, eds. *The Hiden Election*. New York: Pantheon Boks, 1982.

First City Bank of Korea. *A History of the First City Bank of Korea*. Seoul: Kwangmyong, 1969.

Fitzgerald, E. V. K. *The State and Economic Development: Peru Since 1968*. Cambridge: Cambridge University Press, 1976.

Fitzgerald, E. V. K. "The Limitations of State Capitalism as a Model of Economic Development: Peru 1968–1978." The Wilson Center Latin American Program Working Papers, no. 27.

Fitzgerald, E. V. K. "The Fiscal Deficit and Development Finance: a Note on the Accumulation Balance in Mexico." The Centre of Latin American Studies Series, no. 35, Cambridge University.

Fitzgerald, E. V. K. "The State and the Management of Accumulation in the Periphery." In Diana Tussie, ed., *Latin America in the World Economy*. New York: St. Martin's Press, 1983.

Foster-Carter, Aidan. "Standing Up: the Two Korean States and the Dependency Debate—a Bipartisan Approach." Paper presented at the Conference on the Dependency Issue in Korean Development, June 5–9, 1985, Seoul.

Foxley, Alejandro. *Latin American Experiments in Neo-Conservative Economics*. Berkeley: University of California Press, 1983.

Frank, André Gunder. "The Unequal and Uneven Historical Development of the World Economy." *Contemporary Marxism* (Fall 1984), vol. 9.

Frank, Charles, Kwang Suk Kim, and Larry E. Westphal. *Foreign Trade Regimes and Economic Development: South Korea.* New York: National Bureau of Economic Research, 1975.

Fransman, Martin. "Explaining the Success of the Asian NICs: Incentives and Technology." *IDS Bulletin* (1984), 15(2): 50–56.

Frenkel, Roberto and Guillermo O'Donnell. "The 'Stabilization Programs' of the International Monetary Fund and Their Impacts during Bureaucratic Authoritarian Periods." In Richard Fagen, ed., *Capitalism and the State in US-Latin American Relations.* Stanford: Stanford University Press, 1979.

Frieden, Jeff. "The Brazilian Borrowing Experience." *Latin American Research Review* (1987), 22(2): 95–131.

Frieden, Jeff. "Classes, Sectors, and Foreign Debt in Latin America." *Comparative Politics* (1988), 21(1): 1–20.

Frieden, Jeff. "Third World Indebted Industrialization: International Finance and State Capitalism in Mexico, Brazil, Algeria, and South Korea." *International Organizations* (1981), 35(3): 407–431.

Friedman, David. *The Misunderstood Miracle: Industrial Development and Political Change in Japan.* Ithaca: Cornell University Press, 1988.

Friedman, Milton. *A Program for Monetary Stability.* New York: Fordham University Press, 1959.

Fry, Maxwell. "Financial Structure, Monetary Policy, and Economic Growth in Hong Kong, Singapore, Taiwan, and South Korea, 1960–1983." In Vittorio Corbo, Anne Krueger, and Fernando Ossa, eds., *Export-Oriented Development Strategies.* Boulder, Col.: Westview, 1985.

Fry, Maxwell, Jr. "Money and Capital or Financial Deepening in Economic Development?" *Journal of Money, Credit, and Banking* (1978), 10(4): 464–475.

Galbis, Vincente. "Financial Intermediation and Economic Growth in Less Developed Countries." *Journal of Development Studies* (1977), 13(2): 58–72.

Galbis, Vincente. "Inflation and Interest Rate Policies in Latin America, 1967–1976." *International Monetary Fund Staff papers* (1979), 26(2): 334–366.

Galenson, Walter, ed. *Economic Growth and Structural Change in Taiwan: The Postwar Experience fo the ROC.* Ithaca: Cornell University Press, 1979.

Galvez, Julio and James Tybout. "Microeconomic Adjustments in Chile during 1977–1981: The Importance of Being a Grupo." *World Development* (1985), 13(8): 969–994.

Gardner, Lloyd. "Commentary." In Bruce Cumings, ed., *Child of Con-*

flict: The Korean-American Relationship, 1943–1953. Seattle: University of Washington Press, 1983.

Gerschenkron, Alexander. *Economic Backwardness in Historical Perspective*. Cambridge: Harvard University Press, 1946.

Gerschenkron, Alexander. *An Economic Development That Failed: Four Lectures in Austrian History*. Princeton: Princeton University Press, 1977.

Gilbert, Stephen. *Northeast Asia in U.S. Foreign Policy*. Beverly Hills: Sage, 1979.

Gilpin, Robert. *The Political Economy of International Relations*. Princeton: Princeton University Press, 1987.

Gilpin, Robert. *U.S. Power and the Multinational Corporation: The Political Economy of Foreign Direct Investment*. New York: Basic Books, 1975.

Gold, Thomas. "Colonial Origins of Taiwanese Capitalism." In Edwin Wickler and Susan Greenhalgh, eds., *Contending Approaches to the Political Economy of Taiwan*. Armonk, N.Y.: M. E. Sharpe, 1988.

Gold, Thomas. "Entrepreneurs, State, and Multinationals in Taiwan." In Edwin Wickler and Susan Greenhalgh, eds., *Contending Approaches to the Political Economy of Taiwan*. Armonk, N.Y.: M. E. Sharpe, 1988.

Gold, Thomas. *State and Society in the Taiwan Miracle*. Armonk: M. E. Sharpe, 1986.

Gold, Thomas. "Dependent Development in Taiwan." Ph.D. diss., Harvard University, 1981.

Goldsmith, Raymond W. *Financial Structure and Development*. New Haven: Yale University Press, 1969.

Gourevitch, Peter. "The Second Image Reversed: the International Source of Domestic Politics." *International Organization* (1978), 32(4): 881–911.

Grajdanzev, Andrew. "Korea Under Changing Orders." *Far Eastern Survey* (1939), 8(25): 291–297.

Grajdanzev, Andrew. *Modern Korea*. New York: John Day, 1944.

Granovetter, Mark. "Economic Action and Social Structure: The Problems of Embeddedness." *American Journal of Sociology* (1985), 91(3): 481–510.

Greider, William. *Secrets of the Temple*. New York: Simon and Schuster, 1987.

Gurley, John. *The Financial Structure of Korea: Preliminary Draft*. Seoul: USOM/Korea, 1965.

Haggard, Stephan. "The Institutional Foundations of Hegemony: Explaining the Reciprocal Trade Agreements Act of 1974." *International Organization* (1988), 42(1): 91-119.

Haggard, Stephan. "The Newly Industrializing Countries in the International System," *World Politics* (1986), 38(2): 343–370.

Haggard, Stephan. "Pathways from the Periphery: the Newly Industrializing Countries in the International System." Ph.D. diss., University of California at Berkeley, 1983.

Haggard, Stephan and Chung-in Moon. "Industrial Change and State Power: The Politics of Stabilization and Structural Adjustment in Korea." Paper presented at the American Political Science Association Meeting in Washington, D.C., August 27–August 31, 1986.

Haggard, Stephan and Chung-in Moon. "The South Korean State in the International Economy: Liberal, Dependent, or Mercantilist?" In John Ruggie, ed., *The Antinomy of Interdependence*. New York: Columbia University Press, 1983.

Haggard, Stephan, Byung-kook Kim, and Chung-in Moon. "The Transition to Export-Led Growth in Korea, 1954–1966." Paper presented at the Conference of the Role of State in Economic Development: Republic of Korea, University of California in Los Angeles, Ausust 14–16, 1987.

Hall, Peter. *Governing the Economy: The Politics of State Intervention in Britain and France*. New York: Oxford University Press, 1986.

Hall, Peter. "Patterns of Economic Policy: An Organizational Approach." In Stephen Bornstein, ed., *The State in Capitalist Europe: A Casebook*. London: G. Allen and Unwin, 1984.

Halliday, Jonathan. *A Political History of Japanese Capitalism*. New York: Pantheon Books, 1975.

Halliday, Jonathan and Gavan McCormack. *Japanese Imperialism Today*. New York: Monthly Review Press, 1973.

Hamilton, Alexander. *On Public Credit, Commerce, and Finance*. New York: Liberal Arts Press, 1957.

Hamilton, Gary and Nicole W. Biggart. "Market, Culture, and Authority: A Comparative Analysis of Managment and Organization in the Far East." *American Journal of Sociology* (1988), 94 (Supplement): S52–S94.

Hamilton, Clive. *Capitalist Industrialization in Korea*. Boulder, Col.: Westview, 1985.

Hamilton, Clive. "Class, State, and Industrialization in South Korea." *IDS Bulletin* (1984), 15(2): 38–43.

Hanguk ûnhaeng. *Financial System in Korea*. Seoul: The Bank of Korea, 1983.

Han Sungjoo. *The Failure of Democracy in South Korea*. Berkeley: University of California Press, 1974.

Harberger, Arnold C. "The Chilean Economy in the 1970s." In Karl Brunner and Allen H. Meltzer, eds., *Economic Policy in a World of Change*. Amsterdam: North-Holland, 1982.

Hasan, Parvez. *Korea: Problems and Issues in a Rapidly Growing Economy*. Baltimore: Johns Hopkins University Press, 1976.

Hawley, James. "Interests, State Foreign Economic Policy, and the World

System: the Case of the U.S. Capital Control Program." In P. Mc-Gowen and C. Kegley, eds., *Foreign Policy and the Modern World System.* Beverly Hills: Sage, 1983.

Hayes, Peter. "Pacific Powerkeg: American Nuclear Dilemmas in Korea." Ph.D. diss., University of California at Berkeley, 1989.

Hilferding, Rudolf. *Finance Capitalism.* Boston: Routledge and Kegan Paul, 1981.

Hintze, Otto. In Felix Gilbert, ed., *The Historical Essays of Otto Hintze.* New York: Oxford University Press, 1975.

Hirsche, Joaquim. "The State Apparatus and Social Reproduction: Elements of a Theory of the Bourgeois State." In J. Holloway and Sol Picciotto, eds., *State and Capital: A Marxist Debate.* London: Edward Arnold, 1978.

Hirschman, Albert O. *A Bias for Hope—Essays on Development and Latin America.* New Haven: Yale University Press, 1971.

Hirschman, Albert O. *Foreign Aid—A Critique and a Proposal.* Essays in International Finance, no. 69, Department of Economics, Princeton University, 1968.

Hirschman, Albert O. *Journeys Toward Progress: Studies of Economic Policy Making in Latin America.* New York: 20th Century Fund, 1963.

Hirschman, Albert O. *National Power and the Structure of Foreign Trade.* Berkeley: University of California Press, 1945.

Hirschman, Albert O. "Notes on the Political Economy of Keynesianism." Paper (no date).

Hirschman, Albert O. "The Political Economy of Import-Substituting Industrialization in Latin America." *The Quarterly Journal of Economics.* (1968) 82:1–32.

Hirschman, Albert O. "The Political Economy of Latin American Development: Seven Exercises in Retrospection." Paper for the 8th International Congress of the Latin American Studies Association, Boston, October 23–25, 1986.

Hirschmeier, Johannes and Tsunehiko Yui. *The Development of Japanese Business.* Cambridge: Harvard University Press, 1975.

Ho, S. P. S. "Colonialism and Development: Korea, Taiwan, and Kwantung." In R. Meyers and M. Peattie, eds., *The Japanese Colonial Empire, 1895–1945.* Princeton: Princeton University Press, 1984.

Ho, S. P. S. "The Development of Japanese Colonial Government in Taiwan, 1895–1945." In Gustav Ranis, ed., *Government and Economic Development.* New Haven: Yale University Press,'1971.

Ho, S. P. S. "South Korea and Taiwan: Development Prospects and Problems in the 1980s." *Asian Survey* (1981), 21(12): 1175–1196.

Hong, Kittack. "Monetary Policies in Semi-Industrialized Countries: Theory and Evidence from Korea and Taiwan." Ph.D. diss., Stanford University, 1984.

Hong, Wontak. "Economic Development of Korea: Development Mechanism and Consequences." Paper presented at the Workshop on Trade and Growth in Pacific Asia, Seoul, April 16–17, 1985.

Hong, Wontak. "Import Restriction, Import Liberalization in Export-Oriented Developing Economies: the Light of Korean Experiences." Paper (no date).

Hong, Wontak and Lawrence Krause, eds. *Trade and Growth of the Advanced Developing Countries in the Pacific Basin.* Seoul: KDI Press, 1981.

Hong, Wontak and Anne Krueger, eds. *Trade Development in Korea.* Seoul: Korea Development Institute, 1975.

Hsiung, James, ed. *The Taiwan Experience, 1950–1980.* New York: Praeger, 1980.

Huntington, Samuel. *Political Order in Changing Societies.* New Haven: Yale University Press, 1968.

Huntington, Samuel. "Foreign Aid: For What and for Whom." *Foreign Policy,* 1971(1–2): 161–189.

Im, Hyug Baeg. "The Rise of Bureaucratic Authoritarianism in Korea." *World Politics* (1987), 39(2): 231–257.

Jackman, Robert. "Dependence on Foreign Investment and Economic Growth in the Third World." *World Politics* (1982), 34(2): 175–196.

Jacobs, Norman. *The Korean Road to Modernization and Development.* Chicago: University of Illinois Press, 1985.

Jacobsson, Staffan. "Industrial Policy for the Machine Tool Industries of South Korea and Taiwan." *IDS Bulletin* (1984), 15(2): 44–49.

Jacoby, Neil H. *U.S. Aid to Taiwan.* New York: Praeger, 1966.

Jansen, Marius, "Modernization and Foreign Policy in Meiji Japan." In Robert Ward, ed., *Political Development in Modern Japan.* Princeton: Princeton University Press, 1968.

Johnson, Chalmers. "East Asia: Another Year of Living Dangerously." *Foreign Affairs* (1984), 62(3): 721–746.

Johnson, Chalmers. "Introduction—the Taiwan Model." In James Hsiung, ed., *The Taiwan Experience, 1950–1980.* New York: Praeger, 1980.

Johnson, Chalmers. *MITI and the Japanese Miracle.* Berkeley: University of California Press, 1984.

Johnson, Chalmers. "Political Institutions and Economic Performance: the Government-Business relations in Japan, South Korea, and Taiwan." In Frederic Deyo, ed., *The Political Economy of the New Asian Industrialism.* Ithaca: Cornell University Press, 1987.

Jones, Homer, *Korean Financial Problems.* Seoul: USOM/Korea, 1968.

Jones, Leroy P., and Sakong, Il. *Government, Business, and Entrepreneurship in Economic Development: The Korean Case.* Cambridge: Harvard University Press, 1970.

Jones, Randall. "The Economic Development of Colonial Korea." Ph.D. diss., 1984.

Kahin, George McT. *Intervention—How America Became Involved in Vietnam.* New York: Knopf, 1986.

Kahler, Miles. "Politics and International Debt: Explaining the Crisis." *International Organization* (Summer 1985), 39(3): 357–382.

Kahler, Miles. *The Politics of International Debt.* Ithaca: Cornell University Press, 1986.

Kant, Immanuel. "Perpetual Peace." In Lewis White Beck, ed., *Kant on History.* New York: Macmillan, 1986.

Katzenstein, Peter J. *Small States in World Markets: Industrial Policy in Europe.* Ithaca: Cornell University Press, 1985.

Katzenstein, Peter J., ed. *Between Power and Plenty: Foreign Economic Policies of Advanced Industrial States.* Madison: University of Wisconsin Press, 1976.

Kaufman, Robert. "Democratic and Authoritarian Responses to the Debt Issue: Argentina, Brazil, Mexico." *International Organization* (1985), 39(3): 473–503.

Kawaguchi, Hiroshi. "Over-Loans and the Investment Behavior of Firms." *The Developing Economies* (1970), 8(4): 386–406.

Kawata, Tadashi. "The Asian Situation and Japan's Economic Relations with the Developing Asian Countries." *The Developing Economies* (1971), 9(2): 133–153.

Kennan, George F. *George F. Kennan: Memoirs, 1925–1950.* New York: Pantheon Books, 1967.

Keohane, Robert O. "The Big Influence of Small Allies" *Foreign Policy,* 1971(2): 61–182.

Kim Byông-kuk, *Central Banking Experiment in a Developing Economy.* Seoul: Korean Research Center, 1965.

Kim Chuk Kyo and Lee Chul Hee "The Growth of the Automotive Industry." In Chong Kee Park, ed., *Macroeconomic and Industrial Development in Korea.* Seoul: KDI Press, 1981.

Kim, E. Han. "Financing Korean Corporations: Evidence and Theory." In Jene K. Kwon, ed. *Korean Economic Development.* Westport, Conn.: Greenwood Press, forthcoming.

Kim, Eun Mee. "From Dominance to Symbiosis: State and the Chaebol in the Korean Economy, 1960–1985." Ph.D. diss., Brown University, 1987.

Kim, Hak-su. "Monetary Policy and Foreign Capital Inflows in a Dependent Economy: the Case of Korea." Ph.D. diss., University of South Carolina, 1977.

Kim, Hosup. "Policy Making of Japanese Official Development Assistance to the Republic of Korea, 1965–1983." Ph.D. diss., University of Michigan, 1986.

Kim, Jong-kil. "The Incentive Structure for Industrialization in a Developing Economy: The Case of Korea." Ph.D. diss., University of Connecticut, 1981.

Kim, Joungwon A. *Divided Korea: The Politics of Development, 1945–1982.* Cambridge: Harvard University Press, 1975.

Kim, Kwan-bong. *The Korea-Japan Treaty Crisis and the Instability of the Korean Political System.* New York: Preager Publishers, 1971.

Kim, Kwang Suk and Roemer, Michael. *Growth and Structural Transformation.* Cambridge: Harvard University Press, 1979.

Kim, Kyong-dong. "Political Factors in the Formation of the Entrepreneurial Elite in South Korea." *Asian Survey* (1976), 16(5): 465–477.

Kim, Myung Soo, "The Making of Korean Society: the Role of the State in the Republic of Korea." Ph.D. diss., Brown University, 1987.

Kim, Se-jin. *The Politics of Military Revolution in Korea.* Chapel Hill: University of North Carolina Press, 1971.

Kim, Seok Ki. "Business Concentration and Government Policy: SA Study of the Phenomenon of Business Groups in Korea, 1945–1985." Ph.D. diss., Harvard University, 1987.

Kim, Seung Hee. *Foreign Capital for Economic Development: a Korean Case Study.* New York: Praeger, 1970.

Kim, Soo-young, "Transmission of International Economic Fluctuations to a Small Open Economy: The Case of Korea." Ph.D. diss., Michigan State University, 1978.

Kim, W. Chan and Philip K. Y. Young. *The Pacific Challenge in International Business.* Ann Arbor, Mich.: UMI Research Press, 1987.

Kindleberger, Charles P. *The World in Depression, 1929–1939.* Berkeley: University of California Press, 1973.

Kindleberger, Charles P. *Manias, Panics, and Financial Crashes,* rev. ed. New York: Basic Books, 1989.

Kissinger, Henry. *The White House Years.* New York: Little, Brown, 1979.

Kobayashi, Ushisaburo. *War and Armament Loans of Japan.* New York: Oxford University Press, 1922.

Kojima, Kiyoshi. *Japan and a New World Economic Order.* Boulder, Col.: Westview, 1977.

Koo, Hagen. "The Political Economy of Development in South Korea and Taiwan: The Interplay of World System, Class and State." Paper presented at the annual meeting of the American Sociological Association in San Francisco, September, 1982.

Kraft, Joseph. *The Mexican Rescue.* New York: Group of 30,1984.

Krasner, Stephan D. *Defending the National Interest.* Princeton: Princeton University Press, 1978.

Krasner, Stephan D. "Power Structures and Regional Development Banks." *International Organization* (1981), 35(2): 303–328.

Krasner, Stephan D. "State Power and the Structure of International Trade." *World Politics* (1976), 28(3): 317–347.

Krasner, Stephan D. *Structural Conflict: The Third World Against Global Liberalism.* Berkeley: University of California Press, 1985.

Krauss, Ellis S. and Muramatsu Michio. "Japanese Political Economy Today: The Patterned Pluralist Model." In Daniel Okimoto and

Thomas P. Rohlen, eds., *Inside the Japanese System: Readings in Contemporary Society and Political Economy.* Stanford: Stanford University Press, 1988.

Krueger, Anne. *The Developmental Role of the Foreign Sector and Aid.* Cambridge: Harvard University Press, 1979.

Krueger, Anne. "Export-Led Industrial Growth Reconsidered." In Wontack Hong and Lawrence Krause, eds., *Trade and Growth of the Advanced Developing Countries in the Pacific Basin.* Seoul: KDI Press, 1981.

Krueger, Anne. *Foreign Trade Regimes and Economic Development: Liberalization Attempts and Consequences.* New York: National Bureau of Economic Research, 1978.

Krueger, Anne. "The Political Economy of the Rent-Seeking Society." *American Economic Review,* 64(3): 291–303.

Kurth, James. "The Political Consequences of the Product Cycle: Industrial History and Political Outcomes." *International Organization* (1979), 33(1): 1–34.

Kuznets, Paul. *Economic Growth and Structure in the Republic of Korea.* New Haven: Yale University Press, 1977.

Kuznets, Paul. "Government and Economic Strategy in Contemporary South Korea." *Pacific Affairs* (1985), 58(1): 44–67.

Kwak, Byông-sob. "A Study of Government Revenue from Money-Creation in South Korea." Ph.D. diss., City University of New York, 1978.

Landes, David. "Japan and Europe: Contrasts in Industrialization." In William W. Lockwood, ed., *State and Economic Enterprise in Japan.* Princeton: Princeton University Press, 1965.

Landsberg, Martin. "Export-Led Industrialization in the Third World: Manufacturing Imperialism." *Review of Radical Political Economists* (1979), 11(6): 50–63.

Lee, Chae-jin. "South Korea: The Politics of Domestic-Foreign Linkage." *Asian Survey* (1973), 13(1): 94–101.

Lee, Changsoon. "Technological Dependence in a Developing Country: The Case of South Korea." Ph.D. diss., The University of Chicago, 1985.

Lee, Chong-sik, *Japan and Korea: The Political Dimension.* Stanford: Hoover Institution Press, 1980.

Lee, Hahn-been. *Korea: Time, Change, and Administration.* Honolulu: University of Hawaii Press, 1968.

Leff, Nathaniel H. "Entrepreneurship and Economic Power: The Problem Revisited." *Journal of Economic Literature* (1976), 17(1): 46–64.

Leff, Nathaniel H. "Industrial Organization and Entrepreneurship in Developing Countries: The Economic Groups." *Economic Development and Cultural Changes* (1978), 426(4): 661–675.

Leff, Nathaniel H. "Monoply Capitalism and Public Policy in Developing Countries." *Kyklos* (1979), 32(4): 718–738.

Lee, Hyock Sup. "The US-Korea Textile Negotiations of 1969–1972." Ph.D. diss., University of Michigan, 1964.

Leite, Sergio Pereira and Reza Vaez-Zadeh. "Credit Allocation and Investment Decisions: The Case of the Manufacturing Sector in Korea." *World Development* (1986), 14(1): 115–116.

Levi, Margaret. *Of Rule and Revenue*. Berkeley: University of California Press, 1988.

Lim, Hyun-chin. "Dependent Development in the World System, 1963–1979: The South Korean Case." Ph.D. diss., Harvard University, 1982.

Levy, Brian. "The Perils of Partnership: Dow in Korea." In Karl Moskowitz, ed., *From Patron to Partners: The Development of U.S.-Korean Business and Trade Relations*. Lexington, Mass.: Lexington Books, 1984.

Linz, Juan. "Fascism, Totalitarianism, and Authoritarianism." In Fred Greenstein and Nelson Polsby, eds., *The Handbook of Political Science*. Reading, Mass.: Addison-Wesley, 1975.

Lipson, Charles. "Bankers' Dilemmas: Private Cooperation in Rescheduling Sovereign Debt." *World Politics* (1985), 38(1): 220–225.

List, F. *National Systems of Political Economy*. Philadelphia: Lippincott, 1856.

Little, I. M. D., T. Scotovsky, and M. Scott. *Industry and Trade in Some Developing Countries*. London: Oxford University Press, 1970.

Lockwood, William. *The Economic Development of Japan*. Princeton: Princeton University Press, 1968.

Lockwood, William, ed. *The State and Economic Enterprises in Japan*. Princeton: Princeton University Press, 1970.

Loriaux, Michael. *Reforming the Overdraft Economy: U.S. Hegemonic Decline and Financial Liberalization in France*. Ithaca: N.Y.: Cornell University Press, 1990.

Loriaux, Michael. "States and Markets: French Financial Interventionism in the 1970s." *Comparative Politics* (1988), 20(2): 175–193.

Lowi, Theodore J. *The End of Liberalism: the Second Republic of the United States*. New York: Norton, 1979.

Lowi, Theodore J. "Toward a Politics of Economics: the State of Permanent Receivership." In Leon Lindberg, ed., *Stress and Contradiction in Modern Capitalism*. Lexington, Mass.: D. C. Heath, 1975.

Luedde-Neurath, Richard. *Import Controls and Export Oriented Development: A Reassessment of the South Korean Case*. Boulder, Col.: Westview Press, 1985.

Luedde-Nuerath, Richard. "State Intervention and Foreign Direct Investment in South Korea." *IDS Bulletin* (1984), 15(2): 18–25.

McKinnon, Ronald. "Financial Policies." In Soha Cody et al., eds., *Policies for Industrial Progress in Developing Countries*. New York: Oxford University Press, 1982.

McKinnon, Ronald. *Money and Capital in Economic Development*. Washington, D.C.: Brookings Institution, 1974.

McKinnon, Ronald. "The Order of Economic Liberalization: Lessons from Chile and Argentina." In Karl Brunner, ed., Economic Policy in a World of Change. Amsterdam: North-Holland, 1982.

McKinnon, Ronald, ed. Money and Finance in Economic Growth and Development. New York: Marcel Dekker, 1976.

McKinnon, Ronald and Donald Mathieson. How to Manage a Repressive Economy. Princeton Essays in International Finance, no. 145. Princeton: Princeton University Press, 1981.

McNamara, Dennis L. Colonial Origins of Korean Enterprise. New York: Cambridge University Press, 1990.

Mak, Juliet Cheng-Leng. "Alternative Approaches to Industrialization: A Comparative Analysis of the Philippines, South Korea, and Taiwan." Ph.D. diss., University of Wisconsin, Madison, 1978.

Malloy, James, ed. Authoritarianism and Corporatism in Latin America. Pittsburgh: University of Pittsburgh Press, 1977.

Marshall, Byron. Capitalism and Nationalism in Prewar Japan: The Ideology of the Business Elite, 1868–1941. Stanford: Stanford University Press, 1967.

Marx, Karl. In Luccio Colletti, ed., Early Writings. New York: Vintage Books, 1975.

Mason, Edward S. et al., The Economic and Social Modernization of the Republic of Korea. Cambridge: Harvard University Press, 1980.

Maxfield, Sylvia and James Nolt. "Protectionism and the Internationalization of Capital: United States Sponsorship of Import Substitution Industrialization in the Philippines, Turkey, and Argentina." International Studies Quarterly, forthcoming.

Meyer, John. "The World Polity and the Authority of the Nation-State." In Albert Bergesen, ed., Studies in the Modern World System. New York: Academy Press, 1980.

Meyers, Ramon and Mark Peattie, eds. The Japanese Colonial Empire, 1895–1945. Princeton: Princeton University Press, 1984.

Middlebrook, Kevin and Carlos Rico, eds. The United States and Latin America in the 1980s. Pittsburgh: University of Pittsburgh Press, 1986.

Migdal, Joel. Strong Societies and Weak States: State Society Relations and State Capabilities in the Third World. Princeton: Princeton University Press, 1988.

Mitchell, Tony. "Administrative Traditions and Economic Decision-Making in South Korea." IDS Bulletin (1984), 15(2): 1–18.

Mitsubishi Economic Research Bureau. Japanese Trade and Industry, Present and Future. London: Macmillan, 1936.

Miyamoto Matao, "The Position and Role of Family Business in the Development of the Japanese Company System." In Akio Okochi and Shigeaki Yasuoka, eds., Family Business in the Era of Industrial Growth: Its Ownership and Management. Tokyo: University of Tokyo Press, 1983.

Mizoguchi Toshiyuki and Yamamoto Yuzo. "Capital Formation in Taiwan and Korea." In R. Meyers and M. Peattie, eds., *The Japanese Colonial Empire, 1895–1945.* Princeton: Princeton University Press, 1984.

Moffit, Michael. *The World's Money: International Banking, From Bretton Woods to the Brink of Insolvency.* New York: Simon and Schuster, 1983.

Monthly Review Editors. "Production and Finance." *Monthly Review* (1983), 35(1): 1–10.

Moon, Seong Rae. "Economic Impact of Multinational Investment in the Korean Economy." Ph.D. diss., American University, 1987.

Moore, Barrington. *Social Origins of Dictatorship and Democracy.* Boston: Beacon, 1981.

Morgan Guaranty Trust Company of New York, "Korea: Adjustment Model for the 1980s?" *World Financial Markets* (March 1984).

Morishima, Michio. *Why Japan Has "Succeeded"?: Western Technology and the Japanese Ethos.* New York: Cambridge University Press, 1982.

Morley, James. *Japan and Korea: America's Allies in the Pacific.* New York: Walker, 1965.

Morley, Sam. "Inflation and Stagnation in Brazil." *Economic Development and Cultural Change* (1974), 19(2): 184–203.

Moskowitz, Karl. "Current Assets: The Employees of Japanese Banks in Colonial Korea." Ph.D. diss., Harvard University, 1979.

Moskowitz, Karl, "Introduction." *From Patron to Partners: The Development of U.S.-Korean Business and Trade Relations.* Lexington, Mass.: Lexington Books, 1984.

Moskowitz, Karl, ed. *From Patron to Partners: The Development of U.S.-Korean Business and Trade Relations.* Lexington, Mass.: Lexington Books, 1984.

Moulder, Frances. *Japan, China, and the Modern World Economy.* New York: Cambridge University Press, 1977.

Nam, Choo-hong, *America's Commitment to South Korea: The First Decade of the Nixon Doctrine.* New York: Cambridge University Press, 1986.

Najita, Tetsuo and J. V. Koschman, eds. *Conflict in Modern Japanese History.* Princeton: Princeton University Press, 1982.

Nakagawa, Keiichiro. "Business Strategy and Industrial Structure in Pre-World War II Japan." In Nakagawa Keiichiro, ed., *Strategy and Structure of Big Business.* Tokyo: Tokyo University Press, 1976.

Nakamura, Takafusa. *Economic Growth in Prewar Japan.* New Haven: Yale University Press, 1983.

Naya, Seiji, "The Vietnam War and Some Aspects of Its Economic Impact on Asian Countries." *The Developing Economies* (1971), 9(1): 31–57.

Newfarmer, Richard, ed. *Profits, Progress, and Poverty.* Notre Dame, Ind.: University of Notre Dame Press, 1985.

Noguera, Ceso Garrido. "Financial Relations and Economic Power in Mexico." In Sylvia Maxfield, ed., *Government and the Private Sector in Contemporary Mexico*. San Diego, Cal.: Center for US-Mexican Studies, 1986.

Nordhaus, William. "The Political Business Cycle." *Review of Economic Studies* (1975), 42(2): 169–190.

Nordlinger, Eric. "Taking the State Seriously." In S. P. Huntington, ed., *Understanding Political Development*. Boston: Little, Brown, 1984.

Norman, E. H. *Origins of the Modern Japanese State*. New York: Pantheon, 1975.

O'Connor, James. *The Fiscal Crisis of the State*. New York: St. Martin's Press, 1973.

Odell, John S. "Growing Trade and Growing Conflict between the Republic of Korea and the United States." In Moskowitz, ed., *From Patron to Partners: the Development of US-Korean Business and Trade Relations*. Lexington, Mass.: Lexington Books, 1984.

Odell, John S. "The United States and the Emergence of Flexible Exchange Rates." *International Organization* (1979), 33(1): 57–81.

O'Donnell, Guillermo. *Bureaucratic Authoritarianism: Argentina, 1966–1973, in Comparative Perspective*. Berkeley: University of California Press, 1988.

O'Donnell, Guillermo. *Modernization and Bureaucratic Authoritarianism*. Berkeley: Institute for Latin American Studies, 1973.

O'Donnell, Guillermo. "Reflections on the Patterns of Change in the Bureaucratic Authoritarian State." *Latin American Research Review* (1978), 13(1): 1–38.

Offe, Claus. "Advanced Capitalism and the Welfare State." *Politics and Society* (1972), 2(4): 479–488.

Offe, Claus. "The Capitalist State and the Problem of Policy Formation." In Leon Lindberg et al., ed., *Stress and Contradictions in Modern Capitalism*. Lexington, Mass.: D. C. Health, 1973.

Offe, Claus. "Structural Problems of the Capitalist State: Class Rule and the Political System. On the Selectiveness of Political Institutions." In Klaus von Blyme, ed., *German Political Studies*. Vol. 1. Beverly Hills, Cal.: Sage, 1974.

Okimoto, Daniel. *Between MITI and the Market: Japanese Industrial Policy for High Technology*. Stanford: Stanford University Press, 1989.

Okimoto, Daniel. "Japan the Societal State." In Daniel Okimoto and Thomas P. Rohlen, eds., *Inside the Japanese System: Readings in Contemporary Society and Political Economy*. Stanford: Stanford University Press, 1988.

Okimoto, Daniel and Thomas P. Rohlen, eds. *Inside the Japanese System: Readings in Contemporary Society and Political Economy*. Stanford: Stanford University Press, 1988.

Okimoto, Daniel, Takao Sugano, and Franklin Weinstein, eds. *Compet-*

itive Edge: the Semiconductor Industry in the United States and Japan. Stanford: Stanford University Press. 1984.

Olsen, Edward A. " ' Korea Inc.': The Political Impact of Park Chung Hee's Economic Miracle." *Orbis* (1980), 24(1): 69–84.

Ozawa, Terutomo. *Multinationalism Japanese Style: The Political Economy of Outward Dependency.* Princeton: Princeton University Press, 1979.

Packenham, Robert A. *Liberal America and the Third World.* Princeton: Princeton University Press, 1973.

Park, Chung Hee. *Korea Reborn: A Model for Development.* Engelwood Cliffs: Prentice Hall, 1979.

Park, Chung Hee. *To Build a Nation.* Washington, D.C.: Acropolis Books, 1971.

Park, Chung Hee. *Major Speeches of President Park.* Seoul: Samwha, 1974.

Park, Chong Kee, ed. *Macroecomic and Industrial Development in Korea.* Seoul: KDI, 1980.

Park, Chung-hoon. "The Second Economic Plan in General View." *Korea Quarterly* (1969), 11(1): 1–20.

Park, Sonwon. "The Emergence of Factory Labor Force in Colonial Korea: A Case of the Onoda Cement Factory." Ph.D. diss., Harvard University, 1985.

Park, Young Chul. "Export Growth and the Balance of Payments in Korea, 1960–1978." In Wontack Hong and Lawrence Krause, eds., *Trade and Growth of the Advanced Developing Countries in the Pacific Basin.* Seoul: KDI, 1981.

Park, Young Chul. "Korea's Experience with External Debt Management." Paper for the International Monetary Fund (April 1984).

Park, Young Chul. "Financial Repression, Liberalization and Development in Developing countries." Paper (no date).

Park, W. H. and J. L. Enos. *The Adoption and Infusion of Adopted Technology: The Case of Korea.* London: Routledge, Chapman and Hall, 1985.

Patrick, Hugh. "External Equilibrium and Internal Convertibility: Financial Policy in Meiji Japan." *Journal of Economic History* (1965), 15(2): 124–156.

Patrick, Hugh. "Financial Development and Economic Growth in Underdeveloped Countries." *Economic Development and Cultural Change* (1966), 14(2): 174–189.

Patrick, Hugh. "Japan, 1968–1914." In Rondo Cameron, ed., *Bankings in the Early Stages of Industrialization.* London: Oxford University Press, 1967.

Payer, Cheryl. "Pushed Into the Debt Trap: South Korea's Export 'Miracle.' " *Journal of Contemporary Asia* (1975), 5(2): 153–164.

Payer, Cheryl. *The Debt Trap: IMF and the Third World.* New York: Monthly Review Press, 1979.

Peattie, Mark. "Introduction." In R. Meyers and M. Peattie, eds., *The Japanese Colonial Empire, 1895–1945*. Princeton: Princeton University Press, 1984.

Pempel, T. J. *Policy and Politics in Japan: Creative Conservatism*. Philadelphia: Temple University Press, 1982.

Pempel, T. J. "Japanese Foreign Economic Policy: The Domestic Bases for International Behavior." In Peter Katzenstein, ed., *Between Power and Plenty*. Madison: University of Wisconsin Press, 1978.

Pion-Berlin, David. "Political Repression and Economic Doctrines: The Case of Argentina." *Comparative Political Studies* (1983), 16(1): 37–66.

Piore, Michael and Charles Sabel. *The Second Industrial Divide*. New York: Basic Books, 1984.

Polanyi, Karl. *The Great Transformation*. New York: Beacon Press, 1944.

Poulantzas, Nicos. *The Crisis of the Dictatorships*. London: New Left Books, 1976.

Poulantzas, Nicos. *Fascism and Dictatorship: The Third International and the Problem of Fascism*. London: New Left Books, 1974.

Poulantzas, Nicos. *Political Power and Social Classes*. London: New Left Books, 1973.

Poulantzas, Nicos. *State, Power, Socialism*. London: New Left Books, 1978.

Przeworski, Adam. "Some Problems in the Study of the Transition to Democracy." In O'Donnell, Schmitter, and Whitehead, eds., *Transition from Authoritarian Rule: Comparative Perspective*. Baltimore: Johns Hopkins University Press, 1987.

Przeworski, Adam. "The State and the Economy under Capitalism." In manuscript (no date).

Pye, Lucian. *Asian Power and Politics: the Cultural Dimension of Authority*. Cambridge, Mass.: Belknap Press, 1985.

Ranis, Gustav. "Challenge and Opportunities Posed by Asia's Superexporters: Implication for Manufactured Exports for Latin America." In Malcolm Gillis and Werner Baer, eds., *Export Diversification and the New protectionism*. Champaign: University of Illinois Press, 1981.

Ranis, Gustav. *East Asia and Latin America: Constrasts in the Political Economy of Development Policy Change*. New Haven: Yale University Press, 1987.

Ranis, Gustav. "The Financing of Japanese Economic Development." *Economic History Review* (1959), 11(3): 440–454.

Ranis, Gustav and Kazushi Ohkawa. *Japan and Developing Countries: A Comparative Analysis*. Oxford: Basil Blackwell, 1985.

Redford, Lawrence, ed. *The Occupation of Japan: Economic Policy and Reform*. Norfolk, Va.: The Memorial, 1980.

Reilly, Charles A. "Intergovernmental Relations in Austere Times: Mexico and Brazil." Paper presented at the meeting of American Political Science Association, Washington, D.C., August 30–September 2, 1984.

Robert R. Nathan Associates. *An Economic Programme for Korean Reconstruction.* Seoul: UNKRA, March 1964.

Robison, Richard. "Authoritarian States, Capital Owning Classes, and the Politics of Newly Industrializing Countries: the Case of Indonesia." *World Politics* (1988), 41(1): 52–74.

Roll, Eric. *A History of Economic Thought.* London: Faber and Faber, 1973.

Rostow, W. W. *The Stages of Economic Growth.* Cambridge: Cambridge University Press, 1960.

Rostow W. W. *The United States and the Regional Organization of Asia and the Pacific: 1965–1985.* Austin: University of Texas Press, 1986.

Rostow, W. W. *Eisenhower, Kennedy, and Foreign Aid.* Austin: University of Texas Press, 1985.

Rotter, Andrew J. *The Path to Vietnam: Origins of the American Commitment to Southeast Asia.* Ithaca: Cornell University Press, 1987.

Ruggie, John., ed. *The Antinomy of Interdependence.* New York: Columbia University Press, 1983.

Sampson, Anthony. *The Money Lenders.* New York: Penguin Books, 1981.

Samuels, Richard J. *The Business of the Japanese State: Energy Markets in Comparative Perspective.* Ithaca: Cornell University Press, 1987.

Schaller, Michael. *The American Occupation of Japan: The Origins of the Cold War in Asia.* New York: Oxford University Press, 1985.

Schmitter, Philip. *Interest Conflict and Political Change.* Stanford: Stanford University Press, 1971.

Schmitter, Philip. "Portugalization of Brazil?" In Alfred Stepan, ed., *Authoritarian Brazil.* New Haven: Yale University Press, 1969.

Schmitter, Philip. "Still the Century of Corporatism?" In F. Pike and T. Strich, eds., *The New Corporatism: Social-Political Structure in the Iberian World.* Notre Dame, Ind.: University of Notre Dame Press, 1974.

Schumpeter, E. B. *The Industrialization of Japan and Manchukuo.* New York: Macmillan, 1940.

Schumpeter, Joseph A. *Capitalism, Socialism, and Democracy.*

Schumpeter, Joseph A. *History of Economic Analysis.* New York: Oxford University Press, 1986.

Schurmann, Franz. *The Grand Design: The Foreign Politics of Richard Nixon.* Berkeley: Institute of International Studies, University of California at Berkeley, 1987.

Schurmann, Franz. *The Logic of World Power.* New York: Pantheon, 1973.

Sheu, Jia-you Joe. "Dependency, Development, and State Action in Hong

Kong, Singapore, South Korea, and Taiwan: 1950–1975." Ph.D. dissertation, Indiana University, 1980.

Shaw, Edward. *Financial Deepening in Economic Development.* Oxford: Oxford University Press, 1973.

Shaw, Edward. *Financial Patterns and Policies in Korea.* Seoul: USOM/Korea, 1967.

Shin, Chang-kyun. "General Trading Companies: A Study of Their Development and Strategies." Ph.D. diss., George Washington University, 1984.

Shin, Hyunchul. "Monetary Policy in an Open Economy with Particular Reference to the Recent Korean Experience." Ph.D. diss., University of Utah, 1977.

Silberman, Bernard. "The Bureaucratic State in Japan: The Problem of Authority and Legitimacy." In T. Najita and J. V. Koschman, eds., *Conflict in Modern Japanese History.* Princeton: Princeton University Press, 1982.

Skocpol, Theda. *States and Social Revolutions.* Cambridge: Cambridge University Press, 1978.

Smith, Adam. *The Wealth of Nations.* New York: Modern Library, 1937.

Smith, Gordon and John T. Cuddington, eds. *International Debt and Developing Countries.* Washington D. C.: The World Bank, 1985.

Sogang University Research Institute for Economics and Business. *A Study of Money Market and Industrial Investment Financing in Korea.* Seoul: Sogang University Press, 1970.

Song, Dae-sung. "National Development of South Korea and Taiwan: A Different Case of Dependency Theory." Ph.D. diss., University of Michigan, 1984.

Stallings, Barbara. *Banker to the Third World.* Berkeley: University of California Press, 1987.

Stallings, Barbara. "Peru and the U.S. Banks: Privatization of Financial Relations." In Richard Fagen, ed., *Capitalism and the State in U.S.-Latin American Relations.* Stanford: Stanford University Press, 1979.

Stepan, Alfred. *Rethinking Military Politics: Brazil and the Southern Cone.* Princeton: Princeton University Press, 1988.

Stepan, Alfred. *The State and Society: Peru in Comparative Perspective.* Princeton: Princeton University Press, 1978.

Stepan, Alfred. "State Power and the Strength of Civil Society in the Southern Cone of Latin America." In Peter Evans, etc., eds., *Bringing the State Back In.* London: Cambridge University Press, 1985.

Stepan, Alfred. ed., *Authoritarian Brazil.* New Haven: Yale University Press, 1969.

Strange, Susan. "Protectionism and World Politics." *International Organizations* (1985), 39(2): 233–269.

Suh, Sang Chul. *Growth and Structural Changes in the Korean Economy, 1910–1942.* Cambridge: Harvard University Press, 1978.

Suh, Sang Mok. "The Evolution of the Korean Economy in Historical Perspective." Paper presented at the Conference on Structural Adjustment in a Newly Industrialized Countries: Lessons from Korea, sponsored by the World Bank. June 17–18, 1986.

Suzuki, Yoshio. *Money, Finance, and Macroeconomic Performance in Japan.* New Heaven: Yale University Press, 1986.

Sweezy, Paul. *The Theory of Capitalist Development.* New York: Monthly Review Press, 1968.

Thayer, Nathaniel. *How the Conservatives Rule Japan.* Princeton: Princeton University Press, 1969.

Therborn, Goran. *What Does a Ruling Class Do When It Rules?* London: Verso Books, 1982.

Tiedemann, Arthur. "Big Business and Politics in Prewar Japan." In James Morley, ed., *Dilemmas of Growth in Prewar Japan.* Princeton: Princeton University Press, 1971.

Trimberger, Ellen Kay. *Revolution from Above. Military Bureaucrats and Development in Japan, Turkey, Egypt, and Peru.* New Brunswick: Transaction Books, 1978.

Tullock, Gordon. "Rent-Seeking as a Negative-Sum Game." In James Buchanan, ed., *Toward a Theory of the Rent-Seeking Society.* College Station: Texas A & M Press, 1980.

Tullock, Gordon. "The Welfare Costs of Tariffs, Monopolies, and Theft." In James Buchanan, ed., *Toward a Theory of the Rent-Seeking Society.* College Station: Texas A & M Press, 1980.

Veblen, T. *Imperial Germany and the Industrial Revolution.* New York: Macmillan, 1915.

Vernon, Raymond. *The Promise of Privatization.* New York: Council on Foreign Relations, 1988.

Vogel, Ezra. "Japan: Adaptive Communitarianism." In George C. Lodge and Ezra Vogel, eds., *Ideology and National Competitiveness.* Boston: Harvard Business School Press, 1987.

Vogel, Ezra. *Japan as Number One.* Cambridge: Harvard University Press, 1979.

Vogel, Ezra, ed. *Modern Japanese Organization and Decision Making.* Berkeley: University of California Press, 1975.

Wade, Robert. "Dirigisme Taiwan-Style." *IDS Bulletin* (1984), 15(2): 65–70.

Wade, Robert. *Governing the Market: Economic Theory and the Role of Government in Taiwan's Industrialization.* Princeton: Princeton University Press, 1990.

Wade, Robert. *Irrigation and Agricultural Politics in South Korea.* Boulder, Col.: Westview, 1982.

Wade, Robert. "The Role of Government in Overcoming Market Failure: Taiwan, South Korea, and Japan." Paper for the World Bank (no date).

Wales, Nym. "Rebel Korea," *Pacific Affairs* (June 1938), vol. 8.

Walker, Richard. "The Future of U.S. Trans-Pacific Alliances." *Orbis* (1975), 19(3): 904–924.

Wallerstein, Immanuel. *The Modern World System: Capitalist Agriculture and the Origins of the European World Economy in the Sixteenth Century.* New York: Academic Press, 1974.

Wallerstein, Immanuel. "The Rise and Future Demise of the World Capitalist System: Concepts for Comparative Analysis." *Comparative Studies in Society and History* (1974), 16(4): 387–415.

Ward, Robert, ed. *Political Development in Modern Japan.* Princeton: Princeton University Press, 1968.

Ward, Robert and Dankwart A. Rustow, eds. *Political Modernization in Japan and Turkey.* Princeton: Princeton University Press, 1964.

Watanabe, Toshio. "An Analysis of Structural Dependence between Japan and Korea." In Wontack Hong and Lawrence Krause, eds., *Trade and Growth of Advanced Countries in the Pacific Basin.* Seoul: KDI Press, 1981.

Watanabe, Toshio. "Heavy and Chemical Industrialization and Economic Development in the Republic of Korea." *The Developing Economies* (1978), 16(4): 385–407.

Weaver, Frederick Stirton. *Class, State, and Industrial Structure: The Historical Process of South American Growth.* Westport, Conn.: Greenwood Press, 1980.

Weiner, Myron and Samuel Huntington, eds. *Understanding Political Development.* Boston: Little, Brown, 1987.

Wellons, Philip A. *Passing the Buck: Banks, Governments, and the Third World Debt.* Boston: Harvard Business School Press, 1987.

Wellons, Philip A. "International Debt: The Behavior of Banks in a Politicized Environment." *International Organization* (1985), 39(3): 441–471.

Whang In-jong. "Korea's Economic Management for Structural Adjustment in the 1980s." Paper presented at Conference on Structural Adjustment in a Newly Industrialized Countries: Lessons from Korea, The World Bank. June 17–18, 1986.

White, Gordon. *Developmental States in East Asia.* London: Macmillan, 1988.

Whitehead, Laurence. "Debt, Diversification, and Dependency: Latin America's International Political Relations." In Kevin Middlebrook and Carlos Rico, eds., *The United States and Latin America in the 1980s.* Pittsburgh: University of Pittsburgh Press, 1986.

Whitings Jr., Van R. "Financial Populism or Responsible Statism: State Intervention in Brazil and Mexico." Paper presented at the meeting of the American Political Science Association, Washington, D.C., 1984.

Wilber, Charles and Steven Francis. "The Methodological Basis of

Hirschman's Development Economics: Pattern Model vs. General Laws." *World Development* (1986), 14(2): 181–194.

Wilcox, Robert. *Japan's Secret War.* New York: William Marrow, 1986.

Wildavsky, Aaron and Carolyn Webber. *A History of Taxation and the Expenditure in the Western World.* New York: Simon and Schuster, 1986.

Williamson, J. F. "Why Do Koreans Save 'So Little'?" *Journal of Development Economics* (1979), 6(3): 343–362.

Winkler, Edwin and Susan Greenhalgh, eds. *Contending Approaches to the Political Economy of Taiwan.* Armonk, N.Y.: M. E. Sharpe, 1988.

Wolfren, Karel van. *The Enigma of Japanese Power.* New York: Knopf, 1989.

Yamamura, Kozo. "General Trading Companies in Japan—Their Origins and Growth." In Hugh Patrick, ed., *Japanese Industrialization and Its Social Consequences.* Berkeley: University of California Press, 1976.

Yamazaki, Makoto. "The Japanese Model in Korean Economic Development after 1953." Ph.D. diss., Duke University, 1984.

Yamazawa, Ippei and Hirohisa Kohama. "Trading Companies and the Expansion of Foreign Trade: Japan, Korea, and Thailand." In Kazushi Ohkawa, Gustav Ranis, and Larry Meissner, eds., *Japan and the Developing Countries.* New York: Basil Blackwell, 1985.

Yasuda, Ryuji. "Politics of Industrial Financing Policy: Korea and Japan." Ph.D. diss., University of California at Berkeley, 1979.

Yasuoka, Shigeaki. "Capital Ownership in Family Companies: Japanese Firms Compared with Those in Other Countries." In Akio Okochi and Shigeaki Yasuoka, eds., *Family Business in the Era of Industrial Growth: Its Ownership and Management.* Tokyo: University of Tokyo Press, 1983.

Yasutomo, Dennis J. *Japan and the Asian Development Bank.* New York: Praeger, 1983.

Yoffie, David. "The Newly Industrializing Countries and the Political Economy of Protectionism," *International Studies Quarterly* (1981), 25(4): 569–599.

You, Jong-il. "Is Fordism Coming to Korea?: Changing Capital-Labor Relations in Korea." Paper prepared for WIDER Project on Capital-Labor Relations, March 1989.

Young, Walter. *Japan's Special Position in Manchuria.* Baltimore, Md.: Johns Hopkins University Press, 1931.

Zysman, John. *Governments, Markets, and Growth: Financial Systems and the Politics of Industrial Change.* Ithaca, N.Y.: Cornell University Press, 1983.

Zysman, John. *American Industry in International Competition.* Ithaca, N.Y.: Cornell University Press, 1983.

Books and Articles in Korean

Chaejông kûmyung samsipnyônsa p'yônchan wiwônhoe. *Chaejông kûmyung samsipnyônsa* [The Thirty Year History of Financial and Fiscal Policies]. Seoul: Samwha ch'ulpansa, 1978.

Chin, Tôkkyu, Han Paeho, Kim Hakjun, Han Sungju, Kim Taehwan, etc. *1950 nyôndae ûi inshik* [Understanding the 1950s], Seoul: Hankilsa, 1980.

Cho, Sun. *Hanguk kyôngje ûi hyônshil kwa chillo* [Current Position and Prospects of Korean Economy]. Seoul: Pibong ch'ulpansa, 1981.

Cho, Sun et al., eds. *Hanguk kyôngje ûi ihae* [Understanding Korean Economy]. Seoul: Pibong ch'ulpansa, 1987.

Chu, Chong-hwan. *Chaebôl kyôngjeron* [Theories on the Chaebol Economy]. Seoul. Chongum munwha, 1985.

Chunghwahak kongôp ch'ujin wiwônhoe kihoekdan. *Hanguk kongôpwha paljôn e kwanhan chosa yônku: chunghwahak kongôp paljônsa* [The Study of Industrial Progress in Korea: The History]. Seoul: 1979.

Chunghwahak kongôp . . . *Hanguk kongôpwha paljôn e kwanhan chosa yônku: chungwhahak kongôp chôngchaeksa* [The Study of Industrial Progress in Korea: the History of Policies on Heavy Industries]. Seoul: 1979.

Chunghwahak kongôp . . . *Hanguk kongôpwha paljôn e kwanhan chosa yônku: chôngchaek kyôljông kwajông ûi imyônsa*. [The Study of Industrial Progress in Korea: The Background]. Seoul: 1979.

Hanguk ilbosa kyôngjebu. *Hanguk ûi 50 tae chaebôl* [Korea's 50 Largest Chaebôls]. Seoul: Kyôngje nung-yul yônkuso ch'ulpanbu, 1986.

Hanguk kidokkyo sahoe munje yôngguwôn, ed. *1986 Hnaguk kyôngji sajông* [Economic Situation in Korea, 1986]. Seoul: Minjung-sa, 1987.

Hanguk kûmyung yôngguwôn. *Hanguk kûmyung yûngam* [Korean Financial Yearbook]. Seoul: Hanguk Kumyung Yônkuwôn, 1982.

Hanguk sahoe yônggu [Studies of Korean Society]. Seoul: Hangilsa, 1983.

Hanguk ûi chôngch'i palchôn kwa kyôngje palchôn [Political and Economic Development of Korea]. Seoul: Asea chôngchaek yôngguwôn, 1979.

Im Myo-min, ed. *Ilbon chabon ûi sangryuk* [The Arrival of Japanese Capital]. Seoul: Chaekye yôngguso, 1966.

Isogaya Sueji. *Uri ch'ôngchun ûi chosôn* [Korea of Our Youth]. Seoul: Sagyejôl, 1988.

Kang Man-gil. *Chosôn huggi sangôp chabon ûi paldal* [The Development of Commercial Capital in the Late Yi Dynasty].

Kang Man-gil. *Hanguk kûndaesa* [The Modern History of Korea]. Seoul: Ch'angjak kwa pipyôngsa, 1984.

Kang Man-gil. *Hanguk hyôndaesa* [The Contemporary History of Korea.] Seoul: Ch'angjak kwa pipyôngsa, 1984.

Kang Sin-ch'ôl, etc., ed. *80 nyôndae haksaeng undongsa* [Student Movements in the 1980s]. Seoul: Hyôngsôngsa, 1988.

Kim Byông-ju and Pak Yông-chôl. *Hanguk kyôngje wa kûmyung* [Korean Economy and Finance]. Seoul: Pakyôngsa, 1984.

Kim Chung-ung and Nam Sang-wu. *Chônwhanki ûi hanguk kyôngje wa kûmyung chôngchaek.* [Korean Economy and Financial Policies in Transition]. Seoul: KDI, 1985.

Kim Chun-hyông. *Hanguk ch'ôlgang gongôp ûi sôngjang.* [The Development of Korean Steel and Iron Industry]. Seoul: KDI, 1976.

Kim Sông-du. "Hanguk ûi tokjôm kiôp" [Monopoly Enterprises in Korea], *Sedae* (December 1967).

Kim ûn-tae. *Ilbon chegukjuûi ûi hanguk t'ongchi.* [The Reign of Japanese Imperialism in Korea]. Seoul: Pakyôngsa, 1986.

"Kûmyunggye lûl chibaehan inmaek p'ando" [Lineages of Men Who Dominated Banking], *ûnhaengga* (March 1971).

Nam Sang-wu, *Hanguk kiôp ûi chaemuhaengtae* [Financial Behavior of Korean Firms]. Seoul: KDI, 1979.

Nishimura, Toshio. *Taeman kwa hanguk kyôngje pikyo* [Economic Comparison of Korea and Taiwan. Seoul: Tadok ch'ulpansa, 1983.

Pak Hyôn-chae. *Hanguk kyôngje ûi kujowa nolli* [The Structure and Logic in Korean Economy]. Seoul: P'ulbit, 1982.

Pak Yông-ho. *"Hanûn t'ûkyung"* ["Special Rescue Loans of the Bank of Korea"]. *Shindonga.* August 1985.

P'ûleijô poggosô [The Frazer Committee Report]. Seoul: Silchôn sinsô, 1986.

Sagong Il. "Kyôngje sôngjang kwa kyôngje-ryôk chipjung." *Hanguk kaebal yônku* ["Economic Development and Economic Concentration." Korean Development Studies]. Spring 1980.

Yi Chong-nam. *Chaebôl: Kyôngje sôngjang ûi p'ilsoyôn ingga p'ilyoak ingga* [Chaebôl: The Necessary Virtue or the Necessary Evil in Economic Development?] Seoul: Hyônje, 1985.

Yi Man-ki. *Shinhanguk kyôngje ron.* [New Theories on the Korean Economy]. Seoul: Ilshinsa, 1982.

Index

Studies of the East Asian Institute

The Ladders of Success in Imperial China, by Ping-ti Ho. New York: Columbia University Press, 1962.

The Chinese Inflation, 1937–1949, by Shun-hsin Chou. New York: Columbia University Press, 1963.

Reformer in Modern China: Chang Chien, 1853–1926, by Samuel Chu. New York: Columbia University Press, 1965.

Research in Japanese Sources: A Guide, by Herschel Webb with the assistance of Marleigh Ryan. New York: Columbia University Press, 1965.

Society and Education in Japan, by Herbert Passin. New York: Teachers College Press, 1965.

Agricultural Production and Economic Developments in Japan, 1873–1922, by James I. Nakamura. Princeton: Princeton University Press, 1967.

Japan's First Modern Novel: Ukigumo of Futabatei Shimei, by Marleigh Ryan. New York: Columbia University Press, 1967.

The Korean Communist Movement, 1918–1948, by Dae-Sook Suh. Princeton: Princeton University Press, 1967.

The First Vietnam Crisis, by Melvin Gurtov. New York: Columbia University Press, 1967.

Cadres, Bureaucracy, and Political Power in Communist China, by A. Doak Barnett. New York: Columbia University Press, 1968.

The Japanese Imperial Institution in the Tokugawa Period, by Herschel Webb. New York: Columbia University Press, 1968.

Higher Education and Business Recruitment in Japan, by Koya Azumi. New York: Teachers College Press, 1969.

The Communists and Peasant Rebellions: A Study in the Rewriting of Chinese History, by James P. Harrison, Jr. New York: Atheneum, 1969.

How the Conservatives Rule Japan, by Nathaniel B. Thayer. Princeton: Princeton University Press, 1969.

Aspects of Chinese Education, edited by C. T. Hu. New York: Teachers College Press, 1970.

Documents of Korean Communism, 1918–1948, by Dae-Sook Suh. Princeton: Princeton University Press, 1970.

Japanese Education: A Bibliography of Materials in the English Language, by Herbert Passin. New York: Teachers College Press, 1970.

Economic Development and the Labor Market in Japan, by Koji Taira. New York: Columbia University Press, 1970.

The Japanese Oligarchy and the Russo-Japanese War, by Shumpei Okamoto. New York: Columbia University Press, 1970.

Imperial Restoration in Medieval Japan, by H. Paul Varley. New York: Columbia University Press, 1971.

Japan's Postwar Defense Policy, 1947–1968, by Martin E. Weinstein. New York: Columbia University Press, 1971.

Election Campaigning Japanese Style, by Gerald L. Curtis. New York: Columbia University Press, 1971.

China and Russia: The "Great Game," by O. Edmund Clubb. New York: Columbia University Press, 1971.

Money and Monetary Policy in Communist China, by Katharine Huang Hsiao. New York: Columbia University Press, 1971.

The District Magistrate in Late Imperial China, by John R. Watt. New York: Columbia University Press, 1972.

Law and Policy in China's Foreign Relations: A Study of Attitude and Practice, by James C. Hsiung. New York: Columbia University Press, 1972.

Pearl Harbor as History: Japanese-American Relations, 1931–1941, edited by Dorothy Borg and Shumpei Okamoto, with the assistance of Dale K. A. Finlayson. New York: Columbia University Press, 1973.

Japanese Culture: A Short History, by H. Paul Varley. New York: Praeger, 1973.

Doctors in Politics: The Political Life of the Japan Medical Association, by William E. Steslicke. New York: Praeger, 1973.

The Japan Teachers Union: A Radical Interest Group in Japanese Politics, by Donald Ray Thurston. Princeton: Princeton University Press, 1973.

Japan's Foreign Policy, 1868–1941: A Research Guide, edited by James William Morley. New York: Columbia University Press, 1974.

Palace and Politics in Prewar Japan, by David Anson Titus. New York: Columbia University Press, 1974.

The Idea of China: Essays in Geographic Myth and Theory, by Andrew March. Devon, England: David and Charles, 1974.

Origins of the Cultural Revolution, by Roderick MacFarquhar. New York: Columbia University Press, 1974.

Shiba Kōkan: Artist, Innovator, and Pioneer in the Westernization of Japan, by Calvin L. French. Tokyo: Weatherhill, 1974.

Insei: Abdicated Sovereigns in the Politics of Late Heian Japan, by G. Cameron Hurst. New York: Columbia University Press, 1975.

Embassy at War, by Harold Joyce Noble. Edited with an introduction by Frank Baldwin, Jr. Seattle: University of Washington Press, 1975.

Rebels and Bureaucrats: China's December 9ers, by John Israel and Donald W. Klein. Berkeley: University of California Press, 1975.

Deterrent Diplomacy, edited by James William Morley. New York: Columbia University Press, 1976.

House United, House Divided: The Chinese Family in Taiwan, by Myron L. Cohen. New York: Columbia University Press, 1976.

Escape from Predicament: Neo-Confucianism and China's Evolving Political Culture, by Thomas A. Metzger. New York: Columbia University Press, 1976.

Cadres, Commanders, and Commissars: The Training of the Chinese Communist Leadership, 1920–45, by Jane L. Price. Boulder, Colo.: Westview Press, 1976.

Sun Yat-Sen: Frustrated Patriot, by C. Martin Wilbur. New York: Columbia University Press, 1977.

Japanese International Negotiating Style, by Michael Blaker. New York: Columbia University Press, 1977.

Contemporary Japanese Budget Politics, by John Creighton Campbell. Berkeley: University of California Press, 1977.

The Medieval Chinese Oligarchy, by David Johnson. Boulder, Colo.: Westview Press, 1977.

The Arms of Kiangnan: Modernization in the Chinese Ordnance Industry, 1860–1895, by Thomas L. Kennedy. Boulder, Colo.: Westview Press, 1978.

Patterns of Japanese Policymaking: Experiences from Higher Education, by T. J. Pempel. Boulder, Colo.: Westview Press, 1978.

The Chinese Connection: Roger S. Greene, Thomas W. Lamont, George

E. Sokolsky, and American-East Asian Relations, by Warren I. Cohen. New York: Columbia University Press, 1978.

Militarism in Modern China: The Career of Wu P'ei-Fu, 1916–1939, by Odoric Y. K. Wou. Folkestone, England: Dawson, 1978.

A Chinese Pioneer Family: The Lins of Wu-Feng, by Johanna Meskill. Princeton University Press, 1979.

Perspectives on a Changing China, edited by Joshua A. Fogel and William T. Rowe. Boulder, Colo.: Westview Press, 1979.

The Memoirs of Li Tsung-Jen, by T. K. Tong and Li Tsung-jen. Boulder, Colo.: Westview Press, 1979.

Unwelcome Muse: Chinese Literature in Shanghai and Peking, 1937–1945, by Edward Gunn. New York: Columbia University Press, 1979.

Yenan and the Great Powers: The Origins of Chinese Communist Foreign Policy, by James Reardon-Anderson. New York: Columbia University Press, 1980.

Uncertain Years: Chinese-American Relations, 1947–1950, edited by Dorothy Borg and Waldo Heinrichs. New York: Columbia University Press, 1980.

The Fateful Choice: Japan's Advance Into Southeast Asia, edited by James William Morley, New York: Columbia University Press, 1980.

Tanaka Giichi and Japan's China Policy, by William F. Morton. Folkestone, England: Dawson, 1980; New York: St. Martin's Press, 1980.

The Origins of the Korean War: Liberation and the Emergence of Separate Regimes, 1945–1947, by Bruce Cumings. Princeton University Press, 1981.

Class Conflict in Chinese Socialism, by Richard Curt Kraus. New York: Columbia University Press, 1981.

Education Under Mao: Class and Competition in Canton Schools, by Jonathan Unger. New York: Columbia University Press, 1982.

Private Academies of Tokugawa Japan, by Richard Rubinger. Princeton: Princeton University Press, 1982.

Japan and the San Francisco Peace Settlement, by Michael M. Yoshitsu. New York: Columbia University Press, 1982.

New Frontiers in American-East Asian Relations: Essays Presented to Dorothy Borg, edited by Warren I. Cohen. New York: Columbia University Press, 1983.

The Origins of the Cultural Revolution: II, The Great Leap Forward, 1958–1960, by Roderick MacFarquhar. New York: Columbia University Press, 1983.

The China Quagmire: Japan's Expansion of the Asian Continent, 1933–1941, edited by James William Morley. New York: Columbia University Press, 1983.

Fragments of Rainbows, The Life and Poetry of Saito Mokichi, 1882–1953, by Amy Vladeck Heinrich. New York: Columbia University Press, 1983.

The U.S.-South Korean Alliance: Evolving Patterns of Security Rela-

tions, edited by Gerald L. Curtis and Sung-joo Han. Lexington, Mass.: Lexington Books, 1983.

Discovering History in China; American Historical Writing on the Recent Chinese Past, by Paul A. Cohen. New York: Columbia University Press, 1984.

The Foreign Policy of the Republic of Korea, edited by Youngnok Koo and Sungjoo Han. New York: Columbia University Press, 1984.

State and Diplomacy in Early Modern Japan, by Ronald Toby. Princeton: Princeton University Press, 1983.

Japan and the Asian Development Bank, by Dennis Yasutmo. New York: Praeger Publishers, 1983.

Japan Erupts: The London Naval Conference and the Manchurian Incident, edited by James W. Morley. New York: Columbia University Press, 1984.

Japanese Culture, third edition, revised, by Paul Varley. Honolulu: University of Hawaii Press, 1984.

Japan's Modern Myths: Ideology in the Late Meiji Period, by Carol Gluck. Princeton: Princeton University Press, 1985.

Shamans, Housewives, and Other Restless Spirits: Women in Korean Ritual Life, by Laurel Kendell. Honolulu: University of Hawaii Press, 1985.

Human Rights in Contemporary China, by R. Randle Edwards, Louis Henkin, and Andrew J. Nathan. New York: Columbia University Press, 1986.

The Pacific Basin: New Challenges for the United States, edited by James W. Morley. New York: Academy of Political Science, 1986.

The Manner of Giving: Strategic Aid and Japanese Foreign Policy, by Dennis T. Yasutomo. Lexington, Mass.: Lexington Books, 1986.

Security Interdependence in the Asia Pacific Region, James W. Morley, Ed., Lexington, Mass.: Lexington Books, 1986.

Security Interdependence in the Asia Pacific Region, James W. Morley, Ed., Lexington, MA-DC: Heath and Co, 1986.

China's Political Economy: The Quest for Development Since 1949, by Carl Riskin. Oxford: Oxford University Press, 1987.

Anvil of Victory: The Communist Revolution in Manchuria, by Steven I. Levine. New York: Columbia University Press, 1987.

Single Sparks: China's Rural Revolutions, edited by Kathleen Hartford and Steven M. Goldstein. Armonk, N.Y.: M. E. Sharpe, 1987.

Urban Japanese Housewives: At Home and in the Community, by Anne E. Imamura. Honolulu: University of Hawaii Press, 1987.

China's Satellite Parties, by James D. Seymour. Armonk, N.Y.: M. E. Sharpe, 1987.

The Japanese Way of Politics, by Gerald L. Curtis. New York: Columbia University Press, 1988.

Border Crossings: Studies in International History, by Christopher Thorne. Oxford & New York: Basil Blackwell, 1988.

The Indochina Tangle: China's Vietnam Policy, 1975–1979, by Robert S. Ross. New York: Columbia University Press, 1988.

Remaking Japan: The American Occupation as New Deal, by Theodore Cohen, Herbert Passin, ed. New York: The Free Press, 1987.

Kim Il Sung: The North Korean Leader, by Dae-Sook Suh. New York: Columbia University Press, 1988.

Japan and the World, 1853–1952: A Bibliographic Guide to Recent Scholarship in Japanese Foreign Relations, by Sadao Asada. New York: Columbia University Press, 1988.

Contending Approaches to the Political Economy of Taiwan, edited by Edwin A. Winckler and Susan Greenhalgh. Armonk, N.Y.: M. E. Sharpe, 1988.

Aftermath of War: Americans and the Remaking of Japan, 1945–1952, by Howard B. Schonberger. Kent: Kent State University Press, forthcoming.

Suicidal Narrative in Modern Japan: The Case of Dazai Osamu, by Alan Wolfe. Princeton: Princeton University Press, 1990.

Neighorhood Tokyo, by Theodore C. Bestor. Stanford: Stanford University Press, 1989.

Missionaries of the Revolution: Soviet Advisers and Chinese Nationalism, by C. Martin Wilbur Julie Lien-ying How. Cambridge: Harvard University Press, 1989.

Education in Japan, by Richard Rubinger and Beauchamp. Honolulu: University Hawaii, 1989.

Financial Politics in Contemporary Japan, by Frances Rosenbluth. Ithaca: Cornell University Press, 1989.

Thailand and the United States: Development, Security and Foreign Aid, by Robert Muscat. New York: Columbia University Press, 1990.

Anarchism and Chinese Political Culture, by Peter Zarrow. New York: Columbia University Press, 1990.

The Study of Change: Chemistry in China 1840–1949, by James Reardon-Anderson. New York: Cambridge University Press, 1990.

China's Crisis: Dilemmas of Reform and Prospects of Democracy, by Andrew J. Nathan. New York: Columbia University Press, 1990.

Race to the Swift: State and Finance in Korean Industrialization, by Jung-en Woo. New York: Columbia University Press, 1991.